DARKER SIDE OF THE MOON "THEY" *ARE WATCHING US!*

By

Rob Shelsky

and

George Kempland

DARKER SIDE OF THE MOON

"*They*" Are Watching Us!

By

Rob Shelsky

And

George Kempland

PUBLISHED BY: *GKRS Publications*

*****

~ DEDICATION ~

There is one person we would especially like to thank, because she has been such a good friend and loyal supporter for so many years.

DIANE ELIZABETH POWELL

We wish to acknowledge you for your loyalty, dedication, mountains of help, and always just being there for us. Again, thank you, so very much!

*****

TABLE OF CONTENTS

INTRODUCTION
What's Going On?

SOMETHING IS COMING!

The world seems to be entering a strange new era. Whether we like it or not, certain events are combining to rush at us like some impossible juggernaut, seemingly unstoppable, unavoidable, and inescapable. Moreover, this dawning age is one filled with new types of uncertainty, because of all this. It's as if we were aboard a speeding train, one moving ever more rapidly, and we have no idea of what or where our destination will be. We race toward enigmas.

Unlike the 20th Century, which was wracked with mainly ideological and industrial upheavals, this time, events seem to be moving in a different direction. The rising interest in "2012" is just one example. But things are going even further and in a more bizarre way, much more dramatically so. Major social turmoil, there definitely will be as a result, no doubt.

However, this time, the causes will be of a very different nature than just mere governments warring with each other. This time, it won't be just something as simple as "isms" fighting each other for dominance in the world.

SOMETHING IS HAPPENING!

Most of us already know this, can intrinsically "feel" it. Weird events are manifesting themselves, despite our best efforts to ignore them, to pretend they aren't happening, or just don't exist. Consequently, people are uneasy and growing more so by the day.

They are asking questions they've never asked before and lots of them! What's more, people ask these questions with a new intensity. Once, we exercised just a mild curiosity about such subjects, a complacent intellectual interest in certain ideas, and even considered some questions as just a form of party entertainment. Now, things are different. Now, we want to know! We *have* to know! We want answers.

Why? Well, there seems to be a growing consensus among many of us that whatever is coming is getting closer, drawing ever nearer, and is now almost here! Whether it's Christians thinking the End of Days are approaching, New Age believers feeling the coming dawn of a New Age, people wondering about the dire implications of "2012," or just everyday folk trying to deal with the massive technological/social changes flooding in upon them, like some vast tsunami, everyone seems to feel that something huge is impending. A crisis or crises seem to be coming. We sense we're approaching a turning point, a major one!

As a result, our questions are also coming thick and fast. Again, they reach a new sense of urgency. This is because on some level, we truly know time is running out for the answers that we so desperately need, and may have to have just in order to survive. What questions? Well, there are all sorts. But a truly major one, one that concerns the near future of all humankind and our individual places in it, seems to concern a variety of mysterious objects we keep sighting in our skies and seas. These objects, collectively, we call UFOs.

UFOS—WHAT'S GOING ON?

This subject might seem completely unconnected at first glance to the concerns expressed above. Nevertheless, no matter how disparate all these topics seem, or how "out-of-this-world" this last one, UFOs, may first appear, they have one underlying principle in common to them, one general theme that runs throughout them all. That is, these mysteries seem to be looming on the near horizon.

This is true of UFOs no less than the other mysteries. Still, the results of some of these enigmas may envelop us very soon, very soon indeed, and perhaps before most of us are ready to deal with them. Maybe, this is where our real fear lies, in the dread of not being able to cope, of not being ready, of *not knowing what's coming!* We believe this has become a general anxiety, a social angst spanning much of the population of the world.

Well, whether or not any of us are ready, these approaching events will profoundly affect us in our own lifetimes, and already have for many. Furthermore, we don't know what the ultimate outcome of these events will be, but they each constitute an unknown, and so a crisis for us.

Will they fundamentally alter our viewpoint of the world and universe in which we live? Oh, yes. They will unquestionably change how we view what has happened in the past, how we live now, and where we are headed to in the future. These effects will come down upon us as individuals and as a species, like it or not. The very survival of all life on this planet, all of it, may even be at stake!

Worse, it appears we are approaching not just a single crisis, but many, and they all seem to be coming toward us at once. One major definition of the word "crisis" means "turning point." Well, we are coming to a nexus of such turning points. Like multiple threads coming together through the eye of a needle, enigmatic events are about to confront humanity and they may well be of cosmic proportions.

A multitude of related questions about these UFOs plagues us, as well, including even the issue of "2012." Are these things all real? Are aliens truly abducting people? Where do UFOs come from if they exist? Who are they? Have they always been here, or is this a more recent phenomenon? Are they planning to come again in force? Do they represent a threat, a danger, or a promise of something better? What are the implications of such things? *What do they want? Why are they here?*

ARRIVING AT STARTLING CONCLUSIONS

Well, it may just be possible to arrive at some real answers to all this. Moreover, we think we have. By using the abundance of evidence now at everyone's easy disposal and then applying the Principle of Occam's Razor to it, we have, step by step, arrived at certain incredible conclusions. They are profound and disturbing in their nature and implications at the very least, and for some, may be truly frightening in the extreme. We personally found them to be so, and thus felt we should share the conclusions here in this book, partly for this very reason, just because they are so disturbing. Furthermore, they do seem to be the most probable answers based on the Principle of Occam's Razor.

Here in this book, *DARKER SIDE OF THE MOON "They"* Are Watching Us! we intend to show in that same step-by-step process, for the benefit of the readers, just how we arrived at the conclusions we did. We will show from the very beginning the means by which we provide real answers, ones that can be acted upon and tested in the future by anyone. We include scientists in this last, especially scientists (if they ever care to do so), because they really should be turning their attention to these topics, instead of just castigating people in their millions for being just subject to "mass hysteria" and victims of sightings of swamp gas, Venus, etc., instead of genuine, strange objects in our skies and oceans.

The answers we've found might even help us to survive as a species, or at least as individuals, but at the very least, they should make us all more aware of what we are really facing from "out there." And "to be forewarned is to be forearmed," as "they" say. To paraphrase, we feel that in this case, ignorance is definitely not bliss, but rather a very dangerous diversion for one to indulge in, indeed.

And one more thing to support our contentions, we'll provide Internet links to much of this information in the Endnotes of this book, so you can go check all this out for yourself. And if you don't like the links we provide, there are much more available via a simple search of any available search engine, such as Google or Yahoo.

We feel this is a new and better approach in many respects to referencing. Why? Well, most of us don't have the time or wherewithal to check out libraries or to buy such source materials that authors traditionally use in referencing their work. And although we do reference many standard sources in this way, we put particular emphasis on reliable Internet sources, so that the reader can simply copy and paste such links into their browsers, go to these sites, and check much of this out for themselves quickly and easily, if they so wish.

CHAPTER 1

Intention

Make no mistake; *DARKER SIDE OF THE MOON "They" Are Watching Us!* is definitely not just another rehash of accounts about UFOs, UFO abductions, ancient aliens, or the like. Nor is it an attempt to prove their existence. That's been done! And it's been done by many other authors, although admittedly, by some much better than others.

No, simply compiling more evidence isn't our intention here. What we intend to do is to break new ground over the whole alien/UFO controversy. You see, we've sifted through the existing evidence, and have arrived at some startling conclusions. These new conclusions, and just how we arrived at them, we will show in this book.

How will we go about doing this? Well, again by a systematic process. So:

1. First, we'll start by discussing just what "real" evidence for UFOs actually constitutes. This involves what we think evidence constitutes, how we perceive things as evidence, and whether evidence for UFOs and the related subjects is reliable. (We'll tell you right here, we think a lot of it is.) The reason we'll spend some time on this, is that it is such a big issue, such a "bone of contention" between ufologists and scientists.

2. Secondly, we'll explain the phrase "extraordinary claims require extraordinary evidence," why and how this is often used, and the real reasons for it being used, and by whom.

3. Thirdly, and perhaps most importantly, we'll tackle all the issues by using a powerful tool, the Principle of Occam's Razor,[i] a major method invoked by scientists the world over to help find the most probable answers to many questions.

Why is this last considered a new approach to the UFO subject? Well, seemingly hardly ever, or to any real degree, at least, is the Principle of Occam's Razor used or applied by UFO authors or researchers in trying to arrive at conclusions. You see, repeatedly, UFO authors list all the evidence and data very well, but seldom do they really attempt to arrive at answers or conclusions that may be of any real use to the average person, other than their claiming these events are real because of all the available evidence they've given to prove them.

In this book, we now take that much as a given, that much has been proven already. Again, we feel the evidence is there and in abundance to prove the existence of UFOs. However, we can go much further than just this by using the Principle of Occam's Razor, which we'll explain in depth later. We will try to determine what all these phenomena might actually, truly mean for our futures and us, as individuals. The thrust in *DARKER SIDE OF THE MOON "They"* Are Watching Us! is to come up with some real answers, ones we can rely upon and so use to determine reasonable courses of action.

However, we are making one notable exception to the above idea that we will not produce an abundance of evidence to support any claims. This is because our research has taken us in a new direction, as the result of some of our conclusions. Although this topic has been discussed before by others, it has mostly been done so on the Internet, and again, no extrapolations have been made to any real degree as to what it all might mean—until now, here in this book. So, we will produce some solid evidence solicited originally by NASA itself, and more from several other sources.

We believe this will constitute a major step forward in our understanding of the whole UFO question. Because, with so uncertain a future facing us all, we need all the input, all the data and knowledge we can get, to first understand, and then hopefully help us to survive possible coming events. And remember, as "they" say, "knowledge is power." We need to acquire such power for ourselves, as individuals, and use it to our advantage, even to help insure our survival, if need be. So with this in mind, let's get started!

CHAPTER 2

A Preponderance Of Evidence

Before we get into discussing the nature of evidence, what even constitutes evidence, let's make one thing abundantly clear from the very outset. We wish to restate that we are not trying to prove the existence of UFOs. In our opinion, that's already an accomplished fact, a "done deal," as "they" say. We feel UFOs are a real phenomenon. Why? Well, for years, book after countless book, and show after show on television and radio, and even docudramas in the theatres, have repeatedly discussed whether UFOs, alien abductions, ancient aliens, and such, exist.

Authors and researchers have done this through a plethora of books, all citing individual cases in their thousands, even tens of thousands. And these cases are usually just drawn from the ones actually reported to the appropriate authorities. One must assume, therefore, that there are thousands more cases besides these, as well, ones which go unreported, since the stigma of reporting such a "crazy" event stops many from admitting such things even happened to them.

The twin fears of ridicule and ruining one's career loom large as factors in this resistance by many people to the reporting of what they have witnessed.[ii] So many people simply don't report "officially" such events. Thus, we can say with reasonable assurance that the numbers of actually reported UFO sightings thus form only the small tip of a much bigger and mostly submerged iceberg of such strange events.

Even so, the "official" reports made, all combine to form almost a seemingly limitless supply of evidence in their own right. This comes to us in the form of sworn anecdotal evidence, as well as thousands of eyewitness accounts and testimonies. There are countless photos and videos, audio recordings, and other reports often made by very reliable persons, including officials of governments and members of the military of various nations, as well as qualified researchers and trained observers in various fields of endeavors, such as MUFON.

This reporting of evidence has also been made by experienced radar operators, seasoned military pilots, skilled commercial jet pilots, numerous police officers, soldiers, sailors, military investigators, military officers, control tower operators, and just so many others whose bona fides simply can't be credibly questioned.[iii] Moreover, these accounts come to us from all over the world and have done so for decades, if not centuries, and even millennia!

In addition, this same reporting holds true on the government level, as well as for the individual level. Even a former Admiral of England (United Kingdom), Lord Hill-Norton, having been privy to classified information, has insisted there is more to all this than we are led to believe and further research into the matter of UFOs should be a high priority. A former British Ministry Of Defence (MOD) member, Nick Pope,[iv] declares that British airspace is repeatedly "penetrated" by strange and unknown "structured craft.[v] None other than Winston Churchill wanted the matter investigated, as well.[vi]

The top-level, highly acclaimed French government study, COMETA,[vii] thoroughly researched the UFO phenomena by using highly respected, qualified individuals for the government's report, and concerning themselves with only the most reliable accounts of such events. They came to some incredible conclusions, ones with strange implications as to the existence of UFOs. The Swedish, Belgian, Brazilian,[viii] and many other governments have all done similar sorts of investigations to various degrees, and all of them, without exception, made it clear they think something is definitely going on. This "something" seems to be truly extraordinary in nature, and most likely "out of this world" or "other world" in origin. At least, this is so, if we are to believe their reports.

There has even been what some scientists would refer to as "hard" evidence of such events, as well. These include actual video and sound recordings (some ascertained by qualified specialists not to have been tampered with in any way),[ix] and government released radar tracking recordings (as with Belgium), etc., and so certified by those governments as being true and correct.

Moreover, planes, helicopters, etc., have had to take evasive action to avoid midair collisions. In addition, there are other and different forms of evidence available from many other different types of sources. The amount of such evidence in total is simply overwhelming!

All of these things have been revealed to us over the many decades. Taken as individual pieces of evidence, they are incredibly compelling and intriguing items. And yes, some of the reports are stronger in nature as to their probable reality, of being "real" evidence, than others. Mistakes do happen even to the best-trained observers. Misidentifications are made…sometimes. But according to Nick Pope[x] and others, some cases simply can't be refuted in this matter. They stand out from the crowd as being virtually unassailable.

Again, the sheer preponderance of evidence, taken in its totality, is awesome in its size, variety, and content, to say the very least. So although skeptics might (however badly they wish to) refute some individuals' testimonies, and even those of trained specialists and observers on a one-by-one, case basis, how do they then account for the thousands, even hundreds of thousands of remarkably similar cases that have occurred, and are still occurring around the world?

Do we really have that many trained, highly qualified people, ones we entrust to fly our planes and to guide them to safety on the ground, who are so bad at their jobs of reporting what they see that they get it all so unbelievably and so often wrong? Are our astronauts, military pilots, radar operators, commercial jet liner pilots, navigators, police officers, soldiers, government officials, etc., all so extraordinarily poor at their jobs that they are just "seeing things," or misinterpreting what they see that badly? Unlikely! This is unlikely in the extreme.

Therefore, taken together, and despite allowing for a considerable amount of some possible misidentifications, such an enormous abundance of evidence still forms a formidable accumulation of proof, a "preponderance of evidence" in favor of the fact that the UFO phenomenon does exist.

And millions have come to believe the phenomenon of UFOs is, indeed, real, and it does exist. We include ourselves in this last viewpoint. In addition, this viewpoint on our part was only arrived at over several decades of studying this whole subject with a close and jaundiced eye, for we are by nature skeptics.

So whether certain doubters and the United States government wish to deny all this (although, in the case of the US government doing this, and despite having had their own military operators tracking on radar and then scrambling jets on occasions to intercept such so-called "nonexistent" UFOs) is, at this point, of little consequence to us. Who really cares what they say?

After all, the United States government is just one of many governments around the world. And many others think there is something to the phenomenon and publicly have stated so. What's more, some of those governments, by inference, have said they suspect the United States of hiding what it really knows, just as many individuals studying the problem think this, as well.

Whether or not the U.S. is hiding anything, there is just too much other evidence from elsewhere around the world, from decades of sightings just about everywhere, and again, in the form of official reports, radar tracking, and recordings (visual and audio), to continue to ignore this issue any longer.

To reiterate; UFOs exist. It's that simple. In addition, people believe this to be so and in incredible numbers. For instance:

1. Roughly 33 percent of Americans alone, as of the year 2000, believe that UFOs are real and do exist. [xi]

2. Another recent poll, as reported on CNN, reported that figure as apparently having grown until it is now slightly over 50 percent![xii]

3. If that isn't surprising enough, another poll suggests that one in five adults, worldwide[xiii] believe UFOs are real. If we take the world population as being just about seven billion, approximately, at the time of the writing of this book, then this number then translates to close to 1,400,000,000 (one billion, four hundred million) people who believe in UFOs worldwide. This is a truly significant number![xiv]

4. Yet another recent poll done nationally in 2002 by the SyFy Channel cites the fact that now 72 percent of Americans actually feel that our government is not telling the public everything it knows about UFOs. Sixty-eight percent feel our government is more knowledgeable about alien life than it will admit to, as the SyFy Channel also stated.[xv]

So this figure can vary some from poll to poll, depending on who took it, when it was taken, and whatever biases toward administering the poll there might have been (more on biases later), by the various pollsters involved, and even exactly who they chose to poll.

However, irrespective of which poll you choose, when translated into actual numbers, they all still show millions of Americans believing in UFOs and feeling there is enough evidence to give credence to the actual existence of them. This, in itself, is an astounding phenomenon.

On a global scale, it means hundreds of millions of people worldwide (again, even perhaps over a billion), who think enough evidence, that a "preponderance of evidence" exists to prove UFOs are actually real. So they believe in their existence. They are convinced. The current amount of evidence satisfies them, as it does us here.

What's more, this vast number of people wants to know more. They want legitimate investigations done of the phenomena, and they want the answers revealed in their entirety, not just in the form of redacted documents in their thousands, with all the important information carefully blacked out of them! Repeatedly, groups around the world have called for such investigations, and some of the groups are composed of very reputable government officials and other professionals. The United States, more than any other country in the world, has refused to do this to any real degree, the very old and so poorly run Project Bluebook," notwithstanding.[xvi]

Therefore, as stated, for us the debate as to whether UFOs exist is over for us. What their exact nature may be, we'll discuss later on, but as for their actual existence, in our minds, there can be no question of this. For those who would like a quick, short overview of some of the cited cases, just go to http://en.wikipedia.org/wiki/List_of_UFO_sightings. If you don't like Wikipedia then just do a quick search on the Internet and you'll find many other sources.

Also take note of this; either the fact UFOs exist is true, or millions upon millions of people have been in gross error, or consistently lied to authorities on what they saw. This means this last group purposely, endlessly, and repeatedly falsified reports (including government reports of various countries), faked countless photos and videos, and committed an equally countless number of hoaxes, not only over decades, but even centuries, for that matter.

So which of the following three versions regarding beliefs about UFOs seems the most likely to be the simplest answer and so true?

1. There are an incredibly widespread and massive number (and by massive, we mean millions of people here if not more likely hundreds of millions) who make grave and constant mistakes, or terrible errors in reporting what they see, (with many such reports being made by well-educated and trained observers). Or,

2. All these countless reports are just elaborate and unbelievably long-term hoaxes mixed in with elaborate conspiracies that have been perpetrated upon the world repeatedly and for generations. Moreover, these conspiracies and hoaxes would also have to involve lies by many of whom we see as upstanding citizens and so who would have had no obvious reason to do such a terrible thing, since it would only harm their reputations or careers. Or, finally,

3. Alternatively, we are really seeing something very strange in our skies. In which case, is there something "out there?" Apparently, the answer to that is yes. And could the answer be just that simple, that something strange is going on, is real?"

The answer, of course, should be the simplest one, and so should be obvious. That is, the third choice, (Number 3) that we really see something often and its nature is very bizarre, otherworldly, and even frightening to many.

To select the first answer would mean having to invoke the idea of an implausibly huge number of eyewitnesses, many of whom are trained experts, who somehow keep getting what they see terribly wrong, repeatedly and without exception, and have done this over centuries.

Alternatively, as with the second choice, it would involve an incredible number of elaborate hoaxes perpetrated over centuries. It would also have to include an equally elaborate set of conspiracy theories to account for having deliberately hoodwinked the public, not only now, but also throughout history. Again, this would mean a truly gargantuan number of people having deliberately lied and having conspired against the truth for some strange reason. And over and over again!

Another thing to remember about choosing an answer is that sometimes the phenomena have even been dangerous and deadly to those who say they saw UFOs, or encountered them more closely. Please don't forget that in some cases, people have actually died because of such encounters. In one report released from the archives of the Russian Navy, it mentions several divers who died underwater while trying to pursue a UFO (called a "USO" when underwater) through the water.

Now really, can any rational person believe the Russian Navy risked the lives of those men for something as trivial, as just "swamp gas," an "hallucination," or an underwater "optical illusion?" Not hardly! For more on this event, please go to http://rt.com/news/russian-navy-ufo-records-say-aliens-love-oceans/ and if you don't like this particular source, again, simply search under this topic. There are many other available websites, all of which report and corroborate this archived release in almost exactly the same way. We liked this one, because it was so thorough.

Then there is the matter of all those who claimed to have been burned by some type of radiation (often with photographic evidence taken at doctors' offices to support this contention), developed cancers, or strange growths on or in their bodies.[xvii] In some cases, these have also led to untimely and strange deaths. Besides, we're not even including what might be happening to possible abductees here.

Furthermore, one other truly remarkable and tragic item is the death of nine cross-country skiers/mountain climbers in the old Soviet Russia, who died under manifestly extraordinary circumstances before ever having even started their climb. The weird conditions of their deaths, ones that local officials subsequently tried to cover up, angered the primary member of the investigating committee to the point that he resigned in protest.

In addition, this event also has photographs, forensic evidence, etc., to support it actually had happened and just as described. That the nine young people died is an undeniable fact. That they died while racing for their lives, fleeing from their own tent (which tent they had cut to pieces from the inside with sharp implements to aid their quick escape), and that they suffered burns, and all sorts of other unimaginable traumas, is not a matter of contention. This much is also a fact.

That the authorities simply can't account realistically for how they died (some tried to call it simple hypothermia from exposure, but then one must ask, what drove nine people, ones only partially clothed and some shoeless, out of their tent into such frigid "exposure" in the first place?). Again, that these young people are dead is an indisputable fact. It's also a given that their deaths involved massive internal traumas to some of their bodies. What's more, there were no marks visible on the exteriors of their bodies to account for these traumas. Also, there was burning of portions of their corpses, skin turned orange, symptoms such as of apparent premature aging, high radiation levels around the tent and on some of their clothes, etc. None of this can be accounted for by simple exposure to the cold.

Remember, these were well-experienced cross-country skiers and climbers. They had done this sort of excursion many times before. They knew all about the dangers of hypothermia. So they would not flee out into the night, in bitterly cold weather, without a very good reason.

As a strange side note, the mountain they were to climb, was named Otorten, which literally translated means "don't go there" and the place where they set up camp was called Kholat Syakhl Mountain, which in English means, "Mountain of the Dead," both so named by the local Mansi people for some reason, a reason now lost in antiquity, apparently.

How does this involve UFOs? Well, several independent reports from different locations nearby refer to sightings of glowing balls of orange light spotted for several nights in that area, and a flying "circular" disk seen heading that way near the time of the actual event. Certainly, being unidentified, these constitute "UFOs" by the very definition.

For more on this event, go to either of these sites: http://www.forteantimes.com/features/articles/1562/the_dyatlov_pass_incident.html

Or,

http://en.wikipedia.org/wiki/Dyatlov_Pass_incident

You will notice that, as stated in both reference articles, "Soviet investigators determined only that '**a compelling**

unknown force' had caused the deaths." [Emphasis added.] So definitely, yes, the UFO phenomenon has deaths related to it.

To return to our main subject here: we have just illustrated above our first example of the use of the Principle of Occam's Razor to arrive at the most reasonable and simplest conclusion about UFOs. If you remember, we were initially faced with several choices. We had to choose as an explanation one of the following three:

1. A tremendous number of mistaken cases of identity by countless observers over centuries are the cause of these UFO sightings.

2. An elaborate, complex, and improbable scenario of countless hoaxes and lies, ones that also must have been perpetrated for countless decades, perhaps even centuries or millennia. Or,

3. We accept the third and the simplest answer that there is something there in our skies and seas, something extraordinary, and people are seeing and reporting about it on a very regular basis.

The simplest and most straightforward explanation in this case declares that people the world over, now and over long numbers of years/centuries/millennia, have and still are seeing some very fantastic and peculiar things and it isn't always just "swamp gas," folks! Not when it also seems to be able to harm, maim, and kill, or at least result in deaths and sickness as collateral damage in the process of seeing such things. Therefore, by the Principle of Occam's Razor, we should choose the simplest choice—that people are seeing something strange and it's having a real effect on lives. In other words, UFOs are real.

Now, having already used it once, in the next chapter, we'll explain exactly what the Principle of Occam's Razor actually is, why it works so well, and why we should use it always.

CHAPTER 3

The Power And Principle Of Occam's Razor

By repeatedly applying the Principle of Occam's Razor throughout this book, as we just did at the end of Chapter 2, we hope to arrive at some likely, or at least, very probable conclusions, just as scientists would. Then we can try to use these conclusions to advance our knowledge of what all this may mean for us, this whole UFO phenomenon in all its guises, what it may portend for us all.

The conclusion of the last chapter was that most people are actually, truly, and frequently witnessing and encountering something very strange in the skies of Earth. We call these weird objects "UFOs."

By using the Principle of Occam's Razor, and so accepting this simplest and most straightforward of explanations, again, we must conclude these are real phenomena. Therefore, we must reject the more improbable idea that all these sightings simply form an incredibly massive number of cases of mistaken identification of more mundane things. We must also discard the even more implausible idea they are a result of some elaborate and endless series of worldwide hoaxes/conspiracies perpetrated in their thousands or hundreds of thousands and over an incredible amount of time.

So given the possible explanations, the simplest answer is this is really happening. UFOs, to repeat a phrase (and it does bear repeating), really are "out there."

Please remember, we aren't so intent with proving the existence of anything in this book, because we feel that's been done already, and repeatedly. Instead, our focus lies on giving some real answers here as to what this all may mean for us, humanity as a whole, here on Planet Earth. But we did want to illustrate how the Principle of Occam's Razor can be applied to help pick the most likely answers; in this case, do UFOs exit?

The answer seems to be, yes. And if UFOs are actually here, as the Principle of Occam's Razor seems to show, then why are they here? What are they? Are they aliens? If aliens are in our skies, what's their purpose in being here? We need to find answers to these questions.

And like many authors, many pundits make endless suppositions about these phenomena, argue the available evidence, but no methodology ever seems to be applied to attempt to winnow all this down to the most likely, the most probably correct answers as to what it all may really mean for us. We wish to attempt to do this. And we do feel the Principle of Occam's Razor is the best way to find those answers.

Opponents to the idea of the reality of UFOs, those scientists and various government officials, along with others, certainly use the Principle of Occam's Razor readily and quickly enough in their arguments to deny the existence of UFOs, ancient aliens, etc. Scientific skeptics fall back on this very same principle all the time in televisions shows, and interviews to refute such claims.

So why shouldn't we use the same method ourselves, if it works so well for them? Why shouldn't proponents of UFOs apply the Principle of Occam's Razor, too? As the old saying goes, "what's sauce for the goose is sauce for the gander," after all. If a method works so well for them, let's then see if it works equally well for proponents of the existence of UFOs.

Additionally, although evidence is given in abundance, various suppositions made, no one seems to have thought (until this book), to try applying that same principle used around the world by scientists to arrive at the most likely of conclusions. Why have UFO enthusiasts and believers failed to apply this sound principle to any real degree?

Well, there is one very telling reason for this, and it is the statement that "extraordinary claims require extraordinary evidence." Scientists use this all the time when asked why they won't seriously discuss the reality of UFOs. And far too many of us who think there is something to these phenomena then fall into this same trap. Shortly, we will discuss this "trap," why we choose to call it such.

To summarize this section, why is the Principle of Occam's Razor used everywhere and so often by scientists? Why is it so relied upon by them? The answer is simple. They use it because it works most of the time. That's why. Which is why we intend to use it here now, finally, and throughout this book, at every possible turn we can, because the principle does work well, and for anyone who chooses to use it.

The Principle of Occam's Razor

As we illustrated it at the end of Chapter 2, is simplicity itself, literally. **Wikipedia** defines it this way:

"Occam's razor (or Ockham's razor)[1] often expressed in Latin as the *lex parsimoniae*, translating to law of parsimony, law of economy or law of succinctness, is a principle that generally recommends, when faced with competing hypotheses that are equal in other respects, selecting the one that makes the fewest new assumptions…"[xviii]

In case that sounds a bit convoluted, more simply put, the Principle of Occam's Razor means that when given the choice of more than one possible answer to a problem, with all answers seemingly about equal in most other respects, then the best way to go is to pick the simplest, least complicated answer of all of them.

As shown at the end of Chapter 2, when it comes to "theories" as to why thousands are seeing UFOs every year and millions have claimed to be abducted, the simplest answer is not that it's a massive series of complex hoaxes or elaborate conspiracies over countless decades/centuries, or an incredible number of mistakes. It's not mass hysteria, or hallucinations. Those answers are too complicated.

Again, the simplest answer is that *something is going on!* So according to the Principle of Occam's Razor, this is the answer we're going to use here, and as a basis upon which to build. And before skeptics scream we're being too "across the board," we freely admit that many sightings may be mistakes, even the vast majority of them, but even by officials' own admissions, some simply cannot be explained away in any normal way.

Therefore, those sightings, by default, must be real. And if real, that means we have UFOs in our skies. Again, "simple mistaken identification of mundane things" wouldn't cause deaths and injuries to the observers. After all, seeing the planet Venus should hardly be fatal…yet, something killed those nine Russian students and those divers we earlier mentioned, as well as many others.

So step one is complete. To summarize, we have arrived at the simplest conclusion, and that is there is something to all these UFO sightings. UFOs exist. But we need to know more. Now with this Principle of Occam's Razor at our disposal, one so favored by scientists, let's move on and find out just what else this all entails!

CHAPTER 4

Perception of Reality

To understand the process of how we arrived at our conclusions using the Principle of Occam's Razor, it is imperative we first share exactly how we went about doing this. We need to clarify what the premise for our "acceptance of evidence" is, and how we went about doing all this, because it forms the foundation of everything, all of our conclusions. If that evidence is wrong, this means in turn all our conclusions in this book would be wrong, as well, despite using the valuable Principle of Occam's Razor. Therefore, we had to approach the topic of what constitutes evidence very carefully.

The first necessary step was to reorder our perceptions of the world around us before even considering any evidence. We had to decide what really constitutes reality. No, this does not mean we took off into flights of fancy, sailed to another astral plane, or put ourselves in any sort of trances, or other "enlightened" states with or without psychotropic drugs.

Quite the opposite is the fact. We wanted to make sure we were seeing the world as it actually is, not as we think, imagine, or wish it to be. Cold, perhaps an even harsh and gritty reality was our sole goal, and not just a "perception" of some candy-coated version of it all, or anyone's "version" of it, for that matter. This had to hold true for us whether it meant rejecting the UFO enthusiast's perception or the other extreme, and the most skeptical of a scientist's disbeliefs. We just wanted as close to the "real thing" as we could get.

Perception Is Not Reality

This concept is of paramount importance when we look at, examine, and discuss evidence of UFOs and their related subjects. What we "perceive" or want to be true, does not necessarily make something true at all. However, just what is perception, exactly? Well, a good definition of perception is the way we look at things, the way we see the world around us. Again, and we can't say this often enough here, perception is not reality,[xix] no matter how many Hollywood or Madison Avenue advertiser types may tell us it is or should be.

Unfortunately, due to the constant repetition of that now cliché phrase by such hard sell, business types, many people really do think the two things, perception, and reality, equal each other for all practical purposes. Although this may be true in advertising, it is definitely not when it comes to dealing with reality and evidence for it.

But perception is powerful, all too powerful at times. Why? Well, this is because perception controls not only how we see things, but also and MORE IMPORTANTLY, how we react to them, and furthermore, how we then act upon those very reactions, as well. It's a chain of events we've forged and often on a very wrong set of initial assumptions. Moreover, we all do this sort of thing and we do it a lot, daily and even hourly!

The Germans have a marvelous word for our perception of things, "*weltanschauung.*"[xx] Roughly, this refers to our particular world viewpoint and encompasses all our personal belief systems, our own sets of ideas through which we perceive the entire world. It is, therefore, our "worldview" of how we believe things "really are," but again, this is not necessarily, *how* they actually are.

We just can't stress this particular point enough here. For instance, if you already "believe" UFOS exist, you may see a bright object in the sky, Venus, and be inclined to think it's a UFO, when it's really, in fact, just the planet Venus. Even so, you might make a report you saw a UFO. However, the reverse is also true. If your perception is based on a highly skeptical background, and a disbelief in UFOs, you may see an actual UFO, but insist it "had to be" Venus.

You see, to create or construct our personal worldview, our perception of just what reality is, each of us uses many sources and we acquire our perceptions over a long period. Information may come in the form of learning through books or schooling over the years, as well as through our parents, friends, family, and other authority figures. It also comes to us through specific life experiences, or events that happen to us as individuals along our road through life.

All this input, this information or "evidence" of how things are, how life and reality is, helps us to evolve each of our personal and particular worldviews, our *weltanschauung*, if you will. Once we've formed these, once created, they are very strongly held viewpoints, often kept virtually intact in their entirety for a person's lifetime! We may even be willing to kill and/or fight each other in order to preserve such viewpoints, such personal perceptions of how things are, or how we think they should be.

Do you doubt this? Well, just think of how many people are fighting and dying right now because of personal and strongly held religious convictions. Various people have done this sort of thing for millennia, because they are so convinced, their religious viewpoints are the correct ones that they must fight to the death to preserve or spread them.

Yet, in the final analysis, these are just "beliefs" held by them, and ones with little or no empirical evidence to support them. In addition, we're not limiting this to any single religion, either. Almost all religions have had adherents who did this, and some of them still are doing this—killing for the sake of their religious beliefs and convictions. Mind you, we're not trying to say religions are "bad." We're simply pointing out, using religion as an example, what strong beliefs can lead to, and that can be, and many times has been in the past, a life, or death matter.

The same has often held true for political beliefs. Heaven knows, we have had our share of such "isms," political beliefs as to how people should be governed over the last couple of centuries, and literally millions upon millions of people have died directly because of this phenomenon. Again, beliefs can lead to "life or death" matters.

Whether it was Hitler's Germany trying to spread the ideals of Nazism, with their concept of Aryan supremacy, or Stalin's Communist Russia, where dissidents were summarily executed in droves, or any other country's "isms," for that matter, whether fascist, anarchist, or whatever, the average person, it seems, was usually the main victim of them all. Many people died because of others' strongly held political beliefs, beliefs those adherents felt to be "true" at any price—that price being human lives (usually other human lives and not theirs).

Why are we talking about this, here in a book about UFOs? Well, it's to show that our worldviews are incredibly powerful things, terrifying at times in their implications and consequences, literally often resulting in major matters concerning life and death.

Furthermore, can this information or evidence we use to construct our worldviews be a major problem for us when recognizing what's truly real? Can our personal *weltanschauung* form an obstacle when it comes to dealing with the wider subjects of UFOs, alien abductions, and ancient aliens?

The answer is an emphatic YES! Unfortunately, just this sort of thing happens all the time and too often. The first thing that occurs when some type of evidence, any type for that matter with regard to UFOs is submitted, whoever is the recipient of it immediately invokes their personal world viewpoint, again, their *weltanschauung*, to judge the validity of any such evidence presented. And often, that response takes the form of ridicule and extreme skepticism.

CHAPTER 5

What Constitutes Evidence—

"There Be Monsters Here"...Or Not?

So let's examine the idea of so-called evidence, evidence of anything. And we say "so-called," because what constitutes evidence is often just in the eyes of the particular beholder. Two people can look at exactly the same thing and arrive at two very different sets of conclusions about it.

This, as we all know, happens all the time! Have you ever listened to the witnesses' testimony of a crime? Their stories can vary incredibly, and yet they all saw the same thing...supposedly.

Total objectivity is virtually a human impossibility, and this is so whether it is with regard to a scientific experiment under rigorous sets of controls, or just judging the nature of a fellow human being, one we chance to meet at a cocktail party, for example. Precisely because we are human, we see everything through a set of mental and/or emotional filters, which in total, constitute our personal perception of reality. There's that word again, "perception."

Nevertheless, we can't help it. Our shields are always up, if you will, and locked firmly in place. We acquire these shields or filters for very practical reasons. They have value. They help us to survive in this harsh reality. They do this by allowing us speedily to recognize things, so we can quickly respond to them, perhaps in time to save our lives. They help us to function, to go about our daily routine, and to deal with unexpected situations—to a point!

As an example of this, every time we see a dog, we don't consciously think through the whole process of what it looks like, how it sounds, and how it behaves, in order to figure out that it actually is a dog. Our preconceived notions of what canines are kick in quickly, allow us automatically to know a dog when we see one, and we do this just about instantly.

So, these sorts of preconceived notions, these automatic mental filtering processes, which form our perception of reality, are acquired in our lives to save us a lot of time and effort, especially when we may be in danger and so response time is critical. Our shields serve a real purpose. There is no doubt of that. Instantly, we usually know what a "dog" is.

In addition, there can be powerful emotional overtones attached to these shields or filters, as well (which form even more filters through which we perceive reality), often very strong ones, and for much the same reasons. If a dog once savagely attacked you as a child, then when you see another dog, there could well be an emotional reaction tied to your perspective of it.

In such circumstances, we've tagged the idea of "dog" with the added emotional filter of strong fear, even terror, and possibly the idea to act by fleeing upon seeing one, or at least not to go anywhere near it! This emotional tagging or added filtering is to help protect us in the future, whenever we again confront such similar and potentially dangerous situations. This aids us in our personal survival.

Still, sometimes, we're completely wrong in this perception of what constitutes a "dog" or the danger involved. When is a dog, really a dog? Maybe, it's a coyote, or a wolf, or something else entirely. For example, when you walk up to someone's house and ring the doorbell, often a dog barks loudly from inside. If you are afraid of dogs, this instantly gives rise to "real" fear on your part. The sound of a loudly barking dog, one that "sounds big" has driven away many a would-be visitor, door-to-door salesperson, or burglar from someone's door.

So the loud barking of a dog, for all practical purposes, then equals for us a sure signal of a dangerous animal being on the premises. Nevertheless, sometimes, it doesn't mean it's a dog at all, but rather just the sound of one, and nothing more.

Owners, as most of us know, sometimes just use an automatic recording of a barking dog that triggers when someone knocks or rings a bell. They do this purposely to scare away would-be burglars and often this works. For many burglars, the sound of a barking dog does truly equal a real dog, as far as they are concerned, and so they go somewhere else.

In other words, they first "react" and then "act" as if the sound meant there was truly a dog there, even when they aren't sure, which is the whole intent of the recorded trickery perpetrated by the owner. But it's not "reality." For in "reality," there is no dog there.

In this case, our mental filters in how we perceive reality as a whole, have acted to deceive us about what is actually "real." The perception filters automatically did this for our safety, but they were still completely wrong. So such a filter about dogs can constitute an outright bias, an "acquired" prejudice and lead to completely wrong conclusions.

So preconceived notions, our perceptions of reality, can make us look at something new (UFO evidence?) and not see it for what it really is, or perhaps may even make us come to a very erroneous assumption about what we are actually seeing. In addition, what if the dog you think you see is not a dog at all, but something else entirely? Sound impossible? Not so!

As a personal example, if we have never seen a possum before, we might just think we were seeing a giant rat. Does this sound farfetched? I wish it were, but it isn't. I know this possibility to be true, because the first time I ever laid eyes upon a possum, I thought it was a giant rat. Yes, that sounds incredibly naïve, but I was a city boy, in my very early twenties. The thing I saw had a long snout, whiskers, a long ropy tail, and ears that made it look very like a rat to me! More importantly, I had heard urban myths of giant rats that dwelled in sewers in cities, and came out at night. Could this be one of those? I was very much "afraid" it could be. I was convinced I saw a "giant rat."

Therefore, a very strong emotional preconception came into play for me, old evidence I'd experienced and was now applying to this new event, and so it helped to color how I viewed what I actually saw, my "perception" of it. Instead of reality, that is, a harmless possum sneaking in the open back door of my house to eat the cat food set out there, I saw my perception instead, that is, a giant dangerous rat, and so reacted accordingly. When it hissed at me, I ran! And if called upon in court to testify at the time, I'd have sworn I saw a giant rat.

And yes, before anyone questions it, I do have a reasonably high IQ, so that wasn't the cause of the problem. Still, I didn't know what I was "really" seeing, despite this fact. I had never before confronted such a thing. So, who knew?

Of course, now when I see a possum, I know it to be a possum. I won't be fooled twice! However, I can never quite look at a possum without feeling a secret twinge of humiliation….

In any case, here, you see, I saw a monster where there was no monster. But is the reverse true, as well? Yes, sadly, it is. Sometimes there are monsters there, and we just don't see them as such.

The point is, when we see something new, discover new evidence, we automatically try to fit it into preconceived notions of what we've seen before, our original perceptions of reality. In the case of the history of UFOs, ancient witnesses described what they saw based on what they had seen (and so was already known to them) before. So UFOs spotted in the sky by members of Alexander The Great's army (while trying to invade India), saw silvery "flying shields."[xxi] Emperor Constantine saw a "cross" in the sky.

Others in antiquity described UFOs as "flaming chariots" strange "signs from God," "comets" (everything unusual in the sky in times past was often referred to as a "comet"), "magic carpets," "shields," etc.[xxii]. Again, those ancient witnesses' descriptions of what they saw were all based on their already acquired perceptions of things they'd seen, things they had already knew about from their everyday life. And instantly, they related these new things to those old ones, if only for descriptive purposes.

Now, centuries later and partly because of this, we dismiss out of hand their sightings, for who seriously believes these days in "magic carpets," for instance. But we must always remember that this was just their attempt to describe something they'd never seen before. It was just their personal perceptions trying to fit in something new, by comparing it to something they'd already seen in everyday life.

Even recently, we've done this and still do. Over the years, we variously have had such descriptions as "airships," "flying saucers," "disks," "crescents," "triangles," "cigars," etc., for UFOs.[xxiii] Always, it seems, we humans try to relate something new we see to something we've already seen. This, in itself, is a form of giving in to our preconceptions based on personal perceptions. Again, even now, we always try to relate the new to the old, "make it fit in." Whether it's a giant rat that we see instead of a possum or a "flying shield" instead of an alien spacecraft this is so.

In this way, we often try to make new things into something we might *expect* to see, based on prior evidence from other similar and earlier events in our lives. Simply put, when later described (and probably so preserved, ultimately, in our actual memories this way, too), we think we actually saw a "fiery chariot," (if we happen to have been living at the time of the Roman Empire, for example).

The same is true for people who claim to have seen aliens. And because those descriptions often somewhat resemble characters from stories, legends, and myths, those witnesses are then ridiculed by others of us for having seen "little green men," "goblins," or various other fairy folk. Of course, it never seems to occur to those same skeptics those tales of old, of goblins and trolls might just have originated from witnesses of the day seeing such aliens, too.

The same holds true today. Today, rather than seeing a UFO, we are told by scientists who hold their own strongly preconceived and negative notions on the subject, that we are seeing swamp gas, weather balloons, tricks of lighting, the planet

Venus, strange-shaped clouds, or outright optical illusions, and/or mass hallucinations.

Is this possible? Of course, it is. Just about anything seems possible. Moreover, it is true that many people have mistaken mundane things, such as the planet Venus, or odd-shaped clouds for UFOs. Nevertheless, the reverse is true, as well. Many, many people have seen something they simply can't explain with ordinary answers, but then try to make them ordinary; because they simply can't or won't believe, what they saw was a real UFO.

As an example of someone trying very hard to explain UFOs away, one extreme skeptic, who was totally against the idea of the existence of UFOs, and who simply had to find a more ordinary reason for every such sighting reported, was a victim of his own preconceived notions in this regard, and very often, in our personal opinions. He even once claimed it was just a firefly trapped between the panes of glass of the windshield of a major commercial jetliner, which the pilot, copilot, navigator, and various flight attendants then must have mistaken for a UFO!

Really, how sadly desperate can we be to hold on to our current perceptions of reality to such a pitiful, painful, and pathetic degree? To invoke this sort of an explanation was utterly ridiculous. His answer doesn't take into account how a firefly might get in between sealed panes of glass on a jetliner in the first place (incredibly unlikely, because it wasn't a new jet just built, so the firefly should have been dead long ago). Nor does his explanation account for how it somehow managed to survive subzero temperatures for long hours and yet still happily fly around inside those incredibly narrow-spaced panes of glass, and while the jet was cruising at altitudes of 32,000 feet or more.

Neither does such an explanation take into account how three, well-trained, long-experienced professionals could continuously mistake a common firefly for a UFO for such a long period. His theory also doesn't account for how the firefly could have changed dramatically in size and brilliance, as reported of the UFO by the cabin crew. In addition, apparently fireflies can even show up on radar and sometimes even be tracked? Oh, come on!

The old saying, "desperation knows no bounds," certainly seems true in this skeptic's feeble attempts at an explanation for the UFO sightings.

So preconceived perceptions of what reality is can be rigid to the point of utter inflexibility. The more desperate someone is to hang on to their viewpoint, or the more they have vested in such a personal perspective, the more they will resort to such extremes to defend and negate any damaging "evidence" to the contrary.

Our point here? Personal and/or acquired professional perspectives not only make us view everything in a certain way, but they actually dictate to us what we "think" we should see. This result is usually a product of fear. Because it's easier to try literally to force some new evidence, to jam it into our existing belief systems, rather than face the possibility that what we've always "known" isn't necessarily correct at all and may be terribly wrong. And we simply can't have that!

We all fear the demolition of what we believe to be right, true, and valid. If you doubt this, just attack someone's personal religious convictions and see what happens! (We don't mean you should really do this—the consequences could be, literally, dangerous, and besides, we should all respect each other's personal religious beliefs.) What was that old cigarette commercial slogan; "I'd rather fight than switch?" When it comes to our perceptions of reality, what we believe to be "right," this is often all too true for many people.

How does this apply to UFOs? Well, we're told, as children, "there are no such things as monsters," so because of this belief instilled in us at such an early age, how many of us adults now are not seeing monsters where there might actually be ones?

Isn't that a terrible thought? How is this possible? Well, again, it is because of our preconceived notions of reality. If something just doesn't fit well into them, or we are "told" it doesn't exist, we often try to pretend then that those things don't exist when they do. This can be an actual habit, one buried in our deepest, most ingrained subconscious levels. After all, wouldn't we all prefer that there were no monsters? So maybe, we simply don't choose to see them, even if they might be there.

Do you want a very simple example of this phenomenon of not seeing something that's there because of a preconceived notion? Ever have someone make you read a note card aloud, one with a single sentence written on it? As in this example:

> "Nothing is more delightful than the City of Paris in the the spring or fall. You should visit there during those times."

Did you read the sentence as if it had only one "the" and not two, after the phrase, "City of Paris?" Most people actually do. They fail entirely to see the second "the." This is a very standard practical joke, by the way, but one best done when written on a small note card or small piece of paper. But if you did read it that way, check the sentence again. "The" does actually appear twice in a row there.

But why do so many read it as if there were only one "the" there when in reality there are two? The answer is because it is what you *expected* to see, thought you *should* see, but not what you actually saw. Out of habit, you were used to seeing only one "the" in such situations, so despite the evidence being there for any to see, you just did not see it at all! You mentally edited out something that in "reality" was there! You did it automatically.

So one often sees what they *expect* to see, because mental filtering systems tell them this is how it should be, is *supposed* to be. Their, or your world viewpoint, is directly responsible for reading reality wrongly at times.

And what if we're not talking about simply missing seeing a "the" here, but something else, perhaps something much more important? Perhaps, we're missing obvious clues, because our perceptions of reality <u>preclude</u> their existence. If monsters or aliens exist, are we just not "seeing" the evidence for them, because we don't believe it can exist, are told that they can't exist, or just don't want them to exist?

In the sample sentence above, about Paris, if you never realized your mistake, never had the perpetrator of the joke point it out to you, and later you testified in court from memory about the contents of that sentence, you would swear on your honor the way you "thought" it read was how it had actually read. But you would be completely wrong! For more on this sort of thing, there is a marvelous book, author Michael Talbot's, *Holographic Universe*, a one-time New York Best Seller, which discusses this phenomenon in much more depth than we do here. We highly recommend it.

When approaching evidence of anything, if we perceive things wrongly, or don't perceive some things at all (as some do not see "the" appearing twice in a row in that sample sentence above), then our grasp of what constitutes "reality" is fundamentally flawed. We may be missing something important, very important, and what's more, we may be doing this on a regular basis, either consciously or subconsciously.

Are we then prone to maybe missing the fact that there may be an implacable enemy nearby, one much closer to us than we think? You have to grant that it is, at least, a possibility. So could "there be monsters here," as ancient maps described unknown areas of the oceans? There could well be. Or they could be very close by, watching us on a daily or even hourly basis! Moreover, to our detriment, we simply don't see them; don't see evidence for their existence, because we don't believe they can exist and so they just can't be there.

Why do we use the word "monsters" repeatedly here when "aliens" would be a far less emotionally negative term, and so should suffice? Well, it's because we feel there is enough evidence to prove that not only do aliens exist, but also they certainly do not have our best interests at heart! They may not be our "friends." In fact, from our point of view, they may just be "real monsters," after all…

A reporter on a very prominent television network recently interviewed a political expert. When asked why the average person often reacts like an ostrich sticking its head in the sand when witnessing horrible situations, such as rife corruption in governments, major tragedies in the world, his response, or words to this effect was: Because reality is harsh, very harsh, often too much so. People die all the time and in horrible ways and without rhyme or reason, it seems.

Bad things happen to good people. So we build up this fantasy world that love and happiness, and secure lives are possible, when in reality, you can die in a hideous way at any given moment, have that loved one torn from you by death in some random car accident or illness, or be wrongly imprisoned, tortured, or even executed. Life is so tough that we create a fairytale version of it to make it tolerable, palatable to ourselves. We do this so we can go on with our lives. *We just choose not to see some things, even though they are staring us right in the face*. We didn't say this. The political expert did. Nevertheless, we thoroughly agree.

Furthermore, if for some reason you just can't ignore, can't dismiss such evidence, then we just label it as "nonsense." Alternatively, we could just conveniently forget about it altogether. If that, too, isn't possible, perhaps we just brand it as nothing more than a hoax, or a "misinterpretation of the facts, of the available evidence." Yes, we have all sorts of methods for protecting our particular views of reality, how we would really prefer it to be. But it doesn't mean monsters aren't really "there!"

CHAPTER 6

Are Scientists Fallible With Regard To Perception And The Reality Of UFOs?

Oh, yes, they are! And they are, perhaps even more so than the average person might be in some respects. This sounds unlikely, we know, but consider that those who are the most educated among us, scientists for instance, and precisely because of their years of intensive and extensive formal training, often may be most prone to making just these sorts of mistakes, more than many of the rest of us "average" citizens.

Why? Well, this may be because scientists have acquired some of the very strongest mental filters and preconceptions of all, during all those extra years of study and training. They are almost brainwashed as it were, or conditioned over years by their superiors and colleagues in many cases, to believe that certain things "must be true," must be a certain way. Therefore, for those people, those things do hold true and must remain true, regardless of any "anomalous" evidence to the contrary.

But, you say, they're supposed to be more objective than the rest of us—right? That's what all that training was for in the first place, surely? Well, in some ways, important ways, they undoubtedly are more objective. As scientists and researchers, they have to be.

However, they are still human, so their objectivity can be quite focused, quite narrow in its use and extent and sometimes to the exclusion of other facts. What they learned must hold true, you see, or all those years of study might have been just a total waste of time. And they can't have that! Nobody wants to think he or she might have "gotten it all wrong," or that what they've studied for years no longer holds even remotely true. Moreover, nobody likes his or her personal or professional world viewpoint, one slowly and painstakingly acquired over years, to be threatened or even destroyed in an instant.

So despite their trying honestly to be as objective as possible, they, being merely human like the rest of us, already approach things with a certain bias, have a lot of preconceived notions and opinions (extra mental filters?) about things they "expect" to see, or are "supposed" to find, or even worse, <u>don't</u> expect to see.

That last is significant. If they see something that doesn't fit their learned theories, their "acquired" academic expectations, their prior sets of data results, they just might, and more quickly than others, dismiss the evidence as irrelevant, just erroneous results, an anomaly, or a complete hoax. Worse, they might simply dismiss it out of hand, as if it didn't exist!

This has happened more often than the average person might realize. In truth, it happens all the time! There have been numerous cases over the centuries of scientists falsifying results to make them agree with what they *wanted* the outcome of the experiments to be, rather than what they really were. Remember that whole big thing about the discovery of "Cold Fusion?" Nobody else seemed to be able to come up with the same results as those who performed the original experiment found. Some even accused those researchers of falsifying their results. Did they? That's still an open question, one not easily resolved, apparently.

However, mostly, it's not a matter of falsification. Rather, it's just a rigid thinking system barring certain outcomes from seeming plausible, because those outcomes defy "normal" and the then-current scientific doctrine on the subject.

I personally know this last is so, because I have experienced exactly the same thing. So have many others. When I went to college, my astronomy professor, a very good and well-educated man of the times, said it was far more likely for an asteroid to end up in orbit around the Earth than to actually ever hit it. He said this in the early 1970s.

He was trying to reassure us about how very unlikely (his words were "practically impossible") it would be for asteroids of any size to ever impact our planet. We had been studying the Moon's impacted surface, you see. It's covered, of course, in large part by craters. Impacts, it seemed, had been rife on the Moon.

Therefore, we were worried, as new astronomy students would be under such circumstances, that the Earth might also be a form of cosmic target, a constant celestial bull's-eye for asteroid practice. Our professor repeatedly assured us this scenario was very unlikely. He said if it ever happened at all, it was either during the formation of the solar system, or was probably just the one time, perhaps twice at the most, and then only early on in Earth's history, when asteroids were more abundant. Orbital mechanics made such a scenario "highly improbable" for something as large as the Earth was to be hit more than a few times, according to him. Likewise (he asked us), if this weren't the case, then where were all the craters that should be on Earth as "evidence" of such past impacts?

Good point—the Earth's surface does not look particularly pockmarked, as the surface of the Moon does, so we students were duly reassured and so breathed a collective sigh of relief. The professor's perception of reality was a nice, safe, secure one when it came to asteroids hitting the Earth. Now, so was our "scientific" perception of this as students, as well, because we had now adopted the "expert's" viewpoint concerning the possibility of asteroid impacts. We had just been trained, you see, to adopt the idea that such a thing was "highly improbable."

Nevertheless, just a few years later, scientists discovered our professor's reassurances were wrong! Asteroids, big and small, along with comets had hit the Earth and many times, it seems. In fact, there may have been so many comet impacts, that according to one major theory, Earth may have received much of its supply of water from them!

So much for relying upon scientists and "scientific" perceptions of reality!

One more example, then we will let this subject go. In 1596, Abraham Ortelius broached the idea of continental drift, and that continents actually drifted about the surface of the Earth. He was laughed at, ridiculed, and the idea was summarily dismissed by others living at the time, much to his embarrassment and chagrin, not to mention the destruction of his personal reputation as a man of knowledge and science.

Much later, Alfred Weggener promoted a more thorough version of this same idea in the 1920s. However, geologists of the time outright ridiculed him, too, just as others had with Ortelius, centuries before him. The then-current theories of geology did not account for such a thing happening, of being even remotely possible. Whole continents floating? Hogwash! So it just couldn't be. How could continents drift around like ice cubes in a bowl of water?

Therefore, they dismissed Weggener's ideas out of hand, often with severe contempt! They attacked him from all sides. He was the subject of ridicule. His career was utterly ruined. It wasn't until decades later, the 1950s, when other geologists came up with the theory of plate tectonics, that Weggener's ideas were finally resurrected and largely accepted as true. This was, sadly, just a little too late to be of much help to poor old Weggener. He was dead by then, having died in ignominy and defeat, having been terribly ridiculed, and his career shattered.

All this happened just because Weggener had dared to propose something different and new, something "so radical." And poor old Ortelius had been out of the picture so long, nobody even remembered to think to give him credit to any extent at the time for even having had the original idea. And so it goes and continues to go.

Of course, the evidence had been there all along, literally for centuries and much, much longer. It had existed all through human history and long before it. The available evidence for the theory had been there all that time. It was self-evident, in plain sight, and there for anyone to see! Certainly, it should have been so for the "trained eye" of a scientist, especially after the idea had been purposefully brought to their and everyone else's attention several times over, and by more than one person. Yet, still they did not see, or more to the point, *would not see!*

Today, anyone looking at a picture of the continents now can clearly see how well South America seems to fit in almost perfectly with Africa, as if two connecting pieces in a jigsaw puzzle. The same holds true for the other continents. Documentaries about geology on television, when discussing the Theory of Continental Drift, use such graphics as these all the time, and virtually without exception.[xxiv]

Nevertheless, those other geologists of Weggener's time, and before him, had strong, preconceived notions, mental filters, and strong shields against seeing just that! It wasn't that they didn't have enough available evidence. Again, it was there for anyone to see, a "preponderance of evidence," as scientists like to say. And it wasn't that they couldn't easily see the evidence. They just didn't want to, or couldn't! Their mental filters protected their particular and *then-current* world viewpoint of geology, and so heavily reinforced their perception of what they *thought* should be "real" or "right." It was easier to destroy another man's reputation, you see, rather than accept the truth.

Actually, this last ploy is a very clever way to go. If one destroys the reputation of the person who promotes a certain theory, a theory that may question or threaten your world viewpoint, you then effectively have destroyed the validity of the theory (if perhaps only temporarily). Destroy the man's reputation and you have thus destroyed the man's theory.

Does this sort of denial sound familiar to you? It should.

Today, witnesses of UFOs are often ridiculed in the same way. Television anchors usually report such items in the news with a wry twist of a smile on their lips, a smug and deprecating laugh afterwards. Often, they relate the item in their "on the lighter side" section, which says a lot right off as to what they think of the UFO subject from the outset (and more importantly, they are simultaneously giving you clues as to what "you" should think, as well). So ridicule still works, not only to dismiss evidence, but also to keep people from even daring to report it in the first place. Remember, as stated earlier, it is said the vast majority of UFO sightings still go unreported.

Now it's easy to see why, isn't it?

Why is any of this important to us here? Because these examples are powerful lessons of what can happen to one's reputation, if you dare broach an "out there" or "radical" sort of subject, such as UFOs, to your fellow academicians in any given field. We heard one archaeologist on television very recently say, for instance, that he had never discussed the theory of ancient aliens with any other archaeologists, that the subject have never even once come up! His words, not ours. And he seemed inordinately proud of this fact.

One has to ask; why is this? Why did he have such an attitude and why did he sound so proud of it? Why isn't the subject of ancient aliens, UFOs, and such, at least something one should consider if only as a minor possibility? Why shouldn't any subject be a fit subject for serious scientific investigation? Shouldn't all subjects be?

The answer, of course, is that to do so would be to face monumental criticism by his fellow archaeologists, their contempt, ridicule, and academic revulsion. That's most probably, why the subject never came up. All his future work would then be considered suspect, No university would then probably hire him, at least, not a "good" one. His reputation would be effectively at an end through such negative peer-group pressure. He/she would be just another "Weggener" of their times.

And don't kid yourself; the repercussions can be horrendous for such daring scientists, even when they have ample evidence, a "preponderance of evidence," to back their point of view, as with Charles Darwin and his theories on evolution.[xxv] The man was ostracized by many for years, put through the social ringer, had caricatures drawn of him in newspapers, pictures depicting him as an ape. He was the subject of outright and outrageous ridicule. No, to broach anything new, let alone with insufficient evidence, minimal evidence, or evidence that simply will not be believed because of academic peer group pressure, is to self-destruct your career as a scientist for sure. It is to touch that electrified "third rail" in the academic world.

Most scientists simply will not dare to do this, especially if they think there is a chance they might turn out to be wrong. So many questions in the scientific community simply aren't asked. This is often out of fear of political repercussions, religious repercussions, and/or being "politically incorrect." What's more, even if they wanted to ask such questions, they'd never find the funding to do so. Grants for research are hard to come by as it is. They don't exist for many subjects scientists might like to consider researching.

Now, mind you, our purpose here is not to attack the scientific community, geologists, or astronomers included—far from it, because we admire them immensely. I even hold a degree in science. Without scientists, we'd still be in the Dark Ages, and that's the absolute truth!

No, our point here is just to explain that we all have preconceptions, mental and emotional biases, of how we think things are "now," or how we want them to be, or think they should be, and scientists are certainly included in this, and for the reasons shown above, as well as for other reasons. Scientists, then, are no exception to all of us wanting our personal perceptions to be reality. In some cases, they may even be bigger victims of this than the average citizen. When it comes to seriously considering the phenomenon of UFOs, we think this is definitely the case.

Denial Definitely Doesn't Constitute Survival!

"I don't want to hear this!" "I telling you, I don't like hearing that!" Have you ever heard someone say these sorts of things, perhaps have even said something like this yourself? We're betting you have. And that's exactly the sort of thing we must avoid here. When examining the evidence and arriving at conclusions, we must try our best to put away our personal likes and dislikes about what we want to hear, about what we expect or think we should hear, and about how the information put forth may or may not jar with our personal belief systems, our particular world viewpoints. This we can do, if with a lot of effort.

Can we obtain perfect objectivity? No, we cannot, but we can at least listen with a relatively open mind, one that isn't full of automatic rejections of anything new and strange. Yes, those preconceptions are there, but we can try to just put them aside for the moment, say "no, I won't use them today."

So as we approach the following subjects, let us try to keep such an open mind, if only for the time it takes to read this book. Try to put aside those old perceptions of how the world is (should be?), strong as they are, as much as they try to control every aspect of how we view things. We must restrain those acquired mental filters through which we all view our world, or at the very least, try to hold them in some kind of check and abeyance.

Let's endeavor to look at the "evidence" presented here, as if we were seeing it for the very first time, could relate it to nothing prior in our backgrounds, and so possibly have to formulate new and fresh explanations for it. Moreover, before we dismiss something as "utter nonsense," let's actually think about it a little first.

Please remember, we're not asking anyone to put aside his or her reasoning powers. On the contrary, we think a person should maintain a strong and healthy skepticism. In fact, such an attitude would be very helpful in approaching these topics. But if one can view the following subjects with a reasonably open approach, then perhaps a new world may open for those who do. It may not always seem a pleasant new world, one tailored to our personal tastes or liking, but we can guarantee it will be a world filled with new possibilities and much else.

At the very least, not being in automatic denial just might help with our long-term survival, because that may be just what's at stake here. Denial doesn't constitute survival. However, the reverse may well be true. To face "reality" is at least to know where one really stands. Only then can one actually attempt to do something about the situation. But pretending something isn't a problem in the first place just doesn't help.

CHAPTER 7

Ancient Aliens—Starting At The Beginning—

The Evidence

As with UFOs, we think the evidence for the fact of their existence is already abundant. But is it enough? Well, with regard to this, scientists are always falling back on that tired old saw, "for extraordinary claims, you have to provide extraordinary evidence."

"Extraordinary Claims Require Extraordinary Evidence"[xxvi]

Great words! They sound very good. Of course, in reality, the whole concept of what is considered an "extraordinary claim" and what isn't seems to be solely determined by scientists themselves, is highly subjective, and even the concept of what the statement says changes from time to time, and from generation to generation, and subject to subject.

Scientists alone, it seems, get to choose the topics that are to be considered as requiring "extraordinary evidence." They alone then get to set how high the hurdle for this evidence must be, how "extraordinary" in nature and amount, and so how much is needed to meet their requirements for a definition of "extraordinary evidence" for that subject. Rather self-serving on scientists' part, isn't it? Additionally, it's just so incredibly arbitrary, as well, for they can raise the bar or lower it at will, or as we feel, at their whim.

It may be fine, for example, to claim that we might all really exist on a two-dimensional surface at the edge of the universe in a sort of "smear," as one scientist put it. It's equally okay to theorize all they want about reality as we know it being just a holographic projection of this two-dimensional "smear" of existence.[xxvii] Yes, some scientists in the mainstream really do actively promote this theory, despite having VERY little or actually no real evidence to support their contentions. This, they even freely admit themselves.

What's more, this astonishing topic has been aired on such well-respected television shows as **Through The Wormhole,**[xxviii] and discussed there by a respected scientist, as well. This strange theory is also covered in such a well-recognized and respected magazine as ***New Scientist.*** And what do they base this "extraordinary" theory on, what "extraordinary evidence" do they provide for us; use to support their outlandish claims and contentions when discussing this theory in such a broadcast, in print, or on the Internet?

Well, to simplify, apparently the sum total of the evidence for this extraordinary theory is that our universe has a certain quality of pixilation or "graininess" about it, if one looks at things on the very small scale. In other words, everything is made up of particles, which in turn might be made up of "strings."[xxix]

This "might" mean (and we say, "might," and that's a very big "might") that this is some very <u>small</u> evidence for the validity of this theory, since according to them, a two-dimensional existence simply couldn't contain enough data to successfully (perfectly) create a three-dimensional universe, such as we live in. There would have to be some "graininess" to the image on the very small scale. Right!

Truly, this is an extraordinary claim by respected scientists, and certainly seriously discussed and pursued/researched by them, and without any real or "extraordinary" evidence to support it, just some small evidence of supposed "graininess," which even they freely admit might mean anything at all. Hmm…and now, many physicists say this isn't so. Whether it is, or isn't, isn't the point here. The point is it was discussed "seriously" in many legitimate venues.

Get it? Again, it seems perfectly okay to discuss a theory of this particular nature, even pursue and research it with almost no evidence at all, in various academic circles, on television shows, and in respected scientific journals and among researchers at various universities. But let someone mention "ancient aliens," for instance, and they won't even dream of broaching the subject, let alone discussing it, or researching it, because of their excuse that "extraordinary claims require extraordinary evidence."

Odd, that the even more incredible claim of us all living in a holographic projection doesn't require such "extraordinary evidence" in order at least to be discussed, to be promoted, to be delved into at length, or to be studied seriously, and in multiple media formats and academic circles. Very odd, isn't it?

Whereas, we do have an abundance of information and evidence for possible visitations and/or interference by aliens in the ancient past that comes to us in the form of incredibly similar legends and creation myths from cultures all around the world. For example:

Creation Myths

Whether referred to as "Sky Gods," "Star People," "Sky Guardians," "Visitors from the Stars," or whatever, these creation legends span the globe from Egypt to the Americas, from Asia to Australia. For instance, here's just a short list:

1. The Ancient Egyptians. They claim in some of their writings that the "Guardians of the Sky" taught them how to build their pyramids and other such structures. A direct quote says:

"and then Saurid and his people built the great pyramid with the assistance of the Guardians of the Sky..." [xxx]

The Egyptians even believed some ancient race of demigod pharaohs once ruled them, as descendants of, or actual people from the sky. This ruling class was supposed to have overly large and elongated heads. And this constant deference to elongated heads can bee seen in past cultures around the globe, from South America to Asia. Ancient Egyptians also believed and said in some of their writings that a type of "magic" was used to help float the large blocks of stone used for building the pyramids. Is this "magic" as in "science?"

2. The Hopi.[xxxi] The Hopi believe at the end of this cycle of time, that the "star people" and "star knowledge" will return. An interesting and intriguing side note to this is the Hopi end time prophecies also mention that one of the final signs of the end of the world coming is the appearance of a "spider web" that encircles the globe. Could this be referring to the World Wide Web?

3. Ancient Sumerians. Anunnaki[xxxii] "sky gods" or "sky guardians" supposedly created and then ruled humanity. Priests at the time were literally and physically the "servants" of the gods, in that they maintained their households and served as laborers for them. Since they were "picked" for this task of personally serving the gods, the priests were considered special, being above that of those humans who did agriculture, mining, etc. And to this day, don't priests still claim to "serve God?" A remarkable parallel or comparison to this system, and one of much more recent times, can be found in the United States. Prior to the Civil War, in the Old South, those slaves who worked directly inside the household of the plantation owner were often considered generally to have higher status than those slaves who worked the grounds of the plantation as common "field" hands.

4. The Sirius Mystery of the Dogon.[xxxiii] *The Sirius Mystery,* a book by Robert K. G. Temple states the hypothesis that the Dogon people of West Africa have an old myth of contact with intelligent extraterrestrial beings from the Sirius star-system. The "mystery" part of this is the Dogon had somehow gained knowledge of Sirius B, an invisible-to-the-naked-eye companion star of Sirius A, which modern science didn't discover until much more recently. Some modern researchers try to discount this idea, saying the scientists themselves influenced the Dogon accidentally in this matter. The scientists involved contested this claim, and rightly so. Again, when one doesn't like the results of the data, it is often easier to attack how the data was arrived at, or the persons doing it, rather than give the results any real credence.

5. Intelligent Life in the Universe.[xxxiv] In 1966, astrophysicists I.S. Shklovski and Carl Sagan gave an entire chapter over to arguing that scientists, as well as historians, should take very seriously the idea that some form of alien contact happened in our past. Again, the argument for this point of view included "the" famous Carl Sagan, no less, who was a scientist of internationally high repute, and the host for the **Cosmos** series on PBS television.

6. Ramayana and Mahabharata Texts.[xxxv] These ancient Hindu texts of India speak of gods who had immense powers, could fly about the earth, to the Moon, and through deep space in things called Vimanas, otherwise known as flying cars, although these craft apparently differed greatly in size and use. These vehicles are constantly spoken of in the Ramayana texts, ones supposedly compiled around the 5th to 4th century BCE. But they refer to a much earlier time in Indian history.

The Mahabharata describes a great war in the skies over India and in space, a war in which something very like nuclear devices are used. In fact, the description of this weapon and its results are so close to modern nuclear weapons, as to be uncanny!

Not only do the texts describe radiation sickness symptoms incredibly accurately, but in other passages, the texts talk about elephants set ablaze along with soldiers by the thousands, who then ran around maddened with pain. It speaks of soldiers of the army having to wash themselves, and everything else, all their equipment, less they sicken and die from an invisible poison upon them (radioactive fallout?)

According to those same texts, the city of Mohenjo-Daro was apparently attacked with one of these weapons, and archaeologists have noted a higher than normal background radiation in some skeletons from there, and have discovered what appears to be vitrified pottery. Vitrification is the process of turning something to glass. To turn clay pottery to glass requires an intense heat, heat not found in normal fires, such as the type that burn buildings, etc. Here's is an extract from those verses, just as an example:

"…A single projectile charged with all the power of the Universe.

An incandescent column of smoke and flame

As bright as the thousand suns rose in all its splendor...

An iron thunderbolt, a gigantic messenger of death,

Which reduced to ashes the entire race of the Vrishnis and the Andhakas.

The corpses were so burned as to be unrecognizable.

The hair and nails fell out;

Pottery broke without apparent cause, and the birds turned white.

After a few hours all foodstuffs were infected...

To escape from this fire the soldiers threw themselves in streams

To wash themselves and their equipment..."

— From ***The Mahabharata***

These writings, along with various forms of literature of some other countries aren't considered by those people to be myths at all, but rather are considered their actual history, such as with the Hindus, and their Ramayana and Mahabharata epic texts of ancient India. It is only we westerners, with our smugly superior attitudes, that have designated them as "mere legends," and "superstitious" or "religious myths."

Meanwhile, we are often just as smugly and absolutely certain our bible is the literal word of God, aren't we? This almost racist attitude of western beliefs being always superior and so more true, versus those of other non-western cultures as being just tales, legends, myths, and superstitions, is not a good thing, we feel. Such a viewpoint tends to make us automatically discount everything of other cultures in this regard as just rank superstition. In fact, some of it actually may be real and so true, perhaps more than we realize! Again, there is that old problem of preconceived notions and biases again!

And yet, the above texts refer not only to what most certainly seems an incredibly accurate description of a nuclear war (and radiation sickness afterwards), but also speaks of "heavenly" battles in the form of multiple attacks in the skies and in space, the types of air ships, those "vimanas" or "astras," as they are referred to in the verses. The texts even include pages upon pages of how these machines were built, descriptions of different types of them, and even name those various types. They speak of how pilots were to operate them, what to do to avoid midair collisions, and the texts even go on to theorize in minute detail and depth as to how the things could function and how they were designed. Quite an in-depth series of mere "superstitious myths," aren't they? But we'll discuss those more a little later on.

7. The Book of Genesis.[xxxvi] In chapter 6, verses 1 through 4, it says:

"When human beings began to increase in number on the earth and daughters were born to them, the sons of God saw that the daughters of humans were beautiful, and they married any of them they chose....The Nephilim were on the earth in those days—and also afterward—when the sons of God went to the daughters of humans and had children by them. — **Genesis 6:1—4 (New International Version)**

8. Book of Enoch.[xxxvii] The first part of the apocryphal Book of Enoch expands and interprets Genesis 6:1. It explains that the "sons of God" were "Watchers." Against God's wishes, these Watchers descended to Earth to interbreed with humans. Their offspring are the Nephilim, "giants" who "consumed all the acquisitions of men."

The Book of Enoch also says the Watchers taught humankind such things as metallurgy, metalworking, sorcery, astrology, astronomy, and meteorology.

Is there more of this sort of thing? Absolutely! Information of this sort, pertaining to creation myths concerning beings from the sky, stars, etc., comes to us in "extraordinary" amounts from all over the world and a huge variety of cultures. You can find shelves full of books on the subject in just about any bookstore, through Amazon.com, all over the Internet, or elsewhere.

But it doesn't end here. We have actual physical items as evidence. Strange artifacts supporting the theory of ancient aliens, produced as "evidence" come from all over the world. Objects are found in Egypt, South America, Europe, North America, Asia, whether in the form of petroglyphs, cave paintings, or even actual physical objects, and/or other strange discoveries. For a quick overview, this list gives an idea of the diversity and strangeness of some of these discoveries:

1. "**A Mysterious Vase**."[xxxviii] This vase, according to a June 1851, *Scientific American* (a most prestigious science journal then and now) article reprinted from a report from the Boston Transcript speaks of a metallic vase found in two pieces, in a section of dynamited rock from fifteen feet below the earth's surface in Dorchester, Massachusetts.

> "The bell-shaped vase…measuring 4-1/2 inches high and 6-1/2 inches at the base, was composed of a zinc and silver alloy. On the sides were figures of flowers in bouquet arrangements, inlaid with pure silver. The estimated age of the rock out of which it came: 100,000 years." [xxxix]

2. Iron mine discovered in Ngwenya, Africa in 1967.[xl] This mine had tunnels and showed strong evidence of having been mined at some time, and to a great extent. The date of this mining, according to Drs. Dart and Beaumont, is from around 40,000 B.C.E. The discoverers believe that in the neighborhood of 100,000 tons of ore may have been mined. This places the mining operations deep in the Stone Age, when humanity purportedly had no mining tools at all, used only simple stone implements, and used no metals, so why would they mine it? How did they mine it without metal implements? Humanity, according to modern archaeologists, wouldn't have mining tools for thousands of years later, or any use for the metal they mined, it still being the "Stone Age," with all such a name implies.

3. Utah Coal Mine, Wattis.[xli] In the early 1950s, while digging for coal, miners broke into a series of much older tunnels. So weathered was the exposed coal in these tunnels, it couldn't be used for burning. Drs. Wilson and Jennings, upon investigation, found large chambers where the coal was apparently gathered together, before then being taken up to the surface. One tunnel ran for over 8,500 feet, well over a mile, and the two of them never finished exploring its full length! No Native Americans used coal at the time the tunnels must have been dug, this having been done so long ago (the weathering of the exposed coal in the mines was one indication of the tunnels' extreme age). Nor did the Native Americans have the wherewithal to extract and mine for coal at that time.

So who was digging all this, for just what reason, and just how long ago? Again, judging by the extreme weathering of the exposed coal in the tunnels, it had to have been a very long time ago![xlii]

4. Doomsday And The Mayan Calendar.[xliii] Most of us have heard about this one. The Mayans were a Mesoamerican culture and a very notable people for many reasons. Their city-state civilization began around 2000 B.C.E. They were builders of pyramids, observatories, sprawling cities in the jungle, and much else. They also refined their calendar to an incredibly accurate degree. How accurate? Well, it is said to be about 1/10,000th of a second <u>more</u> accurate than our calendar in use today!

Now, this is even more surprising, because despite their many achievements, the Mayans hadn't even invented the wheel. Yet, they developed a calendar that slightly surpasses even our own for accuracy. So accuracy in their dating system is not at question here. The Mayan calendar works and works well! How did they manage this? Also, they predicted to the year when the white man would arrive, and even the detail of them having horses![xliv] Worse, they also predicted the end of the world, as we know it, would come in December of 2012. However, if one discounts such prophecies as being reliable (and we're not sure of that!), then who told them about the white man coming? Was it just an incredibly lucky guess? And how did they know these interlopers would have horses? Why do their myths and legends speak of otherworldly beings, ones who will return? Well, that remains a mystery, although there are many theories. The incontrovertible fact remains that the Mayans had a calendar equal or even superior to our own, made some astonishingly accurate prophecies, and spoke often of beings not of this world, one of which promised to come back.

5. Petroglyphs in Australia.[xlv] Drawings and paintings on stone in Australia bear an eerie resemblance to modern drawings of aliens, and resemble closely such paintings found in the Americas and Europe, as well as Asia.

6. Piri Reis and other maps. [xlvi] This map, a compilation (apparently) of earlier maps, includes some incredible features. Drawn from the collection by Piri Reis, a well-known admiral of the Turkish fleet of the times, the map has been the subject of consternation and conjecture practically ever since. The surviving portion shows the western coast of Africa, and the eastern coast of South America.

Originally thought to be less accurate than current maps, this idea was dramatically revised when M.I. Walters of the U.S. Navy Hydrographic Bureau realized the map was using the projection method and that this accounted for apparent distortions and "supposed" errors in it. He transposed the Piri Reis map onto a globe. The map was completely correct, in proportion and very precise. He also stated that such accuracy could only be the result of aerial surveying, but based on the fact the map showed an ice-free coastline of Antarctica, which supposedly hasn't been this way for 6,000 years, just who created these portions of the map is still a profound mystery.

Mountains now hidden under a mile-thick layer of ice clearly show up on the Piri Reis Map, as well as inland features of South America, such as rivers, mountain ranges, etc., that simply hadn't been explored or mapped at that early date, according to our current historians.

Moreover, the Piri Reis Map is not the only such map of this type and mystery. There are more! The Portolan Maps, seemingly sprung full-blown without any predecessors (to show their evolving process of accuracy), and so just sort of "appeared." They were far beyond other maps in depicting the Mediterranean Region, to the point of looking as if they had used a "satellite" to create them. Again, no other maps of that time and area were nearly as accurate as the Portolan Maps.

7. The Baghdad Battery.[xlvii] A name used for a number of pottery jars that appeared designed for one purpose only: to act as batteries. Repeated tests showed they could easily have been used for electroplating and/or electro-stimulus. That they date back 2,000 years or more, almost two millennia before the discovery of electricity by the West, and the use of it, is a great puzzle.[xlviii] Who was electroplating or using those batteries so long ago, and why? Electroplating is simply the most likely explanation, but since no electroplated jewelry or metal objects have ever been discovered from this time period that, too, is a strange puzzle. And how would such a primitive civilization learn how to build a battery, and then figure out such a use for it?

8. Star Child Skull.[xlix] The Star Child skull was found in Mexico. It is believed to be about 900 years old and is an odd-shaped skull. Again, much controversy rages around this object. However, that it was found and has been dated to about 900 years ago is a fact. It is also a fact the skull has an oversized cranium. DNA studies of the skull have provoked even more controversy. The findings, according to some who have reported on this, show the skull is only half-human. Half the DNA seems to be from an unknown source. If this is true, then the child was a hybrid. It also means something very strange concerning aliens was going on over 900 years ago.

Furthermore, for those who think the skull just might be the symptom of encephalitis that particular idea has definitely already been ruled out. There seems to be no natural cause for the shape of the skull according to known science. Just what does this mean? Well, for many, it means aliens have been interfering in the development of the human race.

9. Boskop People.[l] This is a strange story of a strange people. Shortly after the turn of the last century, bones were dug up in South Africa. These included some over-sized skulls. Moreover, the skulls showed these people had small, child-like faces. They also apparently had very large brains. To this day, they are a controversial subject to the scientific field. However, despite all the arguments, one thing is certain. Skeletons were found. That they show people with a large cranium and small faces is also true. And since a number of such skeletons were found, they came to be known as the Boskop People, Boskop being a small town located nearby the discovery.

Now does this description of these people sound at all familiar to you? Of course, it does. This depiction is similar to those of thousands of witnesses who describe aliens in various UFO encounters. But these are now an extinct people, the Boskop. And they have been for many millennia.

So, just who were they? Were they members of the human race? Were they another type of hominid? Or perhaps, were they members of an alien colony? This last seems unlikely. Since no implements that we would consider advanced tools were found with them, we must assume they were another human people, but a people with overly large craniums and child-like faces.

The very fact that such a people even existed so very long ago, ones that had such large brains, brains that many scientists think might even be bigger than our own, and therefore they were a more intelligent people, is a weird thing indeed. Just who were they? Why did they have such large brains? Why did they then die out? The answers to these questions are yet unknown.

10. Various and sundry objects found embedded in rock and coal.[li] Added to all the above, so-called "anomalies," are numerous, and we mean numerous, objects found the world over embedded *inside* of rocks and coal, often ones dug up from deep in mines, buried far down in ancient strata, or while laborers dug ditches, dug foundations for roads, houses, etc. The finds are impressive and date back incredibly far in many cases! For instance, in the nineteenth century alone, numerous objects were discovered embedded in solid coal, such as nails of all sorts, a strange gold necklace, an iron "pot" of sorts, and many other things.

All these were usually described as being of "quaint," "exotic," or "antique" design in the published accounts of the finds in those times. One woman even found a ceramic sort of "ladle" embedded inside a large chunk of coal. Again, there are many more accounts of these items being discovered where they have no right to be, locked in solid rock and coal that was laid down as strata millions of years ago. Other reports tell of objects, such as an obviously machined cube of metal found in an ancient layer. How did these things get there? When? Why? Who put them there?

When you have this many "anomalies," they simply aren't anomalous anymore. The main definitions of "anomaly," according to the Free Dictionary by Farlex, are:

> ***1.*** *Deviation or departure from the normal or common order, form, or rule.*
>
> ***2.*** *One that is peculiar, irregular, abnormal, or difficult to classify: "Both men are anomalies: they have . . . likable personalities but each has made his reputation as a heavy" (David Pauly).*[lii]

So when people are finding this stuff all over, and in such quantities, it can hardly then be considered "abnormal" any longer, but rather very normal! And isn't that just a little more "evidence" (*incredibly more in our estimation*) than the pittance of evidence offered in the idea by some physicists that our reality seems a little "grainy" on the super-small scale, and so may be "possible evidence" for the fact we live in a holographic projection of the universe? Their "evidence" is simply a matter of minor conjecture, while the evidence cited above can be found in museums, can be handled, inspected, and analyzed!

Again, this double standard, this almost hypocritical requirement for yet endlessly more evidence to be produced for the idea of ancient alien visitations in order to allow it even to be discussed, versus almost no evidence at all for the holographic projection theory of our entire universe just astounds us.

CHAPTER 8

"Extraordinary Evidence"

A Truly Arbitrary And Subjective Thing?

Why isn't extraordinary evidence necessary, required to discuss the above-mentioned theory of our universe being a holographic projection, but is required to discuss anything to do with UFOs? Why is there so arbitrary a delineation between the two subjects? Why is the concept of other intelligent life forms visiting us in the distant past somehow far more outlandish, more "extraordinary" by far than that of our whole universe being just a holographic projection of a two-dimensional "smear" on the edges of the universe?

Of course, the answer is simple enough as to why this double standard exists. It exists because scientists have seen so many people ridiculed for their ideas and beliefs about UFOs that they don't want to touch the subject in any way, unless they can prove it beyond the shadow of a doubt.

Even so, scientists feel perfectly free to wander without restraint into the field of ultimate existentialism, ponder the very nature of reality, that which makes up our universe, etc., and with almost no evidence at all, or only the most tiny, flimsiest, and improbable sorts of evidence to back their lofty points of view. Even so, talk away about those subjects, they will!

What's the upshot of all this? Well, some subjects in science, such as that of ancient aliens, are just taboo no matter what, are considered career wreckers, and so those are ones that are arbitrarily assigned the hurdle of needing "extraordinary evidence" to prove them, while other subjects, even more incredibly outlandish ones, are not. Again, there's that double standard. For us then, this double standard borders on sheer hypocrisy, and the argument that extraordinary evidence is needed for anything related to UFOs, but not other "outlandish" suppositions, borders on the manifestly insincere!

Alternatively, the explanation could be that this is just so against many scientists' ingrained and present world viewpoints, that they just may not want it to be true. Such ideas may just go too strongly against everything they've always been taught, felt they are sure of knowing, so they just can't seriously accept them.

And sadly, again, it's those very same scientists who have the power to arbitrarily declare certain things need "extraordinary evidence," while not other things. And some of those theories, in our opinion, are far more extraordinary in their claims than just entertaining the mere idea of other beings having once visited Earth!

Really, this ability for scientists to choose what they want or don't want to discuss, or even to consider seriously in any way, borders on the arbitrarily random. Random—almost, but not quite, because the real reason is those scientists are, perhaps, "afraid" to touch certain subjects; afraid it will mean the end of their world viewpoints, fearful it could turn their worlds upside down and/or destroy their personal careers and make them laughingstocks, objects of ridicule in the academic world. That's the probable truth in its simplest form, in our opinion.

Need a quick and incredible example? Well, at a convention we attended one year, one scientist on the panel actually admitted to falsifying a UFO photo he had sent to a famous radio host whose program deals particularly with this sort of subject. The host, because the photo had come from a "scientist," accepted it as "real evidence," apparently.

When asked by us why a scientist would "intentionally muddy the waters" like that, his response was something to the effect that he had just "wanted to prove that photographs of such things could be faked." Mind you, we had a good-sized group listening to our panel, and they all heard his words to this effect, from him, the horse's mouth as it were, so it isn't just us saying this for the heck of it.

But that was his sole reason, just to prove photos could be faked? Really? Really? Come on!

Do none of us have Photoshop or similar programs on our computers with which to alter such pictures or any pictures, and any time we feel like it? It's incredibly easy to do, as we all know. The "scientist" somehow didn't know such programs existed, were ubiquitous, were on almost every computer sold nowadays, and had been available to just about everyone for years? He thought he had to, at such a late date in proceedings, try to prove that photos could be faked? Really? And just what program did he use? We're betting it was something very similar in style to Photoshop. Hmm…

What utter and absolute hogwash his excuse was for us! In our opinion, this was the weakest excuse for falsifying data we've ever heard! If any reputable scientist were to do this at his job and was subsequently discovered doing this sort of thing, he or she would be summarily dismissed and rightly so! Nobody, especially scientists, should ever falsify data for any reason under any circumstances whatsoever, if only because it discredits them and their fields of study. Scientists should never participate in hoaxes, ever!

Later admitting to such a hoax, and such a feeble explanation, notwithstanding for it, doesn't make what he did any less damaging! We can't help wondering if he'd like it if someone else falsified data results on some experiment, and he then spent several pointless years as a scientist trying to corroborate such phony results. We can't help but feel he wouldn't be very happy about such an outcome.

To say we were astounded, staggered that any so-called "scientist" would ever do such a thing as to "fake" something is to put it mildly! But you see, it was to do with the subject of UFOs, and so apparently he felt safe enough in doing this, probably felt there would be no real repercussions. After all, it's only UFOs, and it's safe enough to ridicule anyone who might be involved with those…right? However, if he ever did this with his own work, we're betting his colleagues wouldn't be very thrilled! I'm betting he'd soon be out of a job. So this sort of thing, then, is a major form of hypocrisy in our personal opinions.

But this is what bona fide researchers in the field of UFOs have to deal with, to put up with, all the time, just this sort of obtuse mentality, this thinking it's "okay" to do this pathetic sort of thing, because it's only UFOs we're talking about here. This type of behavior often results from those who have a certain mindset, or a superior attitude, an arrogance, and who think they are above the rest and that they alone determine that which should be taken seriously and that which shouldn't be. One has to ask; who made them the arbiters of which fields of study should be given credence and which shouldn't? Who set them up as all-knowing in this regard?

To say this shows little or no respect on his part for those of us who are seriously trying to do our best to determine if ancient aliens or UFOs exist or ever existed, is to say the least. Yes, such behavior infuriates us, because it appears to be open marks of contempt such people seem to have for others, many who are honestly trying to determine the truth of things. They automatically expect respect for themselves as "scientists," because as he put it at the convention, just because "I'm a scientist," but so should they also give that same respect to those honestly trying to find answers on the various topics of UFOs. To say we found this attitude offensive to us, was to say the very least!

And it isn't just the one "extraordinary" theory about holographic projection of our universe that is acceptable to researchers as a legitimate theory to discuss, while the idea of ancient alien visitations is not. There are so many! Superstring Theory,[liii] for instance, now considered the best candidate for allowing for us to finally have a Theory of Everything, as they call it, of all the known forces in the universe, has (according to scientists themselves) not a shred of "real evidence" to support it. "They" say this, themselves! Yet it, too, is discussed seriously and endlessly, even though it involves multiple dimensions, possibly (and even likely), many parallel universes into the bargain.

Physicists have discussed and delved into Superstring Theory, and still do, in every major scientific magazine that covers such subjects. String Theory is spoken of endlessly at times it seems, by various types of physicists around the world, on television and off, in journals, and in research papers. The theory is widely heralded by many quantum physicists as the "probable solution" to the whole question of a Theory of Everything.

Yet, there is no real "evidence" at all given by those same scientists' own admission, to back up this theory. Where is the "extraordinary evidence to justify such an extraordinary claim" here? Moreover, many scientists say it may NEVER be possible to produce any such evidence. Even so, they do go on and on about the subject, don't they? It's hard to watch a science program on physics on television without someone mentioning the subject, at least in passing.

In addition, it is truly an extraordinary claim, is it not, that our universe may be composed of vibrating strings, rather than particles, and require multiple dimensions and perhaps even parallel universes in order to work? However, it doesn't seem to need "extraordinary evidence" to be allowed for as a common topic of serious discussion, or to be taken seriously by scientists around the world as something to research. Again, just why is that? Why doesn't such an extraordinary theory require extraordinary evidence to support it, too?

The answer is obvious…again. The community of scientists has decided this is an "acceptable" topic for serious discussion. So it simply doesn't require much evidence to do this, if any at all, apparently, to be so discussed.

Meanwhile, to discuss the concept of ancient aliens or UFOs is anathema to them, is too dangerous a subject by far to the careers of academicians to dare entertain. Few people want to live life on the third rail, it seems, and scientists, just like the rest of us, are just as afraid of such a fatal "career electrocution" as one put it.

So how do they get around this? Well, again, they do it by arbitrarily demanding extraordinary evidence, using this as a major hurdle before they'll even begin to entertain the idea of discussing it seriously. What's more, they don't accept evidence of testimonies, even by professionals trained to observe, and this despite such "expert testimony" always being sought after in court trials, and used all the time in such a way! In other words, if scientists don't wish to deal with an issue, they can and often do, start by their first demand for "extraordinary evidence," and then discount such evidence as invalid when it is supplied. A real "Catch 22" there, I'd say, a real lose-lose situation for any UFO researcher.

So that's it in a nutshell. They just don't want to touch the subject of UFOs or ancient aliens in any way. Anything to do with UFOs in any shape, or form, is strictly taboo! We also suspect there is an element of snobbery involved here, too. Being so well educated, so well trained, isn't it just a little too easy to look down on the "masses" as being subject to such "silly" beliefs and "ridiculous," "uneducated" notions? Isn't it just a little too easy to indulge in the superiority and arrogance of living high in an ivory tower, roaming about their dreaming spires, and so easily ignore and not find credible the sworn testimony of millions of "ordinary" people, because they are just "average," less educated, and little more than a mob? We think this attitude by some scientists may just figure into this a little, as well.

The testimony of the common person is not to be compared with theirs! Don't agree? Well then, check out the weight that "expert testimony" carries in court (by a psychiatrist, medical doctor, police officer, forensic specialist) versus the testimony of just an average citizen. Often, such expert testimony carries the day. People have been sentenced to death based on such and many times!

Yet, when UFO believers produce recordings of actual astronauts, statements by astronauts, police officers on patrol,[liv] military and commercial jet pilots, and such, these are all discounted as "not hard evidence" and so not sufficient for most scientists to consider studying the UFO phenomenon. Why?

Aren't these also trained people, ones who are "experts" in their chosen fields, and so giving their "expert" testimony, too? Or is it just scientists who can give expert testimony in a court case? Again, that old double standard, that almost hypocritical viewpoint of theirs, shows itself once more!

So here is the crux of the matter: just what is our conclusion to all this? Well, scientists seem to arbitrarily choose (as they wish to and for whatever reasons they might have, personal, professional, or otherwise), what subjects require "extraordinary evidence," and which ones don't.

More to the point, they can then choose to disregard such evidence when it is supplied, for whatever reasons they choose, by simply declaring it invalid, not "hard evidence," just a fluke, an anomaly (this last is a real catch-all phrase used often—"erroneous data—it's just an anomaly," so ignore it!), or an outright hoax.

So although we see many television shows on UFOs,[lv] ancient aliens,[lvi] and such, rest assured they are not produced by scientists and most likely will not be. More importantly, any scientists interviewed on them probably will not only be incredibly skeptical of the whole subject, but will often state that the subject isn't even one they ever discuss, as we mentioned one archaeologist saying earlier on.

Oh well! At least, now we know why. It seems for a variety of reasons, they simply don't wish to go near these topics, and one of the main reasons is fear—fear of ridicule and the ruin of their careers. So it would seem one can't blame them for wanting to stay away from these subjects. Although, we personally don't think anyone should ever be moral cowards in any way when claiming to be in pursuit of the truth.

CHAPTER 9

Born Under An Evil Moon

A thing of darkness, a home of evil, and is it very nearby? We're afraid it's closer than we might want to think or imagine. Are we, from the time we're all born, and then through a lifetime of toil and until the day we die, watched over by an evil, inimical, and implacable presence from a place so close as to be seen by us unsuspecting people all the time, and yet so far away that it still remains almost unreachable? Is there someone, or some "thing," looking down upon us at this very minute? When we gaze up at the night sky, are we seeing the home or base of the "enemy" and not even aware of this fact?

We're often told by some UFO believers to "watch the skies," but has it ever occurred to us that we, in turn, are being closely watched, and even more intimately so than we ever thought, possible? Is there some permanent base in our sky nearby?

I'm talking of the Moon,[lvii] of course, our nominal companion of the night (although it's a daytime companion, too, in reality). Its average distance is just 238,857 miles, just about a quarter million miles from us. This puts it just far enough away to make it difficult and very expensive to get to on any sort of a regular basis, especially to land on, and then from which to return. In fact, it's been so difficult and expensive; we haven't had a manned landing on the Moon in just about 40 years now![lviii]

However, it's still close enough where we can view its surface fairly well, even without the aid of a telescope, just with the naked eye. And we have done so for centuries. So we think we know the surface of the Moon very well.

But have you ever considered something might just be lurking there, hiding, and staring back at us, too, and that "something" may have been doing so for ages? And it might just be with possibly evil intentions toward us?

Yes, we know, it sounds like the stuff of pure science fiction. Doesn't it? But there is considerable evidence "something" just may be there. It may have been there for a very long time.[lix] Just how long exactly? Nobody can be sure, but it might have been for centuries, and possibly even millennia…or more.

Sound ridiculous? Perhaps it even rings strongly of paranoia to you? Besides, who has any real evidence of such a crazy thing, anyway? Well, the answer to that last question might just surprise you! Because, believe it or not, there is a lot of evidence that points to this from a number of different sources. However, much of the evidence for this proposition is compiled into just one document and that document is one of NASA's own. I'm referring to **NASA Technical Report R-277, "Chronological Catalog of Reported Lunar Events**."

This report, a product of a direct request by NASA itself, came out in July 1968, and is a detailed compilation of some 450 years of sightings of strange events on the Moon's surface. Moreover, if you think the document is the result of just "a few" observers, then think again. Three-hundred-plus observers are included in the report, all citing strange events on the Moon. Again, these reported events have taken place over the last 450 years and many of the observers were the top astronomers of their day!

Do such observations actually go back even further in time? Yes, but the creators of **Technical Report R-277** decided 450 years was sufficient. This was for a variety of reasons, one of which, undoubtedly, was the telescope came into general use during the early 1600s, so observers tended to give reliable reports on the various phenomena from that point on, and just because of the telescope's introduction.

Now let us repeat here, this **Technical Report R-277** is a report commissioned by NASA, for NASA's benefit, and includes bona fide observations of some very famous and highly respected astronomers throughout history.

These are not to be considered in any way to be sightings by modern-day UFO buffs, rank amateurs, anyone with a special "axe to grind," or anything of the sort. So, as the term "reputable" is defined, nobody could possibly find fault with most of these observers.

Now, we can't include the entire report here. It's just too lengthy, having a whopping 579 entries in it, but the entire report does form an appendix at the end of this book.

However, we include some of the entries here for very specific reasons. First, they give a comprehensive idea of just what's been sighted on the Moon over the centuries. This sample includes a good representation not only of types of sightings, how often they occurred, when they occurred, but also where on the Moon they tended to occur. This last is very important, perhaps even crucial! We will explain this later.

Nevertheless, since today's scientists demand "extra-ordinary evidence," for extraordinary claims, we include these representational entries to satisfy such demands. The sheer number (and remember these constitute only a small portion of 579 such entries total), made by reputable, some even famous scientists, and over centuries, should satisfy anybody's need for not only "extraordinary evidence, but such evidence in abundance!

We did include certain sightings simply because they occurred so frequently, over such a long duration, and in the same areas so often that we considered them of special interest. We will discuss this last curiosity in more depth later on, as well.

Furthermore, do also remember that many or most of the sightings weren't just something that lasted for a split second, and so could be misinterpreted easily by the observers. Some events went on for hours and others for days, sometimes even weeks! Some kept recurring the same way over months and even years!

Now please bear with us, as we cite some examples here. If you like, you can just quickly skim through them to get a general idea, but do pay attention to the type of event and their locations! This last is very important. And unlike the original report, we have often added explanations, comments, and/or qualifications about such sightings. We have boldfaced the actual descriptions themselves, for the readers who just prefer to skim quickly through these listings.

Example from the 1500's C.E:

1. November 26, 1540, ~05h00m, the Region of Calippus, "**Starlike appearance on dark side of the Moon.**" Observers: at Worms. Reference: Hess 1911.

Please note, by "dark side of the Moon," the observer was referring to a normally visible portion of the face of the Moon, which was temporarily in darkness, and not the far side of the Moon, which often is erroneously referred to as the "dark side of the Moon." This darkness mentioned, could be due to shadows cast by mountains, crater rims, etc. This could also be due to areas of darkness due to the Moon's different phases, or could refer at times to the terminus (the "line") between daylight and darkness on the Moon.

Since the Moon always has one face permanently toward Earth, we cannot see most of its far side, of course. We do get to see a little of it, due to the Moon's librations (a slight rocking back and forth of the Moon over time, as seen from our Earth), and this allows us to see just about 59 percent of the total lunar surface. However, both sides of the Moon do get full daylight and darkness. Still, from Earth, we just see the one. So again, there is no "dark side of the Moon," really, as Pink Floyd says...

Examples from the 1600's C.E:

2. November 26, 1668, Dark Side, "**Bright starlike point.**" Observers: several New Englanders. Reference: Josselyn 1675; Mather 1714; Lowes 1927. (Please note: again, we have a "starlike" event on the Moon. This is over 128 years after the prior event, and yet is described exactly the same way, "starlike!").

3. Three years later, November 12, 1671, Pitatus Crater, "**Small whitish cloud.**" Observer: D. Cassini. Reference: Bode 1792a; Lalande 1792 (1966). (Please note: Cassini is famous for discovering a gap in the rings of Saturn, which was then named for him, the "Cassini Gap" or "Cassini Division.")

4. Two years after the above event, October 18, 1673, Pitatus Crater "**White spot,**" Observer: D.Cassini, Reference: Bode 1792a; Lalande 1792 (1966). (Please note, again we have something "white" in the Pitatus Crater, and two years later!)

Examples from the 1700's C.E:

5. Fifty-two years after the prior event, August 16, 1725, Plato Crater, "**A track of ruddy light, like a beam, crossing the middle of the obscure (shadowed) area (crater in darkness).**" Observer: Bianchini. Reference: Hesp. Phos. Phaenom. 1728; Sirius 1887; Wilkins 1958. (Please note: the Moon, as most people are aware, is totally lacking in an atmosphere. So, "streaks," flashes, glows, etc., cannot be created by meteors streaking through air. There is no air. Without atmosphere, there is no friction, so no heating, and no glows, flashes, or flares possible from such a source until actual impact. What are they, then, these "streaks," "tracks," and "beams?")

6. Thirteen years after prior event, August 4, 1738, 16h31m, Location, N/A. "**During solar eclipse, appearance like lightning on the face of the Moon (Partial eclipse).**" **Observer:** Friend of Weidler. Reference: Phil. Trans. 1739. (Please note: again, there is no atmosphere on the Moon, so no lightning as we know it, and no weather, either.)

7. Thirteen years later, April 22, 1751, Plato Crater, "**Yellow streak of light across crater floor while crater was in darkness.**" Short, Stephens, Harris. Reference: Sirius 1887. (Another "streak!")

8. Again, thirteen years later, September 26, 1788, Near Aristarchus Crater; 30 min "**Bright spot 26" N of main crater.**" Observer: Schroter. Reference: Rozier 1788, 1792; Schroter 1791.

9. December 2, 5:35am, 1788, Aristarchus Crater, "**Extraordinarily bright, like star.**" Observer: Schroter. Reference: Schroter 1791.

10. December 11, 1788, Plato Crater, "**Bright area, like thin white cloud.**" Observer: Schroter. Reference: Schroter 1791.

11. 1788, Aristarchus Crater. "**Brilliant spots.**" Observer: Bode. Reference: Bode 1792b; Houzeau and Lancaster 1964 ed.

12. January 10, 1789, "**Lunar 'volcano.'**" Observer: Seyffer. Reference: Seyffer 1789; Houzeau and Lancaster 1964 ed. (Please note: there are no volcanoes on the Moon today, and haven't been for millions/billions of years according to today's scientists, so this was a misinterpretation of something else seen there, but what, exactly?)

13. March 29-30, 1789, Grimaldi, and near Riccioli, "**Two flickering spots on edge of Grimaldi, and near Riccioli on dark side of Moon a bright spot.**" Observer: Schroter. Reference: Schroter 1789, 1791; Houzeau and Lancaster 1964 ed.

14. March 29-31, 1789, Aristarchus Crater, "**Nebulous bright area.**" Observer: Schroter. Reference: Schroter 1791.

15. March, 1789, Near Aristarchus Crater, "**Brilliant spots near Aristarchus; luminous spots on dark side.**" Observer: Bode. Reference: Bode 1788-89, 1789, 1793; Houzeau and Lancaster 1964 ed. Notice how we see certain areas, which over decades and centuries keep showing up as having strange "anomalies" in or around them? Now let's continue:

16. Almost one year later, January 17, 1790, Aristarchus region, "**Small, hazy spot of light.**" Observer: Schroter. Reference: Schroter 1791.

17. March 19, 1790, Aristarchus region, "**Small, hazy spot of light.**" Observer: Schroter. Reference: Schroter 1791. (Please note: again, these cannot be the results of meteorite impacts, unless they glowed for months in the cold vacuum of space. If so, a crater of some sort would have resulted as well. None was seen. None is seen now. So, if not meteorite impacts, what are they?

18. March 2, 1797, Promontorium Heraclides, vicinity, **"Observations of a volcano on the Moon."** Observer: Caroché. Reference: Caroché 1799; Houzeau and Lancaster 1964 ed. (Please note: again, according to today's scientists, there are no active volcanoes on the Moon and have not been for several billion years.)

19. July 2, 1797, Mare Vaporum, "**Vapors resembling mountain."** Observer: Schroter, Olber. Reference: Klein 1879. (Please note: many observers over the centuries saw hazy-like events, also referred to as "nebulas," "mist," "dark mist," or "clouds," or in this case, "vapors." Again, there is no atmosphere on the Moon, no volcanoes, so what are these phenomena?)

Examples from the 1800's C.E:

20. Moving ahead now in time, February 5-6, 1821, Aristarchus Crater vicinity, "**Luminous appearance on dark side; 6th to 7th mag, 3' to 4' diameter."** Observer: Kater, Olbers. Reference: Browne Kater 1821; Olbers 1822, 1824; Gauss 1874; Houzeau and Lancaster 1964 ed.

21. May 4-6, 1821, Aristarchus Crater, vicinity, "**Bright spot on dark side…."** Observer: Ward, Baily. Reference: Ward 1822; Baily 1822. (Please note: Aristarchus seems to figure prominently, yet again!)

22. January 27, 1822, Aristarchus, vicinity, "**Bright spot like 8th mag star."** Observer: F.G.W. Struve. Reference: Struve 1823.

23. June 22-23, 1822, Aristarchus Crater, "**Lunar 'volcano.'"** Observer: Ruppell. Reference: Ruppell 1822.

24. 1822, **"'Volcanoes'" on the Moon; several occasions.** Observer: Zach. Reference: Zach 1822.

25. 1822, "**Lunar "'volcano.'"** Observer: Zach. Reference: Zach 1822. (Just what are these so-called "volcanoes?"?)

26. May 1, 1824, Near Aristarchus Crater, "**Blinking light, 9th to 10th mag on dark side.**" Observer: Gobel. Reference: Gobel 1826. (Please note: a "blinking light," does not sound anything like a meteor, volcano, or anything natural, for that matter.)

27. December 8, 1824, Plato Crater, "**Bright fleck in SE part of crater.**" Observer: Gruithuisen. Reference: Sirius 1879. (Please note: 1824 seems a very busy year for both Plato and the Aristarchus craters.)

28. April 8, 1825, Plato Crater, "**W part of crater brighter than E part.**" Observer: Gruithuisen Reference: Sirius 1879. (Please note: the question must be asked as to why one side of the crater is brighter than the other, and this is obviously not do to normal sunshine, or it wouldn't have been reported.)

29. April 22, 1825, Aristarchus Crater and vicinity, "**Periodic illumination.**" Observer: Argelander, Gobel. Reference: Argelander 1826, Gobel 1826. (Please note: here we have two observers who are seeing the same thing at the same time. And what can account for a "periodic illumination, naturally? Is this the same phenomenon as the "blinking light?")

30. April 12, 1826, 20h00m, Mare Crisium, "**Black moving haze or cloud.**" Observer: Emmett. Reference: Emmett 1826; Caprilon 1879.

31. Jumping ahead in time some here, December 25, 1832, Aristarchus Crater, vicinity, "**Bright spot.**" Observer: C.P. Smyth. Reference: Smyth 1836.

32. December 22, 1835, 18h30m, Near Aristarchus Crater, "**Bright spot, 9th to 10th mag.**" Observer: C.P. Smyth. Reference: Smyth 1836.

33. February 13, 1836, Messier, "**Two straight lines of light; a band between covered with luminous points.**" Observer: Gruithuisen. Reference: Sci. Amer. Supp. Vol.7. (Please note, one cannot think of any "reasonable" known natural phenomenon to account for this "two straight lines of light" with a "band between covered with luminous points.")

34. June 24, 1839, Grimaldi, **"Smoky-gray mist."** Observer: Gruithuisen. Reference: B.A.A. Mem. 1895.

35. July 19, 1839, Schroter, **"Dark mist."** Observer: Gruithuisen. Reference: B.A.A. Mem. 1895.

36. December 27, 1854, Teneriffe Mountains. (near Plato); 5 hr, **"Two luminous fiery spots on bright side." ...an appearance I had never seen before on the surface of the Moon though I have observed her often these last 40 years.... It appeared to me from the brightness of the light and the contrast of colour to be two active volcanoes or 2 mouths of one in action."** Observer: Hart. Reference: Hart 1855. (Please note: yet again, the interpretation of it being volcanoes or the mouths of them just can't be, so it had to be "something" else.)

37. June 12, 1862, 06h19m, **"During [lunar] eclipse, the E [IAU:W] side dark brick red and something seemed to oscillate before it." At the mid-eclipse on the S side, "a very small meniscus** [crescent-shaped body] **was seen nearly the color of the uneclipsed Moon**." Observer: N/A. Reference: Liais 1865. (Please note: what could account for something oscillating "before it?" Also, definition of "meniscus" added by us.)

38. June 10, 1866, Aristarchus Crater, **"Starlike light."** Observer: Tempel. Reference: Denning, Tel.Work p.121. (Please note: that "starlike light" just keeps appearing there, over the centuries, and again and again. Always it is described as a "starlike" object or "bright" point or spot.)

39. April 9, 1867, 19h30m - 21h00m, Aristarchus Craeter vicinity; 1 hr 30 min, **"Bright spot on dark side, 7th mag, becoming fainter after 20h15m UT.** Observer: Elger. Reference: Elger 1868.

40. May 6-7, 1867, Aristarchus Crater; at least several hours each night, "**Left side of crater, very bright luminous point, appearing like a volcano.**" Observer: FlamMarchion. Reference: FlamMarchion 1884. (Please note: this went on for hours both nights, but apparently not all night long. Meaning; it came and went.)

41. May 7, 1867, Aristarchus Crater, vicinity, "**Reddish-yellow, beacon-like light.**" Observer: Tempel. Reference: Tempel 1867; Astr. Reg. 1868. (Please note: the phrasing: "beacon-like light!" How would a "natural" phenomenon account for this? And this isn't the first such observance; remember the "blinking light" from prior observations?)

42. 1870, "**White spots on the Moon, "lightning.**" Observer: Birt. Reference: Birt 1870. (Please note: again, with no atmosphere, how can there be lightning?)

43. 1870, Godin, "**Purplish haze illuminating floor of crater, still in shadow** Observer: Trouvelot. Reference: Trouvelot 1882; Moore 1963

44. 1871, W of Plato, "**Fog or mist.**" Observer: Elger, Neison. Reference: FlamMarchion 1884.

45. July 16, 1872, Plato, "**NE portion of floor hazy.**" Observer: Pratt. Reference: Caprilon 1879.

46. January 4, 1873, Kant, "**Luminous purplish vapors.**" Observer: Trouvelot. Reference: Trouvelot 1882; FlamMarchion 1884; Moore 1963.

47. April 10, 1873, Plato. "**Under high sun, two faint clouds in W part of crater.**" Observer: Schmidt. Reference: Sirius 1879.

48. February 3, 1881, 19h00m, Aristarchus Crater (on dark side, limb area), "**Very bright (~8.0 mag star) with pulsations.**" Observer: "Gamma." Reference: Sirius 1881. (Please note: this recurring theme for Aristarchus, "blinking lights," "beacon-like" light, light with "pulsations," "flickering," "oscillating" lights, etc.)

49. August 6-7, 1881, Aristarchus Crater region, "**Whole region between Aristarchus and Herodotus and S part of Great Rille (Schroter's Valley) appeared in strong violet light as if covered with fog**." Observer: Klein. Reference: Klein 1902.

50. September 16, 1891, Schroter's Valley, **"Dense clouds of white vapour were apparently arising from its bottom and pouring over its SE [IAU:SW] wall in the direction of Herodotus." Observer:** W.H. Pickering. Reference: Pickering 1903.

Examples from the 1900's C.E:

51. March 1, 1903, Aristarchus Crater, "**Intermittent light "like a little star."** Observer: Rey. Reference: Rey 1903. (Please note, here we go yet again, with blinking lights, beacon-like lights, lights with pulsations, and now an "Intermittent light 'like a little star.'" Remember all those sightings of a "starlike" light, as well, from much earlier? Just what are they?)

52. March 3, 1903, Aristarchus Crater, "**Intermittent light 'like a little star.'"** Observer: Gheury. Reference: Bull. Soc. Astr. France.

53. February 19, 1905, ~19h03m, Aristarchus Crater, "**During eclipse, bright spot shining in the dark as a little star. (Lunar eclipse.)"** Observer: Moye. Reference: Moye and Russell 1905; Fisher 1924. (Please note: Aristarchus, Plato, and a number of others seem to be recurring locations for these similar types of events. One might assume that if they all took place during a lunar eclipse that it was some "trick of the lighting," an optical illusion or something of this type. However, although they do seem to take place often during lunar eclipses, yes, they also, and many other times, appear anyway, as well. Things just stand out better in complete darkness, rather than the full glare of harsh sunlight, as we all know.)

54. 1931, Aristarchus Crater, "**Bluish glare."** Observer: Goodacre, Molesworth. Reference: Goodacre 1931.

55. November 3, 1949, 01h06m, Aristarchus Crater, "**Blue glare, base inner W wall."** Observer: Bartlett. Reference:

Bartlett 1967. (Please note: different observers, at different times of years, in different decades and centuries are observing this "blue glare." What is it? Why is it different from the "starlike" light, or the "beacon-like," "blinking" "pulsations" "flickering," or "intermittent lights? More than one type of activity seems to be going on here. Are they somehow related?)

56. July 31, 1950, 04h50m, Aristarchus Crater, "**Violet glare, E, NE rim.**" Observer: Bartlett. Reference: Bartlett 1967.

57. May 11, 1954, 20h00m, Eratosthenes "**Central mountain group invisible, though surrounding details very clear.**" Observer: Cattermole. Reference: Contrib. by Moore. (Please note: something was obscuring the central mountain group to the point that it made the mountains "invisible," and yet everything around that area was visible. How can this be? Again, no atmosphere or volcanoes, so no clouds, mists, fogs, or haze should normally ever appear on the Moon, right?)

58. November 12, 1954, 02h42m, Aristarchus Crater, "**Blue-violet glare; E wall bright spot and whole length of E wall. Suspected violet tint in N and NE of crater; Certainly on plateau. Greatly faded by 05h07m.**" Observer: Bartlett. Reference: Bartlett 1967. (Please note: although Aristarchus has numerous events of starlike objects, etc., and "blue glare," the events really seem to take off during all of 1954. Sighting after sighting of blue or violet glares are noted by trained astronomers.)

59. September 7, 1955, 04h52m, Aristarchus Crater, "**Strong blue-violet glare; E, NE rim; also E base of central peak. Dark violet, nimbus.**" Observer: Bartlett. Reference: Bartlett 1967.

60. And the decades and centuries roll by, and still observers see the same thing, as here: August 4, 1965, Aristarchus Crater; ~2 min, "**Starlike image, 6th to 7th mag.**" Observer: Bornhurst. Reference: Cameron 1965.

61. September 11, 1967, 00h32m, Mare Tranquilitaties; 8-9 sec., "**Black cloud surrounded by violet color.**" Observer:

Montreal group. Reference: B.A.A. Lunar Sec. Circ. 1967, 2, No. 12.

End of NASA Report Samples

This brings us to the end of our representative sample of sightings on the Moon. Again, the appendix at the end of this book contains the entire and much lengthier report. And yes, we know there were a lot of entries here. However, when you consider they represent only a small fraction of the 579 in the report, then the number of cases cited here isn't really over the top.

In any case, we quite deliberately wanted to show the sheer volume of such reports, how they all were startlingly similar in their descriptions. We also wanted to show how often certain areas of the Moon, such as the Aristarchus Crater, and Plato, seem to figure prominently in so many of these reports. We wanted to impress on you the reader, just how clearly there is "an abundance of evidence" for these events. Also, we wished to show there is a "preponderance of evidence" for something occurring on the Moon that isn't "usual" or "normal" by any means.

At first glance, it may seem like many very different types of events are occurring, and there definitely is variation, but in reality, they are not as different as one might think. The events can be narrowed down to being bright "streaks," "flashes," "glowing," "pulses," "beacons," "mists," "clouds" "volcanoes," "colors" "beams," "stars" "starlike," and "tracks." And these can be narrowed still further, since "mists," "vapours," and "clouds," for instance, are probably referring to much the same sort of phenomenon, just described slightly differently by different scientists (as witnesses in a trial case might differ in their testifying).

The same could be said for "starlike" and "stars," as being the same phenomenon, and "flashes," "beacons," and "pulsations," could all be the same sort of phenomenon, as well, with just different descriptive phrases uses to describe them. This could go for "tracks" and "beams," also. In addition, obviously, "volcanoes," according to our scientists of today, is a misnomer for something else, perhaps something "glowing," or as in "colors." ("Glowing" and "colors" could be mists ionized by solar radiation, but what is the source of such mists, if so?)

As stated above, another reason we resorted to this many samples out of 579 examples is to show the extraordinary abundance of evidence, as supplied by reputable and "scientific" sources. This is to satisfy that need for "extraordinary claims require extraordinary evidence." And again, if anyone wants more of these reputable reports on the happenings on the Moon, they have but to go to the appendix to read the NASA report in its entirety.

Surely then, we have produced an "extraordinary" amount of evidence, from "extraordinarily" reliable sources, and it is a veritable "preponderance of evidence." But what does this all mean? What are these sightings on the Moon? What are they and what do they portend?

Occam's Razor Again.

Well first, let's apply the Principle of Occam's Razor to what we have covered so far. We'll start with the most probable explanations (according to scientists and skeptics) for these sightings:

1. As skeptics may argue (and in some cases, already have), all these sightings, over so much time, are just an incredibly numerous series of mistakes caused by various optical illusions and tricks of the lighting. They would argue the witnesses (although mostly highly qualified scientists and observers), were just constantly mistaken in that they were only seeing optical illusions, etc., and either that, or they just weren't credible witnesses in the first place.

However, if this is so, those many renowned scientists and observers have then been "mistaken" continuously, repeatedly, and for centuries! Moreover, what could cause so many "mistakes" so often, and for such a long duration? Are they just so many idiots? Do they all have terrible eyesight? Not hardly.

Again, many famous astronomers, and groundbreaking scientists in their fields saw these things. So they don't appear to be, and simply all can't be, optical illusions or just "tricks" of the lighting.

2. Another explanation might be (and again, it would certainly be offered by skeptics) that all these sightings are just cases of many mistaken identifications of more mundane things. In other words, something actually occurred, and not just an optical illusion, but it might just be that all those trained astronomers over the centuries, and repeatedly, might be just seeing a mundane event or events.

But what mundane events could account for a "flash," "pulse," "streak," "beacon," "track" or "starlike object," or whatever inside a crater? If it's somehow just meteor impacts, or some other such thing, why in those same areas over and over? And what kind of meteor impact pulses for hours, or behaves as a beacon, or causes a track or beam to appear across the lunar surface, and yet leaves no impact craters?

Well, to be fair, perhaps a few of those observers could be mistaken at times in this way, after all, the hour may have been late when they were observing (it usually was), they may have been tired, etc. Perhaps, even many of them (although considering their credentials this higher number is unlikely in the extreme one would think), may have done just this sort of erroneous reporting, but even so—all of them? Could all of those observers make the same mistakes, describe the same erroneous sightings, and about the same areas of the Moon and over centuries?

That's just not very likely now, is it? In any case, some very reputable observers and scientists saw these same phenomena over hours, days, and even months. Those are some optical illusions! They had staying power, apparently.

And if meteor impacts, those must have been some strange ones to create such weird effects! They must have been huge to glow for such a long period in a cold vacuum, and being often seen in shadowed areas, glowing like this in regions that were as much as a minus 249 degrees Centigrade or just 26 degrees

Kelvin (above absolute zero).[lx] So to retain such heat as to glow for any length of time under such conditions, they had to be either **(1)** large meteors, or **(2)** traveling at very high speeds, thus releasing a great deal of kinetic energy as heat upon impact.

Yet, oddly and again, they do not leave craters as proof they even happened? What kind of meteor could do that? And this answer begs the question of why some regions of the Moon would have so many more such meteor impacts than others. Why would this be? We repeat that this is a very unlikely and farfetched explanation, simply because it isn't satisfactory, requires a great deal of more elaboration to work (such as explaining the fact of no new craters, the persistent heat glows often under such extremely cold conditions, or why these "glows" would pulse, flash, appear "starlike," or as pulses or beacons). This answer just wouldn't begin to sufficiently explain "tracks," "streaks," and such. So again, more explanations are required, making this a ponderous, complicated, and so unlikely solution according to the Principle of Occam's Razor.

3. The third and final explanation is that scientists are actually seeing something real. This explanation says that over centuries, weird phenomena have been seen on the Moon and repeatedly. These phenomena, according to these scientists, also seem to occur in some areas on the Moon much more than others, as if they "clustered" in these particular regions for some strange reason. Although some may be the result of natural occurrences, (the occasional meteor impact for short duration events that appear as a "glow," in a specific region, perhaps), most cannot, as shown above, be explained by this method, and so must be something more. Something "alien" is causing them.

Taking the "extraordinary evidence," as real, the sheer preponderance of it, and having been produced in NASA's own commissioned report, we can now come up with the most likely, the simplest, and so most probable explanation for the events seen.

Applying the Principle of Occam's Razor. We now have to choose the simplest explanation for these real sightings. What do we conclude? Well, the first explanation (Number 1) seems incredibly insufficient to explain the abundance of various types of sightings, and the possible causes stated in the explanation are even further weakened by the various durations of the events themselves, and the fact they've occurred for centuries. Optical illusions and tricks of lighting simply can't account for everything. And to try to do this makes for a cumbersome explanation, one with just too many "holes" in it.

The second explanation (Number 2) seems more probable, on the face of it. Multiple causes for multiple types of events result in mistaken identification of more mundane things. However, again, and here is the crux of the problem with this answer; such an explanation presupposes more than one—in fact, probably many different and unknown causes for such "mundane" phenomena. Again, all things being equal, that answer is cumbersome, and involves an awful lot of "scientific unknowns," yet to be discovered and/or determined.

However, the third explanation would seem the simplest and most straightforward. "Someone" or "*something*" of an intelligent nature is behind most of these sightings. And, no, this answer doesn't have to account for all of such sightings. Some small number of them could be optical illusions, meteor impacts, etc., as argued by the skeptics. Even so, because just so many events on the Moon can't be explained satisfactorily by these arguments, and because they occur so frequently in certain areas, one has to assume that the only all-encompassing answer is that "someone" is responsible for these events.

So the third answer, according to the Principle of Occam's Razor, given that all other things are pretty much equal, is the simplest, most straightforward answer. It requires less reliance on too many unknown factors (requiring only one), and so should be the one chosen. Something is happening on our Moon! And more, "someone" is causing most of what we are seeing. But let's delve into this a little deeper, just to please those rank skeptics out there who might accuse us of just glossing over the first two explanations before settling on what they would believe is our favorite.

CHAPTER 10
Implications And Answers

Please understand that such sightings haven't stopped, either. They are still going on and have been since the arbitrary cutoff date of the NASA report. They didn't "magically" just end with that report being filed, nor did they begin with its initial reported event.

These lunar events were going on for centuries, even millennia before the report began, as this report from Gervase of Canterbury[lxi] shows from the Twelfth Century. This quotation is taken from his Chronicles:

> "About an hour after sunset on June 18, 1178 A.D., a band of five eyewitnesses watched as the upper horn of the bright, new crescent Moon 'suddenly split in two.' From the midpoint of this division a flaming torch sprang up, spewing out…fire, hot coals and sparks. . .The body of the Moon, which was below writhed. . .throbbed like a wounded snake."

Witnesses said this occurred multiple times. NASA refers to this event in one article as a "mystery," because nobody is sure what caused it, although there are various attempts to find answers, none of them very convincing or satisfying.

But the point here is the number of such lunar sightings (often referred to by scientists as "Transient Lunar Phenomena") is overwhelming and has been going on this way for a very long time, indeed! One could say the sheer numbers of them are incredible! Even more incredible are how certain locations seem to be focal points. Aristarchus Crater and the immediate regions around it are among the recurring sites. Some researchers estimate that Aristarchus alone could account for as much as 70 percent of all such sightings. Why is that? Why is Aristarchus Crater[lxii] such an unusual area of the Moon?

Plato is another location that seems constantly to have such sightings associated with it, also, and there are others. For practical reasons, again, we had to limit the number here in the main body of the book, but we did include many of those that showed how often certain lunar regions had so many events.

With Aristarchus, although always well in the sightings' ball game for sure, it was in about 1954 through 1956, that it really kicked off with continuous sightings, with its blue and violet glows and glares being reported all the time. Again, such sightings continue to this day, and are photographed by amateur, as well as professional astronomers. Even Neil Armstrong, on his trip to the Moon on the Apollo 11 mission, verified a sighting along these lines.

Now, as mentioned as one of our "other" explanations, one might attribute all these to certain optical illusions, such as tricks of the lighting during lunar eclipses. However, most event sightings were not occurring during such eclipses, only some few. Many were during periods when the shadows were long, or those areas were in complete darkness, due to the Moon's changing phases.

However, it is expected that lights, glares, luminescent fogs, bright clouds, phosphorescent hazes, blinking, intermittent, pulsating, flickering, and beacon-like events, as well as "starlike" objects, naturally would show better if the surrounding areas were in such darkness, so this would be the expected thing.

As an obvious similar example, it is much easier to see stars in the night sky of our Earth, than during the daytime, although the stars always are there, rising and setting, just as the sun and Moon do. They are simply masked by the brilliance of the sun's light during the daytime, of course. Same with these events; they just tend to stand out better for us when they occur in darker areas.

Furthermore, scientists have often told us the Moon is a "dead" world.[lxiii] It has been called "sterile," on many an occasion, and almost totally lacking in an atmosphere of any sort for all practical purposes. It has been said it has less than one-trillionth of Earth's atmosphere and is for all practical purposes a vacuum.[lxiv] This much we do know, because we've landed there. The Moon has no appreciable atmosphere at all to speak of, certainly nothing anywhere close to what could support "lightning," "clouds," "vapors," "mists," or "haze." So how do we then account for all these bizarre reports and over such a lengthy period? We can't, unless we incorporate a whole series of yet unknown, scientific causes.

In addition, as for bright streaks, bands, horizontal lines, tracks etc., just being a side effect of incoming meteors, well, even being fair here, and saying these oddities are just the result of some such type of meteor showers, we still have major problems with this hypothesis. This is because it is very unlikely meteors are constantly picking out these same areas of the Moon to hurtle over repeatedly, down through the centuries, as somehow they're picking out those regions as being special targets for them of some sort, and far more often than any other areas of the Moon! That would presuppose meteors are doing it on purpose, are singling certain areas out, repeatedly.

We mentioned another consideration earlier. Again, without an atmosphere, there is no friction, so no heating of incoming objects, and therefore no glowing streaks or bands of light from meteors! Meteors on the Moon are not shooting stars! Meteors may cause a glare upon impact from the energy released, but not "streaks" or "bands" of light by just flying over the surface before impact. And what would account for "tracks?" And where are the impact craters such meteors should make? None have been noted.

So if not meteors, what then could explain these moving lights seen sometimes in clusters, sometimes alone or in small numbers, and sometimes "oscillating," "blinking," pulsating," "flickering," or moving slowly about the surface of the Moon?

Meteors just don't behave that way, and most certainly not in a vacuum. And volcanoes aren't mobile.

Moreover, what could account for sightings that were interpreted as volcanoes, some seen for days on end, when we are assured by our scientists that the Moon has no currently active volcanoes, and only had such in extremely ancient times, geologically speaking? Again, for the near side of the Moon, volcanoes supposedly stopped about three billion years ago! So how can anyone in the last 450 years have observed so many nonexistent volcanoes? And wouldn't they have left new craters after erupting, and ones of considerable size that could be seen, if so?

Whatever these events are, they do not seem to do this. And remember, again, we're repeatedly told the Moon is a "dead" world, with little seismic activity, almost all geological activity having ceased long ago, no molten core, and no tectonic plates to move around to trigger volcanoes. It is, simply put, pretty much a solid ball of rock. So we repeat the question: what is causing all these phenomena?

A small group of researchers thinks there might be vents on the Moon that still allow some internal gases to escape. Could these then account for the clouds, fogs, mists, and hazes seen on the Moon? This is possible, of course, but again, there seems to be neither rhyme nor reason to this, as to where these clouds and fogs appear. If these sightings were the results of gases from particular active vents, one would reasonably assume then that this is where one usually would sight such phenomena, and nowhere else, that such sightings would be very consistent in their location in this respect and how they appear.

Such does not seem to be the case, except for a notable few exceptions—Aristarchus being one of them, and even there, the nature of the sightings vary greatly, incredibly so. Mists from vents? Yes, but blinking lights moving about the surface—not hardly!

No, these cloud/mist sightings are seen everywhere, it seems, with sightings obscuring entire mountains, hazes covering huge crater valleys, "black clouds with a violet tinge" seen out on the giant lava flows ("mares")—again, just about everywhere. And in a complete vacuum, how long could they exist in such a state? According to physics as we know it—this couldn't be for very long!

With regard to Aristarchus, we have constant sightings of blue glares, or violet glows, as well as "starlike" lights, along with "beacon-like" ones, etc. Yet, there is no sign of volcanic activity in the crater, nothing new, no lava flows, no plumes, and no new volcanic craters, nothing seemingly changed by all this activity.

If there were that kind of volcanic action there, surely our constant observers from Earth would note this. We now have very powerful telescopes, and as an astronomical object, the Moon is practically in our back yard. If there were such volcanic activity, it would call into question all our ideas about the nature and structure of the Moon as we now think it is. In other words, it would be back to the drawing boards on that topic!

And if not these astronomers observing volcanic activity from Earth, then surely our astronauts, who actually went to the Moon, would see and photograph such activity, or the satellites that now orbit the Moon, would! So if it is somehow, against all current scientific thinking, that there is an active volcano there, why don't we yet know this? It would be a momentous discovery! But there is nothing. Yet, so often has this particular crater been noted to have a blue glow or violet glare, that some now refer to Aristarchus as the "Blue Gem!"[lxv] Hmm…

What's more, some make a case that spectrum analysis of the "blue glow" or "glare" shows it to be almost identical in results with that of a fusion tokomak (a device used to research and create fusion power here on Earth, but still in the research stages).

If this is the case, and that proves to be true, we're talking about a fusion reactor on the Moon, or at least fusion of some sort! And there is another type of radiation that could account for this, one known particularly for its blue glow, as well. This is called Cherenkov Radiation.[lxvi] This is the "blue glow" commonly associated with nuclear reactors, commonly called Cherenkov Blue.

But there is a problem for nuclear fusion reactors on Earth, and that is the ready supply of a material known as Helium-3.[lxvii] This Helium-3 makes a great source of fuel for possible fusion reactors. It occurs naturally on Earth, but is very scarce. However, on the Moon it is far more plentiful. By one estimate, there is has enough Helium-3 there to meet our needs for close to 10,000 years![lxviii] As the article referenced by the endnote here states in its title, "The Moon Was Made For Mining (Helium-3)."

Another interesting coincidence here, isn't it? We have the fact of the blue glow in the "blue gem" crater of Aristarchus perhaps being so close in resemblance to a fusion reactor's spectrum, and looking very much like Cerenkov Radiation of nuclear power plants. Then added to this, the fact that Helium-3 is so very plentiful on the Moon, and just happens to be ideal for fusion reactors? Indeed, this is very coincidental…

Then there are the streaks, the "beams" and "bands" of horizontal light, the lights like a "beacon," "flickering," lights, "intermittent lights," "pulsating lights," and lights appearing here and there all over, even different colored ones. Some of these, according to the NASA report, come in clusters, some are seen over long periods of time and seemingly at random, in and around mountain ranges, as well as in the large areas of solidified lava, so-called mares (Latin for "seas," because they were dark, flat areas that resembled "seas" to ancient astronomers), craters, and elsewhere. And some of these lights move about—some fast, but some slowly traversing the terrain. Are they just super slow and low meteors, perhaps? Such just don't exist. We all know that. Meteors just don't cruise slowly about the surface of planets.

In summary, we are faced with a real set of conundrums. We have volcano-like glows, where we are assured there are no volcanoes. We have strange puffs of vapor, clouds, nebulas, purple and violet hazes, as well as mists, and more where there is no atmosphere. We have "starlike" objects that appear and disappear, some repeating over the centuries in certain locations and for days at a time, and some just blinking and pulsing away.

Other sightings appear, as well, and all over the face of the Moon, seemingly appearing at random. We have streaks of light where there should be none. We also have "beams," "lightning," strange "tracks," and many other phenomena, and all this over a period of centuries, and with some of the sightings made by the top scientists of their day!

They are real enough, as all those scientists reported. There can be no question of their validity. But just what are they? One has to ask, is the Moon a dead world after all? Or is "someone" there, as we have now concluded? Yes, "someone" indeed, is causing many of the observed phenomena, is our emphatic answer.

Still not convinced? Well, let's try a simple comparison to something we do know the answer to and something very similar to this problem in nature. For example, let's apply it to this: say you are looking at the newly discovered Earth from an orbiting space ship. You are an alien flying over a section of the planet that's in total night. You note a myriad of twinkling and blinking lights on the planet's surface. Moreover, your equipment is good enough to show they don't remain lit during daytime, only at night! And this occurs repeatedly. What a mystery!

So you begin methodically to try to apply every natural phenomenon you know that might account for this set of unique observations. Is it bioluminescence on a grand scale? No, it can't be that, because the spectrum analysis shows it's not. You try other explanations. Ultimately, none fits, at least not nearly well enough. What's left? The process of elimination leaves you with two answers:

1. Either completely unknown and strange bits of science are at work here (rather unlikely, given your race's current high level of scientific understanding), or

2. "Someone" is turning those lights on and off and so is responsible for their existence. The principle of Occam's Razor

would say it is "someone," rather than "some natural thing," because the second answer is a currently known explanation, and a much simpler one than trying to contrive some weird new science(s) to answer the problem. Why take such a complicated approach when the simpler one suffices and is probably the correct one? That is, someone is controlling the lights.

Well, this example is very much like what we are seeing on the Moon. So we must apply Occam's Razor to these phenomena in the same way. And just as we did with the lights on Earth, we get the same result.

Therefore, no "natural" explanation or even multiple such "natural" explanations we know of can account for all these things satisfactorily and with the same ease and simplicity as just that one other and "simpler" explanation; again, "someone" is causing many of them. This is so with the lights of Earth, and it is so with the lights of the Moon. Alternatively, are we trying to have two completely different sets of scientific standards/criteria here, because we "know" the answer to the one, the lights on Earth, while not the other, the weird lights, and phenomena on the Moon?

Well, we can't do that. Either the Principle of Occam's Razor works for all, all worlds, or it doesn't work for any, and remember, it is scientists who tout this principle all the time, who make so much of it! Having accepted this conclusion, that "someone" is behind many of these phenomena, we can then go further.

Still using the principle of Occam's Razor, we can then reasonably assume that certain locations are being used on a regular basis, since this is where the majority of sightings keep occurring, although there are many elsewhere, too. But just as city lights on Earth form clusters amidst the scatterings of a sea of lights, and are seen night after night from space, we are seeing odd lights repeatedly more in certain areas on the Moon than others and over long times.

Ultimate conclusion? As unbelievable as it may sound, it would seem that "someone" definitely is on the Moon and perhaps occupying certain regions or doing something in those regions on regular occasions. Furthermore, from that same evidence derived from NASA's report, we see that they may have been there for quite a while, centuries, in fact, or even longer!

But we're not stopping here. This isn't all the evidence we have. In the next chapter, we'll study the evidence of certain NASA photos spoken of by several, well-credentialed people, and their personal testimonies, and even some videos currently available on the Internet and elsewhere that are reliable in their sources (NASA, for one). Let's consider these now.

After all, as valid as the NASA Technical Report R-277, "Chronological Catalog of Reported Lunar Events" is, and its multitude of cited observations are, it's not the only source for such ideas. Again, we have many more. But one thing more to keep in mind; since the lights on the moon come and go, aren't there all the time, we have to either assume the perpetrators of them are coming and going, but not staying there all the time, or that they are doing their best to hide their presence as best they can...

CHAPTER 11

Other Evidence Concerning the Moon

Neil Armstrong reported on his trip to the Moon:

"Hey, Houston, I'm looking north up toward Aristarchus now, and there's an area that is considerably more illuminated than the surrounding area. It seems to have a slight amount of fluorescence."[lxix]

This comment by Armstrong was neither the first nor the last type of such comments on the subject of strange phenomena concerning our lunar neighbor. When it comes to remarks by astronauts about odd things in space, upon the Moon, or even while in orbit around the Earth, we have a number of actual recordings of such events. Among these comments by various members of the crews are several made about alien spacecraft sightings, and they call them just that! These include recorded remarks by astronauts onboard the space shuttle in orbit around the Earth, and on at least one Apollo mission, as well as during the Gemini missions. That there is a long history of such remarks cannot be in doubt. There is even film footage of such.

Nor does it end there. Various people, who have worked for NASA, and along with contractors to them, also have things to say. For a quick rundown, let's consider some of the following:

With regard to remarks about aliens and/or alien objects on the Moon:

1. Sergeant Karl Wolfe,[lxx] who had his security clearance status upgraded, so that he could enter a restricted lab, was surprised to find so many people from other countries when he arrived there. The place was fairly buzzing with them.

To his mind, something very special must be going on. Nevertheless, he was only concerned with his own job, the repair of some photographic equipment. He entered a dark room where there was one lone attendant. After talking with the airman for a while, the man told him, and then showed him photos of the far side of the Moon showed a surface "base" there, one that may have been used for mining operations. (Remember all that Helium-3 and the moon "was made for mining?"). He did not specifically say that it was an alien base; however, the strong implication was that it was, for there were definite structures. And after all, who else could have put it there?

Nobody could launch such a massive operation from the earth without America having been made aware of it. And having foreign scientists present seemed to show the entire world was concerned about this or at least, America's allies were. This is the gist of Sgt. Karl Wolfe's testimony. If he qualified for a high security clearance, why should we then question his competence or veracity? The US Government didn't. He was good enough for them.

2. In a book by Timothy Good, *Above Top Secret*, the author asserts that Neil Armstrong saw UFOs during his Moon landing.[lxxi] Mr. Good said Armstrong saw a strange "light" near a crater. The implication is we were "warned off."

3. Furthermore, in 2006, Buzz Aldrin publicly admitted that the astronauts indeed, had seen UFOs.[lxxii] However, because of the fear of panic, NASA did not want this made public.

4. Donna Hare, a former NASA employee, who received a number of awards for her work, claims NASA covered up and altered photographs of the Moon to rid them of alien objects such as lunar bases, etc.[lxxiii]

5. On May 15, 1963, Gordon Cooper while orbiting the Earth, reported a UFO sighting. He described it as a green-glowing object, one that was approaching his capsule very quickly. This claim was supported by tracking radar on the ground. This was not the first time astronaut Cooper had sighted a UFO.[lxxiv] In 1961, while flying an F-86 over Germany he spotted one. Apparently, a metallic, disk-shaped object, it could outmaneuver American aircraft.[lxxv]

6. Astronauts Ed White and James McDivitt, while orbiting the earth in June of 1965, saw a UFO, as well.[lxxvi] They described it as a metallic object. Its shape was unfamiliar to them. They took a picture of the thing, but NASA has never released that picture. The question is why?

7. Astronauts James Lovell and Frank Borman, in December of that same year, also saw an unfamiliar spacecraft, or UFO.[lxxvii] When they radioed this information to the ground, they were told it was their own booster rocket they were seeing. They responded by saying they did see the booster rocket quite clearly, but they also saw this other spacecraft. It was of unknown origin.

8. Donald Slayton, Major Robert White, NASA Pilot Joseph A. Walker, Commander Eugene Cernan, all reported UFO sightings, as well.

9. NASA's astronaut, Scott Carpenter supposedly said: "At no time when the astronauts were in space were they alone: there was a constant surveillance by UFOs."[lxxviii]

10. NASA's Maurice Chatelain, former chief of NASA's Communication System, in 1979 said that Neil Armstrong had reported seeing two UFOs perched on the rim of crater while on the surface of the Moon. Chatelaine also stated he believed UFOs might be local to our own Solar System. He conjectured they might be from Titan.[lxxix]

Now, either we have a lot of astronauts and people who worked for NASA directly, or in a close relation with it, who are just plain crazy and/or are seeing things, or they are actually seeing things. Alternatively, they could be outright liars.

Or we have some people telling the truth, ones who saw remarkable evidence across extraordinary spectra that support the contention that UFOs are in space near Earth, on our Moon, and in our Solar System. So which are we to believe? We think it is obvious we would not trust the piloting of our spacecraft to insane persons, so therefore, what they reported must be fact and true as far as they are concerned. All these people are not liars, and since they include our best-trained observers in space—astronauts—they weren't mistaken all the time, either.

Now what does this all mean for us? We have evidence given by statements of highly respected individuals from across the board when it comes to NASA and related agencies, all saying not only do the UFOs exist, but they exist in numbers, have been seen by many, and this fact seemingly has been hidden largely by NASA.

We also have evidence in the form of testimony given by highly respected individuals stating there have been UFOs sighted on the Moon during flights there. Is there even more evidence for this contention? Yes, there is. We could probably double the size of this book by adding it all here. However, we will not. It isn't necessary. The abundance of evidence is clear. There is an "extraordinary" amount of evidence, and it is incontrovertible.

Applying The Principle Of Occam's Razor. We now have to decide what the simplest and therefore most likely explanation is for what we've been seeing all these centuries on and around the Moon and Earth.

Our most obvious choices are:

1. All the people mentioned above are lying and/or committing hoaxes and all the evidence given in the NASA Report can be explained away by invoking the idea of some hitherto unknown natural phenomena (definitely plural) that could account for all these things seen on the Moon. This explanation also has to include a reasonable explanation for why such vaunted public figures would lie to the American people so, or how so many trained observers (astronauts, for instance) could be so mistaken in their observations. Or,

2. All these people actually saw what they say they did, and that "someone" is responsible for many of the events witnessed over the centuries on the Moon.

Using the principle of Occam's razor, we can only arrive at one realistic conclusion: the simplest given all things being pretty much equal: that is, these astronauts and other people are all telling the truth as they see it.

Now, let's go a step further. If, indeed, all these people are telling the truth as they see it and to the best of their ability, then we know that (a) UFOs are in space around the earth and (b) UFOs have been sighted on the actual surface of the Moon, and finally (c) UFOs seem to be monitoring our space activities closely.

In addition, we have then to consider NASA may be trying to hide these facts. If one takes into account witness testimony that they have been airbrushing photographs, switching to private channels when communicating with astronauts about UFO sightings, failing to make public photographs they have (ones taken by astronauts), and generally refusing to indulge in any indication for or against the whole subject of the existence of UFOs. Moreover, they are doing this when they must supposedly know better.

The question is why? Why hide all this? Is it truly because they fear a panic by the public? Again, we must go back to the fact that according to the most recent polls, the majority of people in the United States and indeed, around the world, already do believe in the existence of UFOs. So the argument such news would cause a general panic is already moot. Of course, it would not cause a panic at this point, not if we already believe they exist! So the reason for keeping something such as this secret must go much farther than that. But what is this terrible secret they are trying to hide, if it is not just the fact of the existence of UFOs, if most of us already believe that and so wouldn't be frightened by such information?

Let's reiterate what we already know now:

1. We now know that UFOs exist.

2. We know they apparently have been seen here on earth for centuries, if not for many millennia. Judging by some of the evidence cited by ancient alien enthusiasts, it might have been even for a much longer period than that.

3. It seems UFOs not only appear in our skies, but in space, on the Moon, and perhaps generally in our Solar System.

4. UFOs seem to be observing us, especially when we are flying in near Earth orbit or on missions to the Moon and while landing there.

5. And again, NASA seems to be trying to cover all this up to the best of its ability, or at least declaring neutrality on the subject, despite a large number of leaks by various astronauts, agents of NASA, and its affiliated individuals.

Applying the Principle of Occam's Razor. What are some possible explanations that cover all these factors? Let's consider some:

1. Well, as stated above, perhaps NASA is trying to hide this because it fears a general panic. However, we've already established that this probably isn't the real reason, not when most are already convinced they do exist. Another problem with this answer is that it doesn't go far enough, doesn't explain why the UFOs are on the Moon, and in space around Earth, other than invoking the nominal answer that we are being observed. Yet, even this further explanation fails to say why they are observing us so closely and for so very long a time.

2. Our second choice involves a conspiracy theory. This would imply NASA knows what's going on, knows its implications, and is in league somehow with all of this, at least, as far as the cover-up is concerned. This would also imply the powers-that-be also know what's going on, and are involved in it to a certain degree, as well. This means a vast number of people involved in various branches of the government, all in league "with the devil" as it were (meaning those who are aware of the UFOs and/or alien races).

Again, the question arises, why? Why would they do this? Well, there are two possible solutions to the question. The first one involves the fact they must be gaining something from it all in some way. In other words, they're getting something out of this, some payoff of some sort or other by keeping it all secret. This must incur in some way to their benefit.

The second solution to this explanation is they are fearful of something, something very powerful, and so are under some kind of orders to keep this information hidden from the general populace, because they've been told to do this. This would imply that NASA and the powers-that-be are in some way intimidated, under some kind of threat, and we must assume it would be a great one to scare such powerful organizations as the United States Government. Granted, this scenario has an X-Files quality to it. And this, too, means we have a multi-level explanation, which makes for a very complicated one. However, this does not mean that it isn't necessarily true. However, not being the simplest explanation, it would therefore, seem to be more unlikely as far as the Principle of Occam's Razor is concerned.

3. Another possible explanation is the aliens have an agenda. This explanation requires that the government knows what's going on (but may not know the exact nature of the agenda), but is powerless to stop it, and also may not know what the ultimate outcome of it is all meant to be. In other words, it is not so much a conspiracy involving our government, as it is the fact they are just forced to play along, because they have no other choice, and are virtually powerless to interfere.

Now let's once again invoke the principle of Occam's razor. We must choose the simplest of the three answers, all else being equal. Why these particular three and not other answers, you wonder? Well these are the three least involved answers we could find. In other words, of all the explanations available, these were the simplest ones we could come up and some of these, obviously, aren't so simple either.

So which of these three answers is the simplest one? Well, Number One is too incomplete to be a good answer in any case, although it is a relatively simple one. However, it is only simple because it is so incomplete. In other words, the answer is more complex than it first appears. If the reason NASA is hiding the

UFO reports is because they don't want to create a panic is false, then we must look for another "real" reason or multiple reasons.

Or, if they believe it really would cause a panic, then they must have good and sufficient reason to suppose this, which means they are hiding something more, some other evidence we just aren't aware of, as well. Because, again, as it stands, and judging by the polls taken recently, the mere existence of UFOs simply wouldn't cause a panic, and NASA must surely be aware of this fact. So then, one must ask, what are they hiding? Again, in truth, the first explanation makes for a large and unwieldy one, no matter how one looks at it. It really doesn't "explain" anything much and only leads to more questions.

Explanation Number Two implies a vast conspiracy, with our government being part of "the enemy." Many people would have to be involved in this conspiracy, and so this explanation becomes as unwieldy as believing all these sightings are hoaxes perpetrated in their thousands. What a vast and clandestine organization this would have to be, so involved to perpetrate such a "dastardly" conspiracy. Even so, although not the simplest answer, this doesn't mean that it, too, might not be the correct one. But going by Occam's Razor, we simply can't choose such an elaborate explanation for all of this, one that requires so many people lying, covering up, and helping the aliens.

Therefore, by default, we are left with the third and final explanation. This one states the aliens have an agenda, and it is one which our government and NASA are simply powerless to interfere with, or stop.

Therefore, their only role in this whole thing is to try to keep a lid on it, to keep things under control, and moving on an even keel. They may be powerless to stop the thousands of abductions. And citizens knowing this fact actually could cause a panic. What good is a government that can't function to protect us, or won't, and allows a multitude of its citizens to be taken and experimented upon? The answer may be our government basically can't stop it, any of it, but can only try to do what they can to minimize the damage and so allow "life to go on" as we know it, the best they can.

This answer on the face of it would seem to be the simplest one. It implies no elaborate conspiracy on the part of our government. It simply states our government is trying to do its best to keep things appearing normal, so that life can go on as close to usual as possible. Are they hiding facts? Probably, this then would be true, but it wouldn't be out of some vast, complex, and evil conspiracy against humanity. It doesn't mean they are in league with aliens.

What this explanation does state is the aliens do have an agenda. It does not explain what that agenda is. Yet, it does relieve us of the burden of trying to find out why our government and NASA would be involved in some elaborate conspiracy, would be in collusion with the aliens in some horrific way, as with the television series and movies of the X-Files imply.

What's more, this answer does not require we know what the agenda of the aliens might be. It simply states there must be one. And when alien races are observing our earth and activities at such close range, and over so long a time, it is only rational to assume they must have some type of agenda, or why waste all that effort?

So we must choose the third explanation, the one stating the aliens seem to have an agenda and our government is powerless to interfere with it to any real degree. It seems the simplest explanation. We repeat; it does not require elaborate conspiracy theories involving our government or government agencies. It simply states there are aliens. They are observing us. And it would seem they have an agenda of some sort. And our government is just trying to minimize the consequences of a damage about which our government is powerless to do anything. So we choose this answer.

CHAPTER 12

An Alien In-Depth Agenda?

Where does this leave us now? Well, so far, we have concluded there are UFOs, they are watching us, and they have an agenda. But are the UFOs intelligent in themselves, or are they guided by an intelligence? This may seem like a silly question, but it does have to be considered if we are to build on our logic. We can't just assume anything.

In any case, there are two most probable answers to this question. The first is they are a natural phenomenon that is new to science, or at least unknown to science of present-day, as in some type of new strange species deep beneath the ocean that might yet be discovered. Sound farfetched? Perhaps, but even the lights seen can be explained by being the product of bioluminescence or some such thing, so this explanation simply can't be ruled out completely at first glance.

This explanation would also have to include, in order to be correct, the fact there are many different types of UFOs sighted (shapes, sizes, and behaviors) and they seem to be able to travel through the vacuum of space without harm, as well as through atmosphere, and into the depths of oceans. The explanation would also somehow reasonably have to account for why UFOs seem to be buzzing our airplanes and other aircraft constantly, as well shadowing certain of our military bases.

Furthermore, this same explanation would also have to take into account the damage caused to people in the form of radiation burns, and the deaths of those, such as the Russian divers, or those Russian college students, as well as many others around the world, including many people here in the United States. And this is even leaving alone trying to include an explanation for cattle mutilations and all those abductions claimed by so many people, and all those countless crop circles spotted so constantly. It could be said, we suppose, that those phenomena might have nothing to do with UFOs, however unlikely that particular scenario might seem to be.

The second explanation is that, yes, UFOs are intelligently guided. This explanation is in its entirety as stated, because if UFOs are guided by intelligent beings, those beings are capable of doing any of the above things mentioned, whether it is flying around airplanes, military bases, performing abductions, cattle mutilations, or such. This means no further elaboration is necessary with this explanation.

Now by applying the principle of Occam's razor, we can select the simplest explanation of the two. And the second choice is so obviously the simpler one. Why? Because it accounts for all these things without needing extra sub-explanations, more complicated or elaborate ones, to cover all the implications and issues involved.

Apparently, UFOs are unnatural, are artificial in nature (meaning they were designed and/or built by someone or something), and so are somehow intelligently guided (either as drones, robotically, or by beings actually occupying them, or perhaps a combination of these things).

Given that we are not yet capable of doing any of this to nearly such a degree ourselves, and do not have command of such technologies, UFOs must, therefore, be controlled somehow by aliens/extraterrestrials.

So having arrived at this answer using the Occam's Razor method yet again, can we take it even one step further? That is, can we decide if they have truly an actual agenda or not?

Well, again, we have two main possible explanations here:

The first is they have no agenda, that they are just simply watching us to be watching us, like cows calmly watching a person walking by their fence while chewing on their cuds (the cows, not the people), and with about as much interest.

Nevertheless, given the abundance of available evidence, does this seem very likely?

Well, we have concluded they have been observing us closely, and seem to have been doing so for a very long time, indeed. This, in and of itself, implies a real agenda of some sort on their part, if only one of prolonged and close observation. But as agendas go, it would seem reasonably harmless if that's the case. Such an agenda would imply they are merely just incredibly long-term voyeurs of some sort, perhaps watching us as we would watch our favorite reality television show.

The second explanation is they do have a more in-depth agenda. Does this last, perhaps, seem the more likely one? Yes. Why? Because they must consume so much energy and expense in order to watch us this way. It would make for very expensive voyeurism as a pastime, and most likely, too much so for any payoff they might get. To travel from another solar system, or even another planet in our own Solar System (remember, one NASA associated official believes they might be from Titan, although such an inhospitable world seems unlikely to us), and they must travel so often, it must mean a high consumption of energy expenditure on their part.

No matter how one looks at it, it would seem probable, under the circumstances, that even being from another solar system, they would need bases closer to hand here, just in order to alleviate this tremendous energy consumption, to make it easier, quicker, and cheaper to perform their tasks concerning us. Sheer logistics demands this.

And even ignoring the cost of such, one has to ask, what about the enormous amount of time it would take out of their lives in simply observing us this way, watching us so closely all the time? Nobody invests so much time without expecting some sort of payoff, unless they are even more alien in nature than we can imagine (which can't be entirely ruled out). But the more investment one puts into something, usually the more one wants out of it.

Let's be honest here; we already know this idea of them being just observers or voyeurs is most likely simply not true. We have too much evidence to the contrary of their direct interference. Even if one excludes all the claimed evidence of Ancient Alien theorists, modern evidence shows an abundance of interference in human lives. Going by this same evidence, the aliens have done more than just watch us for the fun of it. They have been actively interfering according to all the evidence we've accumulated so far.

The Ancient Aliens theory, along with the evidence its adherents supply in such abundance, suggests a great amount of interference in our culture, civilizations (past and present), and perhaps even in our physical makeup as living beings, has taken place. There does seem to be some very strong evidence of this last idea.

For a review of why we think this, please see Chapter 7. Chapter 7 refers to a great deal of evidence as to why we believe there has been interference throughout our past. Everything from the Anunnaki "sky gods," to the "star child," etc., seems to indicate intervention on a massive scale, and repeatedly on the human individual level, as well.

The seemingly almost endless citing of cases of abductions by other UFO authors would also seem to indicate this sort of thing is still going on to this day. Again, we haven't even really dealt with the subjects or issues of cattle mutilations and/or crop circles. If these things are, in fact, also real manifestations of aliens, then certainly we are being interfered with, often, and to a remarkable degree, and in many ways.

This would seem likely also, because it is in keeping with the enormous expenditure of time and energy the aliens must be undertaking concerning us. Again, if you expend those kinds of resources, it must be for a very good reason. You surely want something and this would probably require interference of some sort on their part to accomplish. Things, after all, don't just happen by magic. Even if one's science appears to us almost as magic.

So of the two explanations, all other things being equal, and according to the Principle of Occam's Razor, we have to take the second explanation. The first explanation, that they are just observers, that this is their only agenda, although possible, simply doesn't seem to fit all the available facts. It, of necessity, ignores a large amount of existing evidence. Besides, it is only superficially simple, because we also then have to ignore the other questions of alien interference and as to why they're interfering. If they have no particular agenda, why are they behaving as if they are? So again, yes, they have a definite and in-depth agenda, it would seem. All the available evidence, past and present, would seem to point to it.

CHAPTER 13

What Is The Nature Of The Alien In-Depth Agenda?

But what exactly is their agenda? That's a much harder question to answer, and again, there are many possible answers, many of which are promoted by various ufologists. However, we know some important things about their agenda, as mentioned above. Let's summarize what we think we know:

1. The agenda seems to have taken place over a very long period (as we measure time, but perhaps not as they do, since we don't know their lifespan). This means the aliens' goals must then be long-term ones, and ones they are willing to wait a great deal of time to achieve.

2. It also means they are willing to invest a great deal of effort and energy to obtain this goal or goals, whatever it or they are, so even not knowing what the payoff is, we can reasonably guess that it has to be a big one, at least in their minds, as they view it.

3. This would also mean, judging by their constant interference, the many abductions that have been claimed, etc., that in order to obtain this goal or goals they are willing to do more or less whatever it takes. We, as human individuals, simply may not matter if we take this idea to be true. It may be that we don't count at all in the cosmic scheme of things, as such, and that we are merely a means to an end in their eyes (assuming they have eyes…). In other words, our value as individuals is severely limited, at least, as far as they are concerned.

Perhaps their goal is for a greater good for the human race, or even for a greater evil. Whatever it is, it must be something they want badly, because they're going through a great deal of trouble to do it. But what is the ultimate goal? We can only guess. We have yet to witness the outcome of all of this.

However, it seems by their actions the aliens simply do not care about us as individuals at all. Their intentions, it seems, preclude asking us if we want to be a part of their agenda, to help to achieve it. In other words, we are not given a choice. When a human is abducted without their say-so, or approval, this means their basic human rights are being constantly violated, as we perceive such rights under international law and American law.

When UFOs buzz our aircraft, fly over restricted air space, cause damage, and yes, sometimes endanger lives, or even cause death, even if it is inadvertently done, then it would seem they hold our lives and us in little regard. At least this must be so compared to them needing to achieve their ultimate goals, and whatever those are, it must be far more important than our personal safety is to them. Their behavior would also strongly imply their agenda is more important even than our rights or lives as human beings in groups, as well as for individuals, when one considers the danger to our planes and other forms of aircraft.

So are the aliens being malevolent toward us by doing this? Are they being benevolent in the long-term, perhaps saving us from some ultimately worse fate? What is their ultimate aim? Is it a good one?

Well, if you were a slave of the Anunnaki in those ancient days of the Sumerians, toiling away under those mysterious sky gods of old, would you really care? Would you be happy to spend your life as a slave doing backbreaking work in mines, and dying young and under miserable circumstances, knowing that someday, centuries later, your race might benefit in some way from this action?

We're guessing the answer to that question is you would probably not be happy, not at all, because to live and die a slave, to have to work under harsh conditions, to never be free, and never to have a choice in the matter at all, would be a terrible thing. Again, such an idea goes against our very concept of basic human rights.

Now let's bring this forward in time. Doesn't exactly the same situation hold true for those who claim to have been abducted now? If you are a modern abductee, one of thousands, or even millions (going by some sets of figures), who are kidnapped, then medically probed in excruciating and humiliating ways, and sometimes have had mysterious alterations made to you, wouldn't you want this to be by your choice? Wouldn't you want the right to opt out of such a thing? And wouldn't most of us choose to opt out of such a horrible event? Of course, we would.

Judging by the often intense and overwhelming need for psychotherapy by many of the victims of this abduction phenomenon, it is not something they would freely choose to do, given the choice in the matter and the resulting mental and emotional damage to them. And according to the descriptions they give, the pain can often be ghastly during these so-called medical examinations.

The fact they, as victims, may be somehow forced to forget it all afterwards, doesn't change the fact they did go through the pain in the first place. And even if they don't remember, it often seems to cause terrible nightmares, and psychological trauma, as well as a tremendous amount of nameless fear that "*they*" may come to do it to them yet again.

Once more, we ask the question: would a person willingly submit to this if they had any choice in the matter? And the answer again is: undoubtedly, the vast majority would not.

Obviously, by all the descriptions given, the abductees do not have a choice in the matter, none at all. And it is doubtful if they will ever be given one in the future. So regardless of the ultimate goal of the extraterrestrials' agenda, for the abductees and many others, it is not something they would willingly choose to be involved in, and so their basic rights are being often and seriously violated to this very day. And what of the long-term consequences to them? Nobody yet knows the answer to this question. Does this sort of thing shorten a person's life? We already know it damages the quality of it severely.

In addition, don't underestimate the problems UFOs cause by buzzing our airplanes. If you were onboard one of those flights, and were to see this happen, wouldn't it frighten you, even terrify you? Wouldn't you worry about the plane's safety under such conditions, be afraid it might collide and then crash? Of course, you would. The pilots certainly do. That's only human to feel this way. So again, their agenda isn't always pleasant for the persons (humans) involved.

We can go further in this vein. If Ancient Alien theorists are correct, many people have been murdered by the thousands, or even in their millions over the millennia. These theorists have sometimes referred to this as the aliens "culling the herd," meaning us being the herd, in this case. The Ancient Aliens theorists contend, given the available evidence, the aliens or extraterrestrials have been interfering for a long time in our genetic makeup. To do this (the theorists claim) has required that periodically, genetic mistakes be expunged from the human race and at regular intervals. Only a certain strain or strains of humans are allowed to continue onward, allowed to flourish. All others must perish. A bit like selecting for a particular strain of bacteria amongst many growing in a Petri dish, isn't it?

The adherents of this theory cite biblical text, as well as many other sources, to prove their point; but with regard to the Bible, in particular, they like to reference the tale of Noah and the Ark. The ancient Babylonians also have this same flood mythology, but in their version, they tell it with their warrior-hero, Gilgamesh playing a significant role, as Noah does in the Bible. Many other cultures have a myth of a great flood, as well, including Native Americans.

Also, Ancient Alien theorists refer to the biblical Exodus (among many other examples), and the fact the Jews were made to wander in the desert until a certain proportion of their group had all died out, before they were allowed to finally enter the Promised Land.

This same sort of thing has also been accomplished (again, according to Ancient Alien theorists) by the use of major floods and other catastrophes, such as plagues, and even through provoking wars. And this would include stopping certain wars at times.

When Alexander the Great wanted to invade India, apparently, the extraterrestrials interfered with his plans by using their vehicles ("flying shields") to buzz the troops, madden the war elephants, and frighten the horses to the point where Alexander's generals and soldiers rebelled shortly after this and wanted to turn back. Thus, India was never taken completely, never conquered by Alexander the Great.[lxxx]

It is said that Alexander was so impressed by this display, and so convinced that these flying shields came from below the surface of the river, that from that day to the day of his death, he had a strong interest in finding out what lay beneath the waters. It is even said he wanted or even did construct a primitive diving bell, and may actually have used it.[lxxxi]

Nor was Alexander alone in seeing such things. Countless times down through the ages, people, often historically famous people, have mentioned sighting such things and they weren't simply meteors they were seeing, because they moved about the sky in ways meteors simply could not do. Greeks, Romans, English, Scots, French, all saw these "flying shields" and often described them in just that way or in very similar ways.

Nor would the Germans and Swiss be exempt from this either. Much later, in late medieval Nuremberg, and in Basil, Switzerland, actual wars seem to play out in the skies over the two cities in broad daylight. Nor were these events short. They lasted for some time. The Nuremberg battle was even immortalized in a woodcut for the newspaper of the time.[lxxxii] Both battles were described in detail, and appeared to involve spheres and long cylindrical objects. They seemed to be shooting at each other, and there were even casualties. Reports of falling cylinders and spheres were made. These apparently disappeared in clouds of steam, evaporating away.

Ancient Aliens theorists even point to the fact of the Black Death, a plague, being a form of "culling." This disease, it is said, may have been responsible for the deaths of as much as half the population of Europe of the day. Ancient Alien theorists refer to statements by a number of witnesses of the time who often claimed to have seen "men" or figures in black robes with hoods, ones who hid their faces, or when seen by accident, were hideous to behold.

They carried scythe-like objects they swung back and forth, and which emitted some form of mist or vapor. Others said they could actually see the plague physically enter their villages or towns as a strange mist drifting through the streets. The Black Death usually followed quickly after these odd reports and occurrences. And these reports are from various places in Europe, not just one small area.

Also, UFO sightings were amazingly common in regions wherever there were new outbreaks of plague. Strange lights were reported in the skies and references to weird comets (again, people of the time always referred to anything strange seen in the sky as a "comet," regardless of what its true nature may have been).

But do the figures in black robes ring any sort of bell to you? They should. This is where our modern-day symbol of death comes from -- a skeletal figure in a hooded black robe wielding a scythe. A frightening thought, isn't it? Have they so scarred our collective psyches, that to this very day, we remember them in our culture as the very image of death itself?

And the Plague continued to return, just about once every generation for a long time after, but less severely, to increasingly diminishing levels until it petered out altogether. Was this a follow-up by the aliens? Were they still culling the herd, still selecting human strains and removing the unwanted ones, until they finally succeeded in having the vast majority of humanity in Europe "breeds true" to their specifications and goals?

And one last thought here; even now, today, strangely, researchers are still unsure what the actual cause or causes of the Black Death may have been. Bubonic Plague seems to have been involved, but judging by some of the reported symptoms, some other disease(s), unknown ones, or different versions, also seem to have been involved, as well, for the transmission of the disease seemed not only to be by flea bites, but often seemed to be airborne.

This is not in character with how a typical plague is usually transmitted. It usually has one main vector, or means of transmission, although, it might have other, more minor means of transmission, as well. Cholera outbreaks, for instance, mostly occur when the disease contaminates potable water. Colds tend to be airborne, or through direct contact with an infected person, or through something they've recently touched. A mosquito transmits malaria.

One simply doesn't see multiple diseases striking all at the same instant, to such a horrific degree and extent, and involving diseases that may not even be related to each other. Yet, some scientists say it must have either been more than one type of the plague, or some other disease was also involved, as well, since not all the described symptoms can be accounted for in any other way.

In any case, never have we experienced in our history, prior to or since this event, the death of half the population of an entire continent through such a terrible way. And this was done by a means that still seems to be mostly unknown, and one, which confounds our scientific researchers to this very day. It is, in short, an enduring enigma.

Also, researchers are puzzled by the way the disease spread geographically. The Plague would seem to have appeared spontaneously on occasion, and simultaneously, often in isolated regions or villages many miles removed from an area of localized contagion elsewhere, thus not giving the needed time for the disease to have been spread by the usual means of transmission and/or transportation of the day (if carried by people or their animals).

Remember, the fastest means of transportation of the day was by horse on land, by boats with sails or using oars on rivers, and wind-driven ships by sea. How then, did the disease suddenly appear in widely isolated locations simultaneously? How is that possible? For more on this, check out the book, *The Gods of Eden* by William Bramley. This is an in-depth and frightening look at how the aliens might have contrived to control us throughout the millennia.

And in more modern times, the same has still held true. If we take those hundreds of thousands of abduction accounts as real, the reports of some people suffering radiation burns when in close proximity to a UFO, the deaths even of some individuals, it would seem the aliens are still "culling the herd."

Why constantly endanger the lives of people aboard jets by buzzing around them like angry insects and thus interfering, at the very least, with onboard instrumentation necessary to our safety while flying? Why not warn people off or just leave them alone by flying away, if we are approaching too close to what might cause radiation sickness, cancer, and even death for us?

What happened to those Russian college students that dark night when they all died on that terrible skiing trip? What happened to those Russian divers that died while investigating a USO? Decades ago, what caused the death of an American military pilot, while his jet was chasing and intercepting a UFO? How did he end up by crashing into a lake? What happened to the young Australian pilot the civilian whose plane disappeared, never to be found again, after he sighted and reported UFOs?

These are hard questions to answer without at least thinking the UFOs' occupants might not care whether we live or die, while they are busy doing what they are doing. Or, even worse, they are deliberately "removing" many of us from life for some reason or other.

So to repeat; whether or not the goal(s) of the agenda of the aliens is a benevolent, or a malevolent one, doesn't seem to matter much for us as humans. What we cherish, as with regard to our lives, our freedom, our health, and our right to choose, seem not only to be terribly unimportant to them, but of no importance at all. In short, they seem to be very Machiavellian, as in the "end justifies the means." And if their goal turns out to be also a malevolent one, as well, so much the worse for us.

We will add one final note to this agenda list. Although apparently ignoring our rights as humans and such, the aliens do not seem to want to destroy us, at least, not yet. This, they could have done at any time. With their advanced capabilities, they could have lobbed a series of asteroids of any size they wished at us, at any velocities, to do just minor or major damage to our world and so us.

There is some evidence that they might have done this on a smaller scale, as in, maybe, to cause (as mentioned above) the "Great Flood" as so many cultures refer to it, or this may have just been a natural event.[lxxxiii] In any case, they would have the capability of wiping us out in this way, and undoubtedly, in many others. So they don't seem to want to make us extinct. However, that doesn't mean they don't have other goals, which we might consider almost as dark, though…

We've covered a lot of territory in this last section. We've examined many issues.

To conclude this chapter, let's say that even if we don't know the exact agenda of the aliens, we know many things about it and they don't seem to be particularly good. Let's summarize them here:

1. The agenda is, by all available evidence, a long-term goal. This idea is based on the abundance of evidence for them having been here for a very long time, and continuing to be here now. We have no reason to think they might not be here for the foreseeable future, at least until they reveal themselves and what they want. Or perhaps, it will be until they have achieved whatever their goal is. And that in itself is a rather unsettling thought.

2. The agenda seems to be involved intimately with us, as humans, as with regard to our physical characteristics, seemingly our genetic makeup perhaps, or something similar. There are many theories on this, any of which might be the correct answer. At this time, there is simply not enough information for us to know for sure.

3. Judging by the constant sightings of their vehicles, the UFOs flying everywhere all over the world, all the time, we can assume they are intent on observing us closely, among "other" things. Whether this has to do with monitoring the results of their interference with us in a genetic or physical sense, or whether it is to monitor us as a culture and our development, or both, or even more items, ones that we may simply not be aware of yet, is still uncertain.

One could reasonably assume that given this is an important experiment to them in some way or other, they would be monitoring it closely, and for multiple factors. To put it more simply, they have a strong stake in seeing how we develop, so they are watching us with a keen eye.

4. Whatever the reason for the aliens' interference, it also seems to involve a Machiavellian approach to humanity, one of perhaps monstrous proportions (no pun intended). The end for them seems truly to justify any means they wish to use to obtain it.

Apparently, if this means abducting people, accidentally killing people, repeatedly placing people's lives in jeopardy, doing things to humans without their right to exercise any choice in the matter, or even "culling the herd," as in killing off on a massive scale, as some noted Ancient Alien theorists argue, the aliens will do it. And they seem to have no compunction about doing it, either, not in the least.

5. However, and this is a large caveat, the aliens do not seem to want us dead as a species, made extinct, at least not entirely, and not yet, anyway. Whatever their agenda, whatever the manipulations going on and to what degree, if they wanted, the aliens could probably easily wipe us out. They could do this in any number of ways. They haven't. Therefore, they do have some purpose or purposes in mind for us, some "ultimate goal," it would seem. Those purposes might involve the "culling of the herd" on a regular basis, though, and for those so "culled," it means their death.

Therefore, here we have it. Aliens are amongst us one way or another. This is so in general, around the world, and on a daily basis. Again, we may not know the exact nature of their agenda, but we know they have one, and it is a big one. The evidence of how they are proceeding toward that goal is also apparent. At the moment, considering the implications, that's probably enough for us to know right now, enough for us to handle. After all, it's hard to imagine the result of their agenda being a benevolent one, especially when they use such terrible tactics to achieve it.

In addition, for us, as humans, this may be the single most important factor of all. Whether their ultimate goal is a benevolent or a malevolent one just doesn't seem too important at this point. Our lives, to us, remain of the utmost importance. And they seem to be treating those lives with all the care that a lazy laboratory researcher might have for his test rats. The aliens are treating us no better than we would common bacteria in a Petri dish. This is, indeed, a very frightening thought.

They are in our skies and they are watching us. Anyone of us could be next as an abductee. And another chilling thought—our human population has just obtained seven billion. Are we about due for another "culling?" Now, perhaps, you can see why we sometimes refer to the aliens as "monsters."

CHAPTER 14
Origin Of The Aliens

So from where do these aliens or extraterrestrials come? Have they always been here? Are they native to our world, and we just don't know it, because they appeared here long before we did and have been hiding ever since our emergence as a species? If so, why do that? Are they from somewhere in our Solar System? Or, are they from somewhere else in outer space? There are more possible solutions to this question of their origin. Maybe, they're from inter-dimensional space. Or perhaps they're from somewhere else in time, possibly the future? So to find the correct answer to this question is not easy. We simply don't have enough information to go on, yet.

Nevertheless, according to the evidence given by witnesses, these vehicles do behave in very strange ways. They seem to defy the known laws of physics or somehow supersede them. Their craft dart about at impossible speeds, use velocities that would kill any human being who might be inside them under normal conditions as we know them. The UFOs seem to suddenly appear and disappear, shoot off at abrupt right angles. They are often seen coming up out of the water, and this can be from lakes, oceans, and sometimes, even rivers.

When seen arising from water, the UFOs are referred to as USOs. This last means "Unidentified Submerged Object." And again, there have been plenty of sightings throughout time with regard to these. We referred to Alexander the Great earlier. He was convinced the "flying shields" came from underwater, and that's where he was convinced they "lived." And remember those Russian divers? They were killed while trying to investigate an underwater USO. American naval vessels have spotted USOs on numerous occasions. Even the aircraft carrier, Franklin D.

Roosevelt, from 1958 through 1960, was widely known for being shadowed by USOs and UFOs while at sea.[lxxxiv] American submarines have tracked objects under the sea that behaved as no then existing submarine could have or even now can. Even Christopher Columbus cited a USO on his first trip to the New World.[lxxxv]

UFOs have been seen coming up from mountains and some coming up from valleys. Whether this means they came from out of the ground is uncertain. Some witnesses claim they do, that they come from caves in the Earth, or hidden bases below ground. We have not seen enough credible evidence to either support or deny this idea.

Could they come from hidden bases below ground? Yes, they conceivably could. The American government has hidden bases underground and even during World War II, both the Allies and Germany had numerous bunkers situated below ground and sometimes whole factories situated beneath the Earth's surface. So this idea is not outlandish in and of itself. Also, they could have hidden bases below the sea or under lakes. With the number of USOs seen raising out of water, out of lakes, out of seas, out of the oceans, and even out of rivers, this idea is not out of the question at all.

Given the supposed capabilities of these UFOs, of being able to travel underwater, why shouldn't they have underwater bases? It would be a great place to hide, because we cannot go to near the depths these things probably can, given their apparent high technological levels and capabilities as described by many witnesses. Although, our technology of late, just in the last two decades, seems to be getting there, a bit. Even though we can't go as far into the oceans ourselves, our robotic equipment can. Still we have so little of such robots available at this point, that any hidden bases by the aliens would hardly be readily found. The oceans are vast. They cover about 70% of the Earth. And with only 20 to 30 deep-sea robotic devices at our ready disposal, we are unlikely to happen on alien bases by sheer chance in the foreseeable near future.

But as to where the UFOs/USOs come from originally, we can only guess. Some UFO theorists suggest a planet orbiting the star Zeta Reticuli,[lxxxvi] since some evidence points toward this. Others look to Orion's Belt, the star, Sirius, or somewhere in the Pleiades. There is some evidence (to some small degree), for each of these as being a possible point of origin.

Others say they come from within our own Solar System, as indeed, the one official claiming they were likely from the Moon, Titan. Or it may be that this is not their original home, but only a base (perhaps one of several or more) of operations, even as our International Space Station is such a base of operations.

One thing seems to be clear, they are here. And they are seen, or manifestations of them are seen, in some areas much more than others. Why this is, is still unknown, although again, various theorists refer to a world grid of power points, or ley lines that provide energy, etc., which they utilize to facilitate the movement of their UFOs. Still others think there might be "star gates" through which they can transport that might exist in certain areas; such gates perhaps being natural or otherwise.

But given the available evidence, the multiple sightings, we have established what we think is a pattern. We think there are possible places, locations from which they are at least operating, although perhaps not places of their original origin. So although they may come from another stellar system, either via a star gate or not, or transport in an interdimensional way from some other parallel universe or dimension to ours, we think the evidence indicates they also have bases here.

Where here? Well, in the next chapter, we'll discuss this.

CHAPTER 15

Look To Your Moon For Warning!

And this chapter title, along with what we've mentioned earlier, pretty much says what we feel. Given the startling contents of the **NASA Technical Report R-277**, the incredible number of strange sightings it so carefully lists, including the number of bizarre variations in such sightings, and those having occurred over such a long time, we feel the aliens may well have a hidden base or bases on our Moon. Further, they may have been there an incredibly long time. This would seem reasonable given the available evidence.

As we mentioned earlier in this book, the Principle of Occam's Razor would have us choose this answer. It is the simplest explanation, rather than trying to come up with a variety of explanations, ones for which our current knowledge of science can't adequately back up. So going by scientists' own adage, "all things being equal, the simplest answer is the best," and using Occam's Razor in this way, we have to go with the idea that aliens are responsible for many of the events we've witnessed on the Moon.

That answer alone can account for all the phenomena witnessed. What's more, although we're sure scientists consider this an "extraordinary claim," the NASA report has a "preponderance of evidence," and an "extraordinary" amount of such evidence, over four centuries of it, to show something very strange is happening on our Moon. For a supposedly "dead world," as many scientists refer to it, it seems pretty lively to us!

Yes, extraterrestrials very well may have bases elsewhere, as well, as with having them underwater here on Earth, for instance, and this wouldn't be at all surprising to us. A good amount of evidence seems to indicate this may be so. After all, America has bases all over the world, and different types of ones at that. We use these to project our power aboard, to influence events around the world.

Why should aliens or extraterrestrials be any different in this regard? In addition, why else would the aliens be seen coming and going so often from under the sea? Unless they are on very expensive fishing expeditions, it must be for some other reason, and that probably is that there are bases below our oceans.

After all, in a world with seven billion people in it, it must be increasingly harder for the aliens or extraterrestrials to hide from us. As a species on the land, we humans are just about everywhere these days and in large numbers. No doubt, this accounts partly for the rise in the number of sightings of UFOs. There are simply more people occupying places where they never did before. More people have cameras and video equipment as we have never had before. So as one would expect, we are capturing more images of the UFOs.

Therefore, if the aliens have bases, where can they put them where they won't be easily discovered? Where could they erect long-term bases where they could reasonably expect not to be found out and then attacked, or their work then interfered with in any real way? Well, the only places we are not occupying are areas deep beneath the Earth, or deep in the oceans, as well as on our Moon, where we have no permanent presence (or even temporary presence, as of this writing).

With regard to our seas, again, our submarines and ships have tracked strange objects, large ones, moving at incredible speeds deep beneath the surface of the waters, and coming and going, back and forth, from them. Those Russian divers died in just this sort of incident. Even so, although it seems likely aliens may have bases in the seas; they must know that eventually, as our technologies develop more, it will be harder and harder to keep them hidden.

Where does that leave us? Well, although "they" may have a while yet where they may consider themselves reasonably safe beneath the waves of our world, the only real place close by where they can still hide with reasonable certainty is the Moon. It is the logical choice. It is close enough for them to observe us very well, and with their technology, to reach us fairly easily, but it is still far enough away for us not to be able to go there anywhere nearly so easily. Logistically, it's perfect in these ways.

And until very recently in our history, just decades ago, as long as they operated from the far side of the Moon, we had absolutely no way of even knowing they were there. But as the technical report from NASA shows, something is also happening on our side of the Moon, the side that always faces us, as well as on the far side. If they wished to observe us directly, they'd need a base or bases there.

Could they have bases there now? If so, they would have to be underground nowadays, to avoid our new capabilities of detection with our lunar orbiters, and such.[lxxxvii] Then that should come as no surprise. After all, many versions of our own plans for bases on the Moon include the idea of possible subterranean shelters. Underground bases are the safest way to live on the Moon. They shield the occupants from harsh solar radiation, cosmic rays, and meteorites. This is why we would probably live that way there.

However, there is one other obvious reason for living underground. That is if you want to hide your presence from any possible observers from the Earth. One can watch, without being watched in this way.

But why a multiplicity of bases? Wouldn't just one well-hidden one be better? Along these lines, some even claim the entire Moon is just that, a gargantuan spaceship in disguise, a massive base of alien operations. Some conspiracy theorists even claim the Moon is hollow. They point to the fact of one statement by NASA, after deliberately crash-landing a satellite on the Moon that the Moon then "rain like a bell." From this, they interpret the idea that NASA implied it was hollow.[lxxxviii]

We don't see this idea as a real possibility, truly feasible, ourselves. First, practically any solid object of a cohesive material can be made to "ring like a bell." When the Earth has a major earthquake, the same thing happens, it "rings like a gong."[lxxxix] It vibrates afterwards. Scientists have measured these seismic shock waves, so we know this to be true.

In any case, even we have figured out the approximate mass of the Moon, and no celestial body of that size, if hollow, could have so much mass, exert the kind of gravitational influence it does, unless perhaps, there was a black hole at its center creating that extra source of missing mass.

Again, using the Principle of Occam's Razor, this idea just seems highly unlikely. The simplest explanation here, all things being equal otherwise, says the aliens would have bases on the Moon, but the Moon itself is not a giant, hollow, disguised spacecraft. If it were, how do we account for the fact the material on the surface of the Moon is identical to that of our own Earth's crust, with regard to composition and age? [xc]

Again, why go through such an elaborate charade, if you have the kind of power it would take to create such a monstrously large spacecraft? Therefore, isn't that just too an elaborate idea, a too farfetched solution? Going by Occam's Razor, we simply don't need to go to such extremes to have someone watch us in secret from a gigantic disguised spaceship, especially when just having a base or few bases on the Moon would suffice, instead.

This would account for what observers are seeing. As the aliens come and go from these bases, one would see, perhaps, periodic flashes of light, streaks, "starlike" objects, etc. Vapors, mists, and clouds could all be waste products, gases resulting from venting of those bases, and/or their craft. Remember, many UFO witnesses claim to have seen similar things coming from alien spacecraft, in the form of mists and even "angel hair," a strange, white, wispy substance that falls to earth and then evaporates.[xci]

There is one other matter to consider here that we haven't really discussed in any depth before. That is, there may be more than one type of extraterrestrial species visiting our Earth.

There is some good evidence for this idea. The Vedic texts of ancient India claimed there were over a hundred different alien worlds and species "out there." Eyewitnesses of aliens describe more than one version of god or alien being, as well, although several types do seem to dominate these testimonies. These are the "grays," the "Nordics," and the squat "blue" ones, as well as an insect-like, or "reptilian" bipeds, among others.

Of course, some of these descriptions may be referring to the same type of creature, just remembered or viewed under different circumstances than some other witness might have seen them. Still, obviously a Nordic-style human looks nothing like a "gray." And since there have been numerous reports of both types of these aliens, one has to wonder if there are not two distinct species of them, or probably even more, as the Indians in their Vedic texts state.

There is further backing for this idea when one considers the various different forms of interference with human life on earth over the ages. So many cases of such interaction seem to be relatively benign, while others smack strongly of the sinister and deadly. This means there may not only be more than one alien base on Earth or near it on the Moon, but there may be more than one species occupying them. This would account for the different sorts of behavior various eyewitnesses and abductees claim, because it is highly likely different alien species would behave just that way—differently.

What's more, they may not always get along. We refer to the Vedic texts again (much in the Ramayana, in this case), and their descriptions of aerial wars, not only on Earth, but in space, and in one case, even one battle on the Moon! Vitrified rock of forts in northern Scotland (although the more-distant, surrounding, native rock in the area made of the same material was not vitrified—just in the area of the stone of the forts), the vitrified pottery found at Mohenjo-Daro, higher than normal radiation levels in some skeletal remains there, all act to form possible evidence of the idea of warring between alien species.

More evidence? Again, how about the evidence supplied by the woodcut of the aerial battle above Medieval Nuremburg, Basel, etc.? Thousands of people witnessed these events. The list seems almost endless in this regard, and all the items on it seem to show the aliens may at times be fighting amongst themselves, perpetrating major wars. The fighting either could be with various factions of the same species, or as postulated by some Ancient Aliens theorists, other species of extraterrestrials, as well.

Are these creatures from another stellar system, another galaxy, from our future, or from some other strange parallel world?

Our answer to this question is another question. "Does it really make a difference?" Because for us, it is more a question of what the aliens are doing to us, rather than where they come from.

When you are being invaded, does it really make a difference where the invaders' homeland is? Would you not be primarily concerned with saving yourself and your loved ones' lives, intent on just driving the enemy out of your homeland once more? It's not as if we could bomb the aliens' homeland, as we bombed enemies during World War II. We don't have transdimensional means of travel to parallel universes, or any spacecraft that can take us to other solar systems. We barely have the means to travel to a limited degree in our own solar system.

Yes, in the end, it would be nice to know where they come from, and it might help in any battle that we may eventually have to wage with them. Nevertheless, our more pressing concerns lie much closer to home. Can we live our lives in relative peace? Must we be afraid of "them?" Is there anything we can do better to safeguard our families and ourselves?

Perhaps, we can do something. Maybe, there are some steps we can take better to insure our survival. We will consider some of the answers to these questions in the next chapter.

CHAPTER 16

The Status Of Us And "Them?"

Here we have come to the crux of the matter. Through the Principle of Occam's Razor, we've shown, step by step, and chapter by chapter that the simplest and most likely scenario is that not only do aliens or extraterrestrial exist, but they most likely have been here a long time.

Countless witnesses and observations (and we mean seemingly countless!), show "they" invade our airspace and our seas with impunity, on a daily basis, and they harass, interfere, abduct and manipulate us, our planes, and vessels, and all at seeming will.

Also, Ancient Aliens theorists have argued effectively that even our history and the lives (and deaths?) of millions over the millennia have been interfered with, as well, and on a massive scale—repeatedly! They cite so-called "anomalies," which are so abundant one can hardly call them anomalies any more, found in mines and dug up in various archaeological digs and from other locations around the world, as proof of their claims.

They also cite directly from just about every ancient religious text we have today, including the Sumerians, Babylonians, Bible Old Testament, Hopi legends, Mayans, and, of course, those incredible Vedic texts of India, among many others.

From around the entire globe, from civilization after civilization, from written texts, as well as oral traditions, people speak of the "sky gods," "angels," "messengers" from heaven, "sky guardians," "sky lords," "star visitors," and such. Many civilizations' histories even tell where in the sky they think the so-called "gods" came from. Others have erected enormous monuments, such as the pyramids, to mirror stellar constellations in the heavens, places where perhaps they think their masters came from and originally resided.

There are towns and villages across Europe and Britain, built along supposed "ley lines" all with the word "star" embedded in their original names centuries ago, as if someone wanted to preserve these names for posterity, and their reference to "star." There is also evidence for their having been a nuclear holocaust in our past. Again, the evidence for interference by "someone" is overwhelming. Since we didn't have such capabilities so long ago, then "someone" else must have had them.

And to reiterate, most importantly, is this last conclusion: We are the victims of their manipulation of us. We are now, have been, and continue to be at their mercy. The interference, apparently, even includes numerous, perhaps countless deaths and injuries.

Please understand this; if it is anywhere near as bad as many Ancient Aliens theorists claim, if only a tiny portion of the thousands of abductions cases reported today are true, if "they" are truly buzzing and interfering with the flights of some aircraft, ocean going vessels, and submarines, then we have much to fear from them. Because even at the smallest level of acceptance of the available reports, taking only the barest minimum of such reports as true, the results still show the aliens, for want of a better phrasing, "just don't give a damn" about us. Worse, it might just be that they do, but not in a good way, not if we are just so many victims of "culling," abductions, and/or other forms of rank interference in our lives and those lives that came before us.

The problem is simple. They are here. Another problem is the government of the United States seems either powerless to interfere on our behalves as its citizens, is perhaps actively covering up the problem, or could be if one wants to go so far as to believe conspiracy theories, even actively in collusion with the aliens in some way.

Why do we wonder about this last? Well, because other governments have been much more forthcoming on these matters, and seem to be much more willing to hide less (although, it seems they are still hiding some information to some degree on many an occasion), but they, too, seem powerless to interfere with the aliens or their agenda.

For instance, as one recent UFO researcher in Israel put it, "In the last twelve years," just about every kind of UFO imaginable has been seen over Israel. Having been in the Israeli Air Force, he claims firsthand knowledge that not only did the military there know UFOs exist, but also that they have repeatedly tried to intercept them. This, despite no public proclamations or comments of any sort regarding UFOs by the Israeli Air Force, either good, bad, or even neutral.

So again, as far as the status of UFOs and aliens/extraterrestrials flitting about our skies and moving beneath our oceans go, they are here. Sightings and/or abductions will continue as they have been, but it is rather obvious now we will receive little or no help from our governments on the matter for whatever the reason(s). Take all the pictures you want, all the videos you like, with the highest resolution camera you can afford, and although those pictures will be of interest to many people, including UFO researchers and the like, they will have no impact on government, at least, not publicly. Our governments, principally the American one, will not assist or help in any constructive or obvious way that is of benefit to you or me, as citizens.

In other words, when it comes to sighting UFOs and whatever may result from such, you're on your own. Oh, you might get some help from the local authorities, but what can they do; chase after UFOs in their patrol cars, when such UFOs can easily outrun our best jets? How can they, then, be of any real aid to you? Many of them have recorded sightings of their own, and/or have been the victims of so-called "missing time," too. And what's our government's response to all this? They claimed the local authorities have just misidentified swamp gas, Venus, or something. Right...we've heard that line before and often enough!

There is one other thing to consider here, as well. Like so many others who did not do this, and so suffered the consequences, be careful about whether you report such sightings or not. The reason for this is the damage it may do to your reputation and career. While in some countries, such as the United Kingdom, where they actively ask their pilots to report such things, here in the United States, quite the reverse seems to be true.

Control tower operators, airline pilots, and other officials who have reported seeing strange objects in the sky, have often, at the very least, been ridiculed, and sometimes even subjected to or been pressured to have psychological evaluations done on them in order to keep their jobs. Some have been suspended from their work, and others transferred. Some were even fired! There is the case of the Japanese pilot who insisted on reporting UFOs tailing his commercial jet over Alaska. This was confirmed by ground radar and another plane's sightings, as well. The result? That pilot now is a "desk jockey," having been "promoted" from being a pilot, a job he loved to do, to that of being a glorified clerk. Get it? Reporting UFOs, insisting upon them being a reality, and even when there is ample evidence to support your contentions, can be a very unhealthy career move.

To put it another way, many people have a good reason to remain silent about what they see that seems unusual in the skies or seas. Even worse, it seems as if our government and/or whatever powers there may be, are actively trying to suppress these reports through such deliberate and negative responses. Remember, people have lost their jobs over reporting such things, including some commercial jetliner pilots. Either that or they are told in no uncertain terms (when they are military people, for instance), that they will obtain no further promotions and/or are sworn to secrecy.

Therefore, many simply do not choose to report such UFO sightings. This last is so obviously true in so many cases, spoken of so often by various people who do not want their identity revealed, or having retired, would only then reveal their identities that we won't even bother to attempt to argue that all this is true. It simply is.

Even people on their death beds have confessed to seeing things, having been involved in things with regard to UFOs, and had kept their silence for years because they'd sworn an oath to do so. We do not feel we are in a position to question or dispute these people or their final confessions. What they say under such circumstances must obviously be true as they see it, at the very least.

So the status on reporting UFOs to official sources being a good idea? No, we don't think it is a good idea to be honest, not if you have "too much to lose." This is the nature of things today. That's what our governments (again, principally the United States Government) seem to want. An intensely negative, even dangerous atmosphere has been created for those who dare to report UFOs. You either can lose your job, career, be called "crazy," ridiculed, or all of these things.

We wish we could say this current sad state of affairs was otherwise, but we simply can't. Of course, the more people who report such things, the more data we collect, the more information we accumulate, and the more we may then be able to arrive at some real, useable answers. Nevertheless, personally, we can't say to people who are in sensitive jobs or are on tricky career paths that they do report such things, that they should go ahead anyway and ignore all the possible repercussions. Because those repercussions can be great and very damaging to their careers, if not lives!

We suggest, instead, that if this is the case with you, and such a thing happens and you do see a UFO or USO, that perhaps instead of contacting official authorities on the matter, you might wish instead to contact MUFON. Even then, depending on your personal circumstances, you may want to do it anonymously. However, anonymous reports simply can't be taken as seriously as those made by people willing to identify themselves and for obvious reasons. There is, of course, the question of all those who like to perpetrate hoaxes still, "muddy the waters," as it were.

In addition, when you are out driving on that lonely road at night and see a strange light in the sky approaching you, please remember that for all practical purposes, you probably will be on your own. Don't expect any military jets suddenly to appear zooming overhead, firing away at the object, to valiantly and heroically intercept the UFO and so save you. Because chances are overwhelming, there will be no such jet, nobody to help you. You are on your own. So the decisions and actions you personally make will help determine what the outcome for you will be. Put bluntly; your fate is partly in your own hands, and the rest is in the "hands" of the occupants of any such UFOs.

If you are abducted, the same holds true. You are on your own. And truthfully? Whatever happens then will happen. You will have little or no choice in the matter as to what, how, and when "they" do something to you, physically, mentally, or otherwise. But judging by the countless reports of abductees, we can be completely certain that the results will not be pleasant, and that they will be painful and perhaps even life altering for you. So think carefully before you approach that "alien spacecraft" sitting in a shadowed meadow, or hovering over a dark forest at night.

If you are the owner of animals, such as a rancher, you must also beware. Your personal lives and those of your animals are subject to the whims of those "others," as well. With the thousands of cattle mutilations being reported, it would seem the aliens/extraterrestrials have no more regard for the animals' lives, than they do for ours, or our rights as humans, for that matter.

So the status of UFOs when it comes to us, as individuals? Again, it's just not good, not good at all. Our advice is if you see a UFO approaching too closely, run! Run as fast as you can away from it, and don't stop until you feel you are safe. We repeat; in this current reality, with the status of things, it seems we are all alone when it comes to facing these things. There will be no or little help from authorities. We can do little ourselves to stop these creatures. So our only alternative, again, is to run. This is true now and we think it's always been true.

This is a bitter truth to learn, we know, but too many have already had to learn it at their high personal cost, and often at a terribly high price. Whether people have had their careers ruined for speaking out, their jobs taken away, been publicly ridiculed and laughed at, this is a truth they have had to learn the hard way. The same goes for those who have been abducted or otherwise been interfered with or hurt by these monsters.

One of the things we can't understand is how some Ancient Aliens theorists think "they" are a kind, benevolent species, and trying to help us "evolve" to their "higher" level. When we see such a researcher on television saying that we have been hybridized over thousands of years and that we have been created and/or altered continually by them until we are, for all practical purposes, just like the aliens now, we cringe. And this is so that when they come again, we won't be frightened, that we will welcome them as celestial brothers and/or sisters? Well, don't we have to ask ourselves how such researchers can possibly think such a thing, think it is a "good" thing?

After all, aren't these the same aliens about whom they also have charged with having committed mass "cullings" (killings) of members of the human race and with impunity? Are these the same aliens that have been supposedly performing medical and DNA experiments on us without our permission? Are these the same extraterrestrials inducing physical changes in us over the centuries, and without our permission?

And now we're supposed to welcome with open arms these creatures when they finally come out in the open and announce their return to us from on high? Really? Really???

Well, we don't think so! If anything, we should run as far and as fast as we can from them. If they arrive and admit to all these charges as having been the truth, we should wage war against them for having killed millions of us over the millennia, for having attempted or even completed genocide upon various races of humanity.

It doesn't matter that they may have done it (by their way of thinking) for "our own good," our ultimate wellbeing. What gives them the right? We've heard that excuse once too often throughout history already and it always meant the deaths of thousand, even millions of us, for "our own good."

No; we are living, breathing, sentient creatures with our own rights, and we should have the right to choose always when it comes to what is done to us. What's more, to kill self-aware, conscious people and as just a means to an end, is unconscionable, and inexcusable! It's a war crime! We're betting that if the tables were turned, "they" wouldn't be thinking nearly so kindly toward us if we'd been perpetrating such crimes over the ages against them in such a terrible way.

Do we sound adamant about this? You bet! The evidence is in. We've sifted through masses of it. We have shown here by repeatedly using the Principle of Occam's Razor what the most likely conclusions are, and those conclusions are not all good by any means.

Through no fault of our own, we are, all of us, victims. We have been victims, and it may well be that we will continue to be victims on a massive scale for a long time to come. And it seems nobody, other than ourselves as individuals, and a few small struggling groups such as MUFON, are doing anything to help us.

So for the third time; what's the status of UFOs and how they relate to us?

THE ANSWER IS: "THEY" ARE HERE!

They've treated us with an incredibly callous disregard for our lives and rights as humans. Worst of all, it seems for all practical purposes we're totally on our own as far as our governments go, when it comes to protecting us!

So what can we do to help ourselves, since we are so on our own? Is there anything we can do? Well, to have answers to this, we need to define the limits of "their" power. Do they have any such limits, or are they, for all practical purposes, omnipotent?

And if not, just how much power do they have? Again, this also is intimately involved with their intentions, for those intentions, meaning the outcome they desire from all of this, defines how much power they can apply to a situation without it resulting in negative consequences for "their" plans or goals. We'll discuss this in the next chapter.

CHAPTER 17

What Is The Extent of The Aliens' Powers And Capabilities?

The above chapter title forms a crucial question for us. Just to what extent are their powers? Some would say we have no way of knowing this answer. They may be right…to a degree. Still, we can make some strong inferences. Let's start with the simple question: Are they all-powerful?

The answer to this is no, they most likely are not. If they were all-powerful, what need would they have for us? Why would they want to interfere with us, literally, even bother with us at all? If they are all-powerful, we would be as insects to them, so beyond us in capabilities would they be. They simply would have no need for us, or anything we might have to offer them. Being all-powerful, they could do whatever they want, whenever they wanted, and anywhere in the universe. They would be as gods.

A good analogy to this would be to reference the movie, **Forbidden Planet**.[xcii] Does this seem like an unlikely place from which to draw a comparison to real aliens? In fact, no, because actually, it's a very good analogy, and is one to illustrate our point here.

The premise of the movie was based on the idea that the original native inhabitants of the planet had developed an instrumentality of the highest order. Using a tremendous, planetary-wide machine, their very thoughts then became real. They had but to imagine something, wish for something, or think of something they desired, and it became real, manifest. They were, for all practical purposes, virtually omnipotent in this respect. They apparently no longer explored space, as humans did in the movie, because they simply had no further need to do so. Everything they wanted, desired, they had right there at home on their own planet. There was no need to go sailing dark interstellar depths of space, to go anywhere else at all. Why bother?

And wouldn't just this sort of behavior apply to our aliens if they were so powerful? If they had everything they needed, everything they wanted, then why would they bother to come here to Earth, to expend the time, energy, and materials to accomplish this feat? They would simply have no need to do such a thing. Again, why bother? So we can safely assume if they are from "elsewhere," then they are not omnipotent. As advanced as they may, they still must have limitations. Otherwise, they simply wouldn't have come here in the first place.

So it then seems very likely they aren't all powerful. This means, by very definition, they have limitations. Just what are these limitations? Well, we know they have fantastic means of traveling. At least, they seem fantastic by the standards of our more comparatively primitive capabilities. Whether they come from other dimensions, the future, or from elsewhere in space, their vehicles still seem to be well beyond ours in technological capabilities.

However, despite such incredible transportation, these ships, too, seem to have their limitations, as well. Judging by the various reports of such alien spacecraft in our skies and seas, we can see they come in many sizes and shapes. Then, why not? Isn't this also true of our own vehicles?

On the ground, we have cars, trucks, vans, motorcycles—you name it, we have variations on the theme of the internal combustion, hybrid, and electric engine. The same holds true for our aircraft. We have propeller-driven planes, jets, rockets, helicopters, dirigibles, air balloons, gliders, again, you name it, and we seem to have it.

Therefore, it isn't such a great leap, such an unusual idea to think the aliens might have the same sort of variations in their vehicles' capabilities, too. Remember, triangular craft, spherical craft, cigar-shaped ships have all been reported, along with many other forms of alien vehicles.

Of course, this also might be indicative that there is more than one type of alien involved. Different aliens might have different types of spacecraft. However, this would be even worse news for us in one respect, because instead of having to deal with just one advanced species, we might well have to deal with many more than just that one. Even so, it would appear the aliens are not omnipotent in nature overall, and their craft do have limitations in their capabilities, and so are designed for different functions.

One further point; rumors abound here and abroad, as well, of "downed" alien spacecraft. If these rumors are at all true to any degree, this also proves the aliens and their vehicles are not omnipotent, that they do have weaknesses. If a great conflict between "them" and us ever arose, these weaknesses, these frailties of theirs would be of paramount importance to us, militarily speaking.

Our belief that the aliens may be using the Moon as a base also enters into this equation. The mere fact one needs bases is a form of limitation itself. Bases, by their very nature, are products of logistics. If you are all-powerful, or if your vehicles are all-powerful, you simply don't need to have bases. If you are capable of projecting your power instantly anywhere you want to, and to any degree you need, and at any time, any distance, why then would you have a need for bases? Under such circumstances, bases would be superfluous, unnecessary.

Following this line of reasoning, the fact the aliens do seem to have such bases, principally on the Moon, and perhaps below the oceans, would suggest they are definitely limited in their abilities, that they have to consider logistics, just as we do. This fact further supports the idea of them being limited in what they can accomplish, what their ultimate capabilities might be. Again, this works to our advantage. It means they must have some vulnerability. In short, although powerful as we measure power, still, they are not God or gods.

However, according to many, their power would still seem to be vast. If one takes into account all the abduction reports by various people, it would seem the aliens can float through walls, take people out of their houses through those same walls, levitate them up into the sky to their ships, and do all sorts of other things that seem to defy the laws of physics. But is this really so? Or do the aliens have limitations even here, in these respects?

Let's look at the facts as reported to us by all these abductees. First, the aliens seem to have to take these people onboard a ship to perform whatever activities they want to upon them. This is a limitation in and of itself. If they were truly all-powerful, they could simply perform these acts from a distance, without the people ever having to be dragged from their homes in the middle of the night and put onboard the ships.

Secondly, many people report they had something inserted into them, somewhere in their bodies. There has even been some evidence of this found, with small bits of matter being removed from some of those who claim such a thing has happened to them.

Those abductees involved, think it is some sort of tracking device, or data gathering instrument, a telemeter device of some kind. If this is so, then again, this shows a limitation on the part of the aliens. The fact the aliens even have to place such devices in people means they cannot monitor them at a distance without such devices implanted in their subjects, just as we have to do ourselves when tracking various species of animals.

This is yet another limitation on the part of the aliens. It would seem they are very much like us humans in these matters. They have to physically interact with people, place certain monitoring devices in or on their person, and then have to monitor these devices, as well as periodically to make physical contact with those people again. Again, all very much the way humans would perform experiments on other people or animals.

Now we come to the matter of their capabilities with regard to abductees. Can the aliens really enter through walls of houses, and then drag their victims out through them? Perhaps this is true, but also perhaps this is not the actual case. You see, we must view abduction reports just as we would many UFO reports. After all, they are also subjective pieces of evidence, and not objective ones. If anything, they are even more subjective in nature than reports of UFOs are. In other words, just as with UFOs reports, we have to discount (unfortunately) a large number of such abduction reports as simply being mistaken, misinterpretations of mundane events, or just outright hoaxes.

Why? Well, the answer for this is there are various reasons. Some people may simply be experiencing an unusual form of sleep paralysis, as some scientists claim. Others, and this would be a sad thing, may simply have deep, personal, emotional problems, or other forms of neuroses, that cause them to claim such a thing—a cry for help, as it were. And we have to be honest here; just as with hoaxes regarding UFOs sightings, some people are going to commit hoaxes with regard to claiming alien abductions.

Certainly, not all such reports are hoaxes, of course. There seems to be too much proof to the contrary in this matter. But just what percentage of the reports are the result of sleep paralysis mistaken for abductions, people with some sort of neuroses who "think" that something has happened to them when it hasn't, or persons just claiming abductions to get into the "limelight" we simply don't know. Do they form a significant portion of the UFO abduction report claims? It would appear they might. The exact percentage, of course, we simply can't determine.

Still, this may account for some of the things reported as being real, but just not being so. Perhaps, people aren't pulled through the walls of their house, and those people just think they were. Can humans be floated up to a spaceship without any physical means, be possible? Well, we've accomplished similar sorts of things in the laboratory with inanimate objects, on a smaller scale, of course. Using magnetism is one way to do this. So the jury is still out on that one, what is actually possible with humans in that regard. The aliens are more advanced than we are, obviously, and so may be able to accomplish this.

We are more inclined to believe those abductee reports that state the victims first saw a UFO, subsequently had memory loss, and/or then claim memories of abductions later. We feel these are probably, for the most part, true. Oh, one could probably quibble over some of the details, but overall, these people are probably telling something close to how it happened. And who knows? Perhaps those others, who claim to have been pulled physically through walls without any problem, are telling the truth, too. We simply don't know.

What we do know is the aliens apparently have limitations even with regard to abductions. Their ships must come near their intended victims. They must perform some actions to get those victims aboard their ships. They then have to do physical inspections and/or examinations, as well as physically implanting items within some of their abductees.

All this implies limitations. They simply can't summon someone from anywhere on the planet to their bases on the Moon or their home planet and have them arrive their in an instant. The aliens must come to them to do what they want to do to them, and they can't just "beam" victims to the Moon or their home worlds.

There is also one final factor to consider; if the aliens have an agenda with us, as they certainly seem to have, then they are probably restricted by this very agenda with regard to what they can do to us. Interfere too much, and their ultimate goals may be subverted or ruined.

As we've said, our government seems to want to keep their existence secret. Oddly, the aliens and despite the constant sightings by witnesses of them, the many abductions of humans they commit, seem to want this same thing. Otherwise, why wipe the memory of the abductees, so they can't remember the abductions? This must be in order to keep it a relative secret.

Let's be practical here. Aliens certainly have the power to appear in force in our skies and perhaps in large numbers, as well, and so make the evidence for their existence incontrovertible, a blatant fact, if they so chose. However, this behavior they seem to avoid. They could make their existence also a well-known fact simply by not wiping the memories of all those abductees, and just let them remember everything.

Instead, "they" go through the effort of removing such memories. It is only years later, or under hypnosis, that most of these people then remember what happened to them. Our government, in some sort of weird collusion, seems to be backing the aliens up with regard to their nonexistence, by using ridicule, disinformation, and by simply ignoring legitimate reports made by people from all occupations.

This means there is a considerable effort being put forth to keep their existence a relative secret. We say "relative," because as mentioned earlier, the majority of Americans now believe UFOs do exist. Still, for decades, this approach has worked pretty well. Of late, it seems to be breaking down. Our trust in our governments on this subject is waning at an alarming rate in recent times. Again, we refer you to the polls taken that show most Americans, and indeed, many people worldwide, often the majority in the countries polled, believe UFOs exist, and do this despite governmental proclamations that aliens and "flying saucers" do not exist.

What can we conclude from all this? Well, obviously, we can deduce there is a need for secrecy on the aliens' part. Whether this is also true on the government's part in order to keep things seemingly "normal," or otherwise, remains an open question.

But why would the aliens collude with our government in trying to maintain such secrecy, unless they, too, need, or want it this way for some reason, unless it aids in achieving their goals, their agenda? What does this mean for us?

Well, it would appear to be another form of limitation on the powers of the aliens, this need to maintain some level of secrecy. This means they must proceed in a certain way in order to obtain their goals, to achieve their agenda. But in having to do so, this limits them and their actions, as with the need to wipe the memories of abductees.

Just how much in this respect does it limit them? Again, we simply do not know. If forced to come out in the open, would it be just a minor problem for them, or would it ruin their agenda completely to do so?

We must keep in mind it isn't just with our modern governments the aliens have been keeping secrets, but throughout our history. Yes, according to Ancient Aliens theorists, they have been interfering with us on a large scale, but still it always seems as if they remain in the background, work their magic through puppet kings and such, etc., according to these same theorists. It appears "they" only come out in the open when they really have to do so.

So the limitation of keeping things secret seems to be an integral part of their agenda. And yes, this does form another and definite limitation on their part.

To conclude this chapter, we have to say that although the aliens are certainly far more advanced than we are, they are not God or gods, as they may have tried to convince our ancestors. They have definite limitations and in many respects. Although it may often seem like they are not, they really are subject to the same laws of physics as we are. They must use ships to get from Point A to Point B, and just as we do. They even seem to be using many different kinds of ships, so no one type of vehicle seems to serve all purposes for them. We do this as humans, because each type of craft serves a different function for us. Logic would seem to dictate that the same must then hold true for "them," as well, given the different types of craft sighted.

Even the Vedic texts refer to many different types of "vimanas."[xciii] Those same texts also refer to different types of aliens, as well. If this is truly so, then this fact could work to our human advantage in some ways, if not others. If these are competing species, then there well may be conflict, as the Vedic texts also seem strongly to imply. Where there is competition, there can be, and often is, discord. And if there is none, perhaps some seeds of discontent can be sown by us. Put another way, we may be able "to divide and conquer." The Vedic texts state conflicts went on and resulted in what appears to have been a nuclear holocaust, a major war that engulfed not only the earth, but even the Moon to some degree, and perhaps the home worlds of many of these aliens. If this is so or just partly true even, it works to our possible future benefit.

Yes, the aliens are advanced. They are very powerful. They have great technological capabilities. However, we have shown here they also have definite limitations in many respects. They are not gods. And they are certainly not the God. And thank God for that! So being limited in power as they are, can we then use this fact to protect ourselves from them? The next chapter takes up this issue.

CHAPTER 18

Can We Protect Ourselves? Do We Need To?

The answers to the above questions are: yes and yes. That is, there is much we can do to protect ourselves, although, as with all such things there are no absolute guarantees. We'll discuss this at length later. As for the second question, we think the entire thrust of this book shows that, yes, it is absolutely necessary to protect ourselves as best we can, and to the reasonable best of our abilities. To do otherwise would be to court possible disaster through sheer inaction.

But let's go back just a little ways first, because to protect ourselves as best we can, we have to remember exactly what we are dealing with here, and just what "they" are capable of doing. As we constantly try to point out, "to know one's enemy is to be forearmed against them," as the axiom goes.

Throughout this book, we have attempted to show by using the Principle of Occam's Razor that we can arrive at certain reasonable conclusions about the aliens. At least, these are the most reasonable, if one goes by the simplest explanations (all other things being equal), as in accordance with that principle. And by using the Principle of Occam's Razor, we have arrived at the following results:

1. Aliens or extraterrestrials, whether they are from another solar system, our own solar system, some other dimension, or future time, do exist. Simply put, they are here and they are not "us." At least not yet, since some theorists claim they are slowly turning "us" into "them."

2. In all likelihood, they have been around for a long time in one form or another. This may mean we have had a succession of visits, which might include different or multiple alien species, or it may simply mean we've had the same ones appearing in our skies for centuries, perhaps even for millennia.

Therefore, Ancient Aliens theorists are correct in that aliens have been here, and have interfered with us in a major way. Although the degree of interference may vary, there can be no doubt that there has been much interference. If it goes as far as some Ancient Aliens theorists suggest, then we are, indeed, the victims of a vast series of manipulations by those "others," in furtherance of whatever scheme or schemes they seem to be trying to fulfill.

3. Worse, the aliens seem to be using just about any means or methods they desire in order to achieve their goals, whatever those goals may be. Again, if certain theorists are right, these goals barely stop short of genocide, if even actually stopping there! We have no way of knowing if certain races of humanity weren't deliberately made extinct by them. If so, this is genocide.

We can only hope this is not the case, but according to those same theorists and a considerable amount of evidence, it is entirely possible. In other words, as far as the aliens are concerned, with regard to us, just about anything goes. Whatever their goals, whatever their ethics or lack of them, they don't seem to include the concept or respect for human rights or even our lives in any real regard. This is an important point.

4. Although the aliens' goals are unknown to us, evidence seems to indicate they might have something to do with genetic manipulation of humanity, as a species. For what purpose they do this, we can only guess, but they seem to have some ultimate goal in this regard, although its exact nature is still manifestly unclear.

5. They also seem to have a callous disregard for us on the individual level, as well as a species, when it comes to achieving their goals. They interfere with our aircraft and ocean-going vessels. They apparently interfere with us as individuals on a grand scale, and anytime they feel like it. In short, they seem to do whatever they want, when they want, and how they want, and their approach is a Machiavellian one, with little regard for human life, possessions, or even our animals, if one is to believe that the aliens are responsible for cattle mutilations, as well.

6. It doesn't stop there. If even a small portion of what Ancient Aliens theorists believe is true, that aliens have been committing vast numbers of murders throughout our history, by way of removing human strains they apparently found undesirable (perhaps genetically undesirable?), then we have much to fear from them.

As just one instance of this, let's remember the stories involving the appearance of the Black Death in various places in Europe, and those strange hooded figures, with their scythe-like objects spewing noxious gases or poisonous vapors. And what leads any of us to believe they've now stopped such practices? When needed, undoubtedly they would still do it, unless their personal mores and ethics have somehow undergone a radical shift of late. We doubt this last.

Judging by the available evidence, their still-constant interference in people's lives without their consent, this just hasn't happened. They still treat us with a callous disregard as rational beings. Aliens may well be amoral creatures for all we know, as we understand the concept of morality. In other words, they simply may have no concept of what we would consider is "right" or "wrong." Even so, this does not bode well for us if this is true. It means they'd have no restrictions on what they'd do to us.

7. Using the Principle of Occam's Razor, we have also concluded the aliens, since they are not omnipotent and must use vehicles, must have bases to project their power/influence. These bases would appear to be in the oceans, possibly underground, and more probably on the Moon, almost certainly so there. On the Moon, they would also be underground bases for obviously practical reasons. This isn't to say that "they" couldn't have bases located in space at the Earth's Lagrange points, very stable places to have such, as well, but we've seen little evidence (so far) for this last. And in days past, they may have had aboveground structures on the moon's far side, as some evidence seems to suggest.

Now knowing these things, helps us think of ways to protect ourselves, and if you don't think people haven't been doing just this, and we're not just talking fringe "survivalist groups" here, then you are sadly out of touch with today's reality.

Not only are individual, so-called survivalists, taking steps to insure their own survival in the event of a major catastrophe, but the wealthy, as individuals, as corporations, and as groups are bunkering down—literally, and it's costing them millions and millions of dollars to do it. We do mean "millions" here, not just a few thousand, or even a few hundred of thousands of dollars. And the rich who are doing this aren't of just one "type." They are across the board, as far as who they are. Need some examples:

Pink Visual, a major adult entertainment company in California announced recently that they are building an "enormous" bunker underground. This bunker is meant to survive any "apocalypse." It is said it will be able to allow up to 1,500 people to survive comfortably there, including the company's sex workers, support staff, administrative staff, families, and even some "fans" of the industry may be allowed to be there. The structure is considered big by any standards, and again according to them, will include bars, microbrewery, living quarters, and much else.

They apparently will not give out the exact location of the bunker to the general populace, though. And, they expect to have it completed well in advance of December, 2012. Keep in mind one thing about all this; it is a very expensive proposition, and although they won't disclose the cost of the bunker project, one can expect it to reach easily into the millions of dollars. [xciv] People don't spend that kind of money, unless they really think they need to! Just why do they think this?

According to an article by Ron Laytner and Martin Ferko and their interview of Brian Camden, who is an owner of the company Hardened Structures (HS) (also shown on

CNBC's Apocalypse 2012 television show), bunkers are now being built at a furious rate here and around the world. [xcv]

Mr. Camden claims the US government is one of the biggest builders of secret bunkers, and according to the article says our government has been on a "binge" of building such secret bunkers for the last 15 years. Hardened Structures is a bona fide company that does contract work for the US government. He also says his company builds bunkers for private and wealthy individuals.

These bunkers come in all sorts of varieties, including ones with generators, battery systems that individuals can even recharge with their exercise cycles, and elaborate filtration systems. Some include the ability of producing oxygen, as with underwater shelters (although some of these are also hidden in "mountains"). The article further states the private owners of such bunkers wish to remain secret, and are accorded this right by the company. Please keep in mind these shelters do not come cheap! The cheapest shelter mentioned in the article, a very modest one that is "disc-like" in shape, but has a protective filtration system costs $38,000. This one can hold six people for a limited duration.

FEMA makes billion-dollar order for dehydrated food.[xcvi] So large is this order that many companies that produce such meals are dedicating virtually their entire output to fulfilling this FEMA order. Furthermore, Mr. Camden and other sources say that FEMA recently has practically cornered the market on dehydrated meals, having purchased some five million meals at one fell swoop alone.

One of the companies even cut loose 99 percent of its regular customers in order to fill the FEMA orders! As Kenneth Schortgen Jr., Finance Examiner at **examiner.com** mentions on his site when he quotes an article from the *Beaufort Observer*, this isn't just an upswing in orders, but "It's a whole new magnitude of business." It's as if FEMA is bent on being the sole customer for all these companies.

And that's not all. FEMA, it is also stated, normally has about six million such meals available on hand for emergencies. This recent order alone is about 426 million meals! That's an incredible increase, and of course, as the article asks, why? Why do they have this sudden need to stock so much! Finally, as the article also asks:

"It almost seems like they're trying to stock a modern day "Noah's Ark," doesn't it?"

For more on this, please go to the **examiner.com** site for a more detailed report on this subject. But that last question is a frightening one, isn't it? Why is FEMA suddenly so intent on maintaining such a huge and so very an expensive stockpile? One has to wonder…

Underground Condos in Kansas can sell for as high 1.75 million dollars. The complex is supposed to comprise 15 underground stories, and have many of the luxuries the wealthy would still want, such as a swimming pool, etc., luxury amenities even desirable in the face of such an event as an apocalypse. It is also said they are turning away new prospective buyers, because the demand is already so great for these condominiums. [xcvii]

Wealthy the worldwide are buying bunkers. Rumors abound, many substantiated, that the wealthy around the world are buying survival bunkers, having them built. From rich Russians to rich Italians, this seems to be so.

"Doomsday Seed Vault" stores millions of seeds.[xcviii] A massive seed vault containing millions of seeds has been built at Spitsbergen Island, inside a mountain on this rock of an island, and situated just over 1,000 kilometers from the North Pole. Bill Gates, according to various sources, had his foundation invest 30 million dollars in this project. There will be or now are air filters, steel-reinforced, dual blast-proof doors, reinforced concrete, motion sensors, and much else. Why such an elaborate and expensive protection system? Why locate it in such an extremely isolated spot, so far from just about anywhere? Why are so many investing large amounts of money to "save seeds?" Are they expecting some planet-wide disaster, because this is an incredibly length to go to just to protect seed diversity.

Why are the rich and our government building bunkers? We must ask this question of ourselves. For decades, individuals, those so-called "fringe" elements of society, have dug and built their own little bunkers, stored them with tools, other implements needed for survival, and various types of preserved foodstuffs and we've thought nothing much of it, have we? These were just "crazies," after all. Right?

But when the extremely wealthy and governments start flocking in great numbers to do this sort of thing, and in droves, and worldwide, then the matter takes on a decidedly different and more ominous tone.

Remember, the wealthy don't get wealthy or stay wealthy by making unwise business decisions. They don't spend/invest large amounts of money unless they feel it will bring them something they want—more money, or something equally important to them, such as their personal survival, perhaps? And, this isn't just a sudden and vast upsurge in "eccentric" millionaires and billionaires doing this. Respectable corporations are doing this, as well, and not just adult entertainment companies, but regular ones, ones we consider "blue chip" companies in many cases.

So, shouldn't we at least be prudent enough to ask ourselves why they are suddenly spending millions upon millions to do this, perhaps even billions in total, *and why now?* Wouldn't one have expected this to occur during the time of the height of the Cold War, rather than lately? Wouldn't one expect this sort of thing more during a highly unstable period of terrorism, but not when such terrorist groups as Al Qaeda have had their organization and ranks so decimated by our governments of late? If it were the lesson of Hurricane Katrina, wouldn't FEMA have upped its supplies sooner than five long years after that event? And why so much food?

Let's be unequivocally clear here; the rich, individually and as corporations, don't throw away millions of dollars on boondoggles. Again, they wouldn't stay wealthy very long if they did. And assuming that most of them have a reasonably astute business sense, one that allowed them to accumulate such wealth in the first place, one then has to conclude that "something is going on."

Now, add in the fact that FEMA is purchasing hundreds of millions of more meals than usual, to the point of drying up the sources for the normal customers of such products all over the country, and they still want more! Add to this fact the government is building bunkers "like crazy" in the last fifteen years, which means they started five years or so before 9-11 occurred, so that wasn't the cause. Finally, add into this all of the wealthy individuals and corporations that are doing the same. Again, ask yourself, why now?

Any reasonable person would have to take notice of all this to some degree, at the very least. In addition, this doesn't really even need to invoke Occam's Razor to come up with an answer. The answer is obvious; the rush is on to protect—to protect one's selves as individuals, as corporations, and on the highest government levels, as well. In short, those with the means and the money are doing what they can to protect themselves from…something.

This is, perhaps, the most frightening thing of all to our way of thinking. We can easily dismiss the odd "survivalist" as a "crazy," "fringe element," or such. But when governments, such as our own, along with millionaires and billionaires, and worldwide corporations are doing this, as well, then the matter becomes a little more chilling to consider. We can dismiss out of hand the "odd" person or small "cult" group as being of no real importance or significance. But how do we dismiss governments, billionaires, millionaires, and corporations when they are doing this "like crazy?"

We don't think we can overlook this. It's too big, too significant, to just ignore. And no matter the public reasons given for some of these things, the answers seem less than believable. Yes, due to the increased risk of terrorism these days, FEMA probably should stock more dehydrated meals. That would seem believable and rational. But again, one would have thought the upswing in this would have occurred immediately after the terrible events of 9-11, and not almost ten years later, when terrorism seems to be moderating and terrorists appear to be in disarray (according to our own government).

Also, remember Mr. Camden said the government has been on a "binge" of bunker building for the last 15 years. Again, this means such bunker building started, predated 9-11 by almost five years! Now, all of a sudden, FEMA is not only increasing its stockpile of meals in a rush, but as mentioned above, "by a whole new order of magnitude." Going from six million meals stockpiled to 426 million meals is incredible, especially when FEMA is drying up the entire market to do this.

We have to ask ourselves—what's up? Why are they doing this? What is the sudden, pressing need to spend a billion dollars right now to do this? Why not farm the purchases out over a number of years? The whole thing is very strange, to say the least. FEMA's public explanation just doesn't seem very convincing, given these huge numbers, and to have done this so suddenly, so massively, and now, but not earlier, when one would have thought it much more likely they'd do something like this, such as a year or so after Katrina, or a few years after 9-11.

Protecting Ourselves As Average Citizens.

But what can we do, as moderate-income individuals and families to protect ourselves, when we don't have such massive resources at our disposal, and can barely make ends meet now in such hard times? Well, we can still do pretty much the same things as the wealthy and governments are doing, to a lesser extent of course, and even can follow the example, if necessary, of those "lone survivalists" so many of us (including ourselves) have so liked to jeer at, and ridicule. We don't necessarily have to go to such an extreme or degree as becoming a virtual hermit in a hole in the desert, but there are steps we can take to help insure our survival when it comes to aliens and/or their intervention in our lives in a more cataclysmic way than they are doing now.

Here are some steps to take, starting with sighting and encountering UFOs:

1. If you see a UFO, capture it on camera/video, but only if you SAFELY can. However, at all times, be mindful your personal safety is paramount, is of the highest importance. Keep your distance. If the vehicle(s) fly towards you, seem intent upon you in any way, run! Get out of there! We can't stress this enough. Run!

Don't hang around and equivocate as to what it might mean. If they seem to be zeroing in on you—just go! Get out of there! It's important to remember that even if "they" aren't out to abduct you, their spacecraft can constitute a hazard in themselves to your health. There have been multiple cases of what appear to be radiation burns. At various supposed landing sites, there are often higher than normal counts of background radiation, as in the encounters by the military in Rendlesham Forest and other places where the native vegetation "won't grow."

Like it or not, you must always consider some people have died from such events, have had sudden strange cancers and tumors appear on their bodies, as a result. And don't forget those skiing students who all died so strangely in Russia, those Russian divers, etc. So keep this all in mind. Their very vessels can cause you great harm, even death, it seems. Yes, we desperately need all the data we can get on UFOs, but it should never be at the risk of your life and health that you obtain such.

2. If you have ever experienced "missing time," feel you have been abducted, we would suggest you undertake a full physical examination. We don't mean to be alarmist about this. In fact, everyone should have a yearly "physical" according to most doctors, anyway. But if you suspect implants, have "scoop marks" on your body somewhere, we suggest you pay particular attention to the idea of having a physical and/or some x-rays done.

If any foreign material is found in your body, have it removed, however small, innocuous, or obscure it may appear to be. Do this if it can safely be done. It may mean nothing more than a simple and cheap extraction as in an outpatient procedure. But our advice is if it can be safely done, and you can afford it; do it! Remember, according to some theorists, these "implants" may be some sort of tracking device or may serve some purpose in an ongoing experiment upon you.

So again, our advice is to have such removed, if you can. This way, "they" may not be able to continue to track your whereabouts and/or abduct you again, if that's been happening. If push comes to shove, and some sort of apocalypse concerning them does occur, then they won't probably be able to track and find you.

3. If you live out in a rural or rural/suburban area, and you sight a UFO, stay hidden from it. Don't worry about taking pictures under such circumstances, because this is simply too unsafe a thing to do, given what we've learned, unless you are certain you can do so safely.

If you are on a relatively deserted road and a strange craft "zooms" over you, you should find a safe and hidden area to park your car immediately! We would further advise leaving the near vicinity of your vehicle, but again, only if safe to do so. You don't want to be doing this on a busy freeway, for instance! But try to find some place where you are hidden from the sky, such as under a bridge, in a culvert underground along the edge of the road, on the porch of a nearby building, or even inside, etc.

The aliens, again, are not omnipotent, as we explained. If they are searching for you, they have to have some type of scanning devices, etc. And the more you can shield yourself from such, the better off you are, probably…

We're not saying you should panic or become hysterical. That wouldn't be of any help in any case and could be downright dangerous, But as in any potentially dangerous situation, you should keep your head and take reasonable safeguards to insure your own well-being. This is just common sense.

4. If you live in an area that suddenly becomes "a hive of activity" for UFO sightings, such as Pine Bush, New York did, or

Gulf Breeze, Florida, and such type locations, stay alert, be careful, and don't allow yourself to be caught out alone somewhere, all by yourself, and with no ready aid nearby. Usually, there is safety in numbers, the more, the better. There is certainly more safety that way than being all alone.

So use common sense. Don't take long lonely walks in isolated areas if UFO sightings have been rampant there. Remember, for millennia, our ancestors were "afraid of the dark." Maybe, there is reason to be still, especially if you are out somewhere all alone, in a location that has experienced recent UFO sightings.

5. Be Prepared! Yes, this sounds very "Boy Scout" in nature and so very cliché and trite, but it's something we should all do anyway. As we mentioned above, rich people, corporations, and governments are doing just this and in huge numbers of late and at the cost of millions of dollars. In any case, just to be prepared is a good idea. Most of us in America, for example, do live in areas that are either prone to hurricanes, tornados, earthquakes, blizzards, or such, so we really should have a "be prepared" attitude anyway. It just makes good sense.

Being prepared usually means having flashlights, plenty of batteries, an emergency radio (preferably one of the hand-cranked ones that never require a battery), blankets, emergency foodstuffs, and water supplies. Keep a well-stocked pantry, for instance, and include packaged goods, dry goods, and canned/preserved items, such as tinned meats, vegetables, and fruits. Having extra vitamin supplements on hand wouldn't hurt any either, as well as a decent first aid kit, etc. Whatever you can reasonably afford, you should try to have. And remember, you can accumulate this stuff over time. It doesn't have to be all at once, as a sudden and huge expense. Just a few extra packages of dried goods and canned foodstuffs added to your weekly grocery purchases will quickly create a well-stocked pantry.

4. A bolt hole? This is in line with the idea of having a bunker and we think is a very good idea to have. True, most of us simply can't afford such hugely expensive things, as the wealthy can and are affording, but you can have alternative plans. You have as much right to survive as employees of a corporation do, wealthy residents, or even government politicians, as far as we're concerned. Remember, it's your taxes, your money paying for those government bunkers! So take some steps to find possible locations of refuge.

For instance, if you know of caves, mines, especially those sightseeing types, which are usually safer), anything underground in your area, keep a route map to them. Some examples of this might be the Carlsbad Caverns in New Mexico, or the Merrimac Caverns in Missouri, Mammoth Cave in Kentucky, etc.

If you live in a city or town with nothing like this nearby, look for a well-constructed, solid building, one with a good, substantial, and preferably deep basement. The bigger high-rises often have several sub basements. An underground parking lot might even do. If you have a basement at home, that works in your favor, or even a storm shelter, if you have one. Consider an air filtration system for those. This might protect you against radiation or biologically dangerous bacteria or viruses. These filters are expensive, so just do what you reasonably can in this regard.

Along these lines, we live in North Carolina, as an example. We know the location of an emerald mine and other types of mines nearby. We also know where we can escape to in the mountains near where we live, and how to get there in a hurry, where there are natural caves and relatively protected areas. Not only does this give us safety in the form of elevation (no flooding), but it is a rugged and relatively unpopulated area.

5. Try to keep a vehicle filled with gas at all times, just "in case." If this means filling your car, van, or truck a little more often than you are used to doing, we suggest this might well be worth the effort. In an emergency, or if there is an "EMP" (Electromagnetic Pulse), power will be knocked out instantly. No power—no gas pumps—get it? At least try to keep a can of gasoline stored in a safe place, just in case. And if the EMP is strong enough, even cars will cease to function, as will phones or anything with electronics in them. So if you have any warning of events, it's best to go to your "safe place" before things actually begin happening. So be watchful. Pay attention to the news, what's said, and often more importantly, what isn't said. If something strange is glossed over on the news, it may be for a reason.

6. As mentioned in passing above, if you need to seek better shelter in an emergency than your home can provide, be sure to have a map of your escape route. And having alternate routes to it marked on the map is always a safe bet, because roads can quickly become jammed with other people who are also fleeing. So using alternate routes may be necessary. Again, just be prepared, in case... Use a paper map or atlas. In a major emergency, satellite GPS devices may cease to function. Mark each route with a different colored marking pen, so you can easily follow them while driving. Avoid freeways if possible. They tend to become stop-and-go nightmares very quickly.

7. Your refuge should be relatively isolated, if possible. You don't want to be competing with hordes of panicked people for a limited space, one right alongside a freeway, for instance. When people are truly panicked they may resort to any (and we mean any) measures to find safety, even if it means pulling you out of your refuge.

8. Take any necessary medications you have with you. If events seem to be deteriorating, try to get extra prescriptions filled, just "in case."

9. With regard to guns—this we feel is strictly up to the individual, their choice alone. We, personally, don't like them at all, but we can see their value in an emergency. So when it comes to firearms, the choice must strictly be your own decision, but we advise that if you have children, you should take long and careful consideration before having a gun anywhere near them. Children have a remarkable way of circumventing parents when it comes to safety in such matters.

So, if you want a gun, think VERY carefully first. It may be of help, or may just add to the overall danger. We repeat;

having a firearm must strictly be the individual's decision. We prefer not to have such for safety reasons, and we don't suggest or encourage anyone to purchase or own them.

10. Avoid likely target areas. If you live in an area you think might be a possible target, as near a military base, major city, etc., then "staying put" may not be a good idea. If you have time, any warning of what may be coming, it might be best to leave the vicinity of such areas. If your emergency route maps take you near to such "target" places, alter your routes accordingly to avoid them as best you can.

11. Have a supply of cash on hand. Credit and debit cards will cease to function if there is an EMP attack, or if power is lost to an area. ATM's won't function. And let's be honest here; money talks! So having some in the form of cash is always a good idea. As far as that goes, things of value may also help. If for any reason you must resort to a barter system, any items of gold, whether jewelry or otherwise, might be advantageous to have. Sound incredible? Not so, because when any government system breaks down, barter systems quickly return to take their place.

12. Have a copy of a medical book. To have a good, comprehensive medical guide included in your survival kit would be helpful, too. Anything that might tell you how to do basics, like setting broken bones, administering CPR, and such, could be very helpful in an emergency. Boy and Girl Scouts are taught just these sorts of things. So this is hardly an outlandish idea.

Please understand that the idea here isn't to become a "crazy," a runaway survivalist, or anything, although, having that sort of an attitude to some limited extent isn't necessarily a bad thing. Just never forget that even when natural disasters occur, it can take several days to even a couple of weeks before government aid can arrive. Do you remember the debacle of timely help reaching victims of Hurricane Katrina? It's happened before, and so it can happen again.

You are, effectively, on your own during such catastrophes, for at least a while. So why not treat the problem of aliens in the same way. The watchwords are always to be careful and prudent—don't rush toward a landed alien spacecraft. Don't go "hunting" for them in isolated places. You just may find them and not in a good way, if you do. Get it?

Do what you can to "reasonably" (and we stress the word, "reasonably," here) to protect yourselves and your loved ones. Keep in mind where you live, the location's strengths and weaknesses in case of any sort of attack or catastrophe, no matter from where it may originate, whether aliens, nature, or human enemies. In other words, perhaps being out in the open, in plain sight, is not the place to be in a national emergency of any sort.

Our advice is you should be able in an emergency to gather your loved ones and emergency supplies, get them into your vehicle (if you are seeking refuge somewhere else other than your home), and be able to be gone from your premises in half an hour. And don't forget to take important documents with you, such as identity papers. You may need them later on.

In times of panic, people panic. That's life. The better prepared you are, the better able you are to deal with a sudden crisis of any sort, the more chance you and yours have of surviving. And being able to make a "quick getaway," instead of just standing around for hours watching the news as the situation deteriorates, and dithering, is the way to go. Remember, your life and the lives of any loved ones you may have, depend on how your react, and how quickly you react.

Again, we stress we aren't trying to be alarmists here! But any intelligent and reasonable person knows well enough that simple precautions for emergencies are always a good thing to have.

Now, with regard to this sudden upswing in bunker building and dehydrated food purchasing, the building of a "Doomsday" seed bank, one can't help but wonder why now? Is "something" coming? And if so, when? In our final chapter, we'll discuss the issue of "2012," and try to understand if there really is anything to the idea of a coming apocalypse.

CHAPTER 19

2012 And The Apocalypse?

Now, almost inevitably, it seems, as if we have no real choice, we have come to the subject of 2012 and the idea that something will happen this year (December 21 is the usual date claimed for this). Given how close we are to that time now, we suppose it is understandable this would be of increasing importance to us all. So of course, the question that now faces us, is there anything to the idea that there is a catastrophe coming, a great change, or alien invasion sometime in December of the year 2012?

Yes, this subject has been talked about repeatedly. It has been the topic of copious television shows, principally on the Discovery Channel and History channels, but certainly not limited to those. The news has even carried stories about it on occasion over the last couple of years. Numerous books have this as their subject matter, and even feature films have been made about this, as in the movie with Nicolas Cage, **2012**. And, if you are one to read such a book as this one is, on the subject of UFOs, you may already have seen some of these shows, have a strong interest, or curiosity about the whole 2012 phenomenon.

So is there anything to this idea of a coming apocalypse? Is there any evidence to support it? Is there a possibility it might actually happen? Well, the answer to this is not an easy one. And we'll tell you right up front, we simply don't know for sure. All we can do is make some educated guesses.

Why is this? Because for us, the Principle of Occam's Razor simply doesn't seem to work well here. Remember, it requires the simplest answer be accepted as most likely, all other conditions being equal in the matter. Well in this case, not all other conditions are equal. Scientists, and almost without exception, say that simply nothing will happen on December 21, 2012, which as it also happens, is the end date of the Mayan calendar.

Those that claim something will happen often have very elaborate theories of the cause, and what the nature of the event will be, or entail. Some say it is the literal end of the world. Some even go so far as to say it is the end of the universe. Others say it's not that sort of ending, but actually is a new beginning. The ushering in of a new age, as in "New Age," is one such belief. Many of these people also believe it is the transcendence of humanity to a new evolutionary level (meaning a higher, more transformative existence).

As for the causes of this event, again, they differ just as widely. One author claims a rogue planet coming into our solar system will badly affect the Earth. This interloper causes earthquakes, and upheavals. Some even theorize the possible flipping of the Polar Regions to the equator (polar shift) with the oceans leaving their beds and flowing over the continents. They claim it has happened before and this is where the idea of there having once been a Great Flood also comes from.

This idea of a rogue planet (Planet X) or star, we personally find rather hard to believe, although the Hopi prophecy is that the end of times will be heralded by the arrival of a "blue star," a former habitat of some sort (International Space Station?).

But why do we doubt this scenario? Because such large objects simply don't just appear "out of the blue." To get close to Earth, to do what proponents of such theories say they'll do, these objects have to move there. And as they move closer, their effects on the Earth would be constant and become continually more severe. If another gravitational body comes so close to the earth where it can cause this kind of damage, we would have early signals of its arrival in our region of space. Yes, there would be earthquakes aplenty, but they wouldn't come and go, they would continue to become more frequent and more severe, much more so.

And we do seem to have had a number of earthquakes this last year, and conceivably that could be an indication of something approaching us. However, scientists assure us that although it seems like we've had more earthquakes than normal, they actually are no more than the usual number.

Moreover, if an object is hurtling toward the earth, and is now close enough to cause such devastating earthquakes, then it should be also causing strange ocean tides, as well. These should come first, even before the earthquakes. If the object can tug at the Earth's rocky crust enough to cause major earthquakes, it can certainly also tug at the Earth's water in its oceans and much more easily. Case in point; the Moon has an effect on our tides, but we don't see undue earthquakes because of the Moon. Yet, the ocean tides rise and fall daily, and significantly, and the Moon is not ripping the Earth apart with earthquakes and volcanoes in the process of raising those tides. Neither is the sun.

The same should hold true for any other large gravitational object. Among the first effects of its approach should be an effect on our ocean tides. The closer the object comes, the greater those tides would be. Ultimately, they would swamp the entire coasts of all the continents on the planet, perhaps even the continents themselves. Yet, unusual tides haven't manifested themselves anywhere on the planet. Therefore, it is unlikely that Planet X is out there, near us. If it were, then one of our many telescopes situated around the world and in space should have noticed it's presence by now.

You see, planets and stars may move quickly, but it still takes time for them to get from Point A to Point B., And in doing so, if they pass anywhere near any other worlds, they disturb their orbits as well. We have seen no sign of this, either. So whether a star, a brown dwarf, or rogue planet, it would seem unlikely to us this would be the cause of an apocalypse in December of 2012. Why? Because such a thing should already have been spotted by us, and that can't be kept secret. There are just too many people, too many amateur astronomers for that to be likely.

Furthermore, although there is some scientific evidence to show the earth may have flipped on its axis in the past (polar shift), this seems to have happened only a couple of times. Additionally, from all available evidence, the process was a very slow one, and not just a matter of hours, days, weeks, months, or even years, but over much longer periods. So that doesn't seem to be a likely event, either.

However, despite all this, there is a compelling oddity. This is the number of sources of prophecies, no less, that all seem to indicate 2012, especially December of 2012, might be the occasion for some major change or Earth event. Here's what we mean:

Doomsday, The Mayan Calendar And Such—More Than Just Hype And Hysteria?

The Mayan calendar ends on December 21, 2011. Most of us know this already. We also know the Mayans were very good at mathematics, and their calendar is actually even slightly more precise than our own, according to some. Moreover, we know the Mayans arranged their calendar in five great cycles. And the last one of these cycles appears to be ending on December 21, 2012. There are no more cycles after that. For the Mayans, it was either the end of time itself, or the starting of an entire new age. We aren't sure which.

But if it is the start of a new age, this is often heralded by major Earth changes according to them. In this case, some Mayan researchers, according to their readings of the hieroglyphics, believe it signifies the coming of a great flood or tremendous rains. Oddly, the idea of a great flood is actually a little disturbing, because our polar ice caps are melting at a much faster rate than even scientists anticipated to be the case. If they collapsed all at once, there would be a fast rising of sea levels around the world, which would constitute a great flood. But scientists assure us it will not happen this quickly. Let's hope they are right.

However, the Mayans are not alone in this sort of prophecy. Modern web bots, searching the web, also have come up with a similar prediction for December 2012. The Sybil Oracle of ancient Rome seems accurately to refer to this as being a time of great change, the end of the world, at least as we know it. The

Oracle of Delphi does, too, and named the date. Merlin, and by this we mean the real Merlin, and not the one of romantic Arthurian legend, but rather the Celtic shaman, Myrddin Wyllt, seems to be predicting much the same sort of thing.

Still, such predictions don't end there. To the contrary, there are many more. Far-seeing psychics, as a group, claim they can't see anything beyond the end of 2012. Researchers working with the ancient prophecy book, *I Ching*, when comparing it to the rise and fall of civilizations and great events in history by using a graph, noticed everything ended in December of 2012. Their graph line, in other words, goes into a flat-line on that date. Edgar Cayce, a famous psychic, predicted great shifting within the Earth's crust (again, polar shift?) and this should be occurring…oh, yeah, right about now, or within a very few years.

Then there is St. Malachy's Pope Prophecy, which says that the current pope is the second to the last, and only one more will follow. It also says the last pope will administer during a time of great upheaval when even the "seven hills of Rome" are destroyed. In Zoroastrian philosophy, *Zand-i Vohuman Yasht*[xcix] described the end times, as well, and seemingly accurately described something very like a nuclear winter, too.

And it doesn't even end there! The Hopi Predictions that the fourth age of the world is coming to an end and the fifth is about to begin, claim one of the final signs will be the wrapping of the Earth in a great spider web (World Wide Web?). Other signs of theirs also already seem to have taken place. The Book of Revelation in the Bible calls for signs and portents of the end times, many of which seem to be occurring now. Nostradamus, that so vague prophet, also seems to refer to our time as the end time. The so-called seer, Mother Shipton,[c] goes to great lengths to describe the final days of humanity, and her prophecies, whatever their real source, are startling on target, uncanny in their predictions.

And there are more such predictions—many more. In fact, it seems we are flooded with ancient predictions and prophecies of this being the end times. Specifically, 2012 is often denoted as the seeming end date in particular, in several cases.

At the very least, this wealth of such predictions from so many diverse sources, over so many centuries and even millennia, all predicting the same or very similar things for the same time period, is certainly strange, exceedingly so... And the quality of the predictions, although often in question, is often seemingly very close to the mark, as well.

When one then adds into this the sudden spate of bunker building around the world, by governments, corporations, and the wealthy, and then combine all this with FEMA buying up seemingly every dehydrated meal in sight, all of a sudden, it does tend to make one concerned, very concerned…

So although real evidence is as yet lacking on this matter of December 21, 2012, we can point to an incredible amount of prophecies and predictions, as well as the behavior of the rich and of the government (including FEMA) that do seem to indicate something may be coming, may be happening on that date or very near it.

Well, is it real and is it going to happen? If not, why do so many think it is, including all those prophets of old? Why is there this seeming groundswell of belief that the end of times are coming, that the very last days of humanity are almost upon us? Is it just mass hysteria and hyperbole, or is there any evidence for it? Will it happen? And if so, how will it happen? Will anyone survive if it does?

Again, these answers are unknowable at present, because we don't have "witnesses," and although the prophecies in many aspects seem just a little too accurate for comfort when describing the present-day world, they are just prophecies after all, and without corroborating witnesses or facts to support them, except other prophets. And yes, this last is very disturbing, but it isn't enough to say if something is or isn't going to happen.

There is one more thing to consider here, though. Many of these people, the Hopi, the Mayan, and such, also have histories (we call them legends and myths—it seems only our history and our religious beliefs are "real" and all the other cultures' histories are not), also speak of those "sky gods," "sky guardians," "visitors" from the stars, etc., and that they will return. This is an odd coincidence, very much so. What's more, many of those same histories claim that those strange beings have promised to return at the end of times.

So does this mean the aliens may have told our ancestors and various native peoples they planned to return at this particular time? Or is it something even stranger, such as visitors from the future visiting the past and warning people? Again, we don't know, so we can't say.

What we can do is notice there are a huge number of prophecies and predictions regarding 2012 and these times as being the "end times." We can also see the strange coincidence that many of the ancients and modern peoples from whom these prophets came, also had strong beliefs about people from the sky interfering in their lives to an enormous extent, such as impregnating human women (many cultures speak of this), and demonstrating their wrath, and having wars among themselves. And remember, many also tell of texts that say the "sky gods" will return. So although we can't say these two things are definitely connected, prophecies about 2012 and aliens, it does form a rather disconcerting and definite link of sorts.

What do we believe as authors about December 21, 2012? Well, we think everyone will wake up on the morning of December 22, 2012, and nothing horrible will have happened the day before. We hope.... We aren't sure of this, but we think this is how it will go.

However, to take the preparations we stated above would still be a wise thing to do. Remember, earthquakes do happen. Hurricanes do occur. Floods deluge huge areas. Tornados and blizzards reoccur every year, so to make simple preparations for emergencies is something we should all do in any case, as a practical matter of course. We restate this, just because it is so important.

However, the December 21, 2012 predictions, for us personally, are just unnerving enough for us to take those precautions we spoke of partly for just that reason. Again, we don't want to be alarmists, but only a fool doesn't at least consider the possibility of problems. If it weren't for that odd linkage between such dire prophecies, such doomsday predictions, and the beliefs of many of those of "sky gods," and all this bunker building and food storing, we'd feel much more comfortable about the whole thing.

CONCLUSION

What Does It All Mean?

We've covered a lot of diverse subjects and topic areas here. In the main, we've concentrated on applying the Principle of Occam's Razor to try to sort through most of the information and see if it is "reasonable," logical to believe if aliens even exist, and if they do, what their motives and agenda might be, if they even have those. And if so, what does it mean for us, and if the agenda is negative, what can we do to protect ourselves.

By applying Occam's Razor, we've shown that in most cases, the simplest explanations support the idea aliens do exist. Moreover, they've quite likely been here for a long while and are still here now. Furthermore, their interference in our history has been great, and often to our detriment when it comes to our lives, property, and basic rights as humans. We've also applied the principle to show abductions probably are happening, although perhaps not in the numbers some claim. These abductions, without our having any say in them, constitute a violation of our rights, and endanger our health and lives.

Past evidence of conflicts involving the aliens and us, or aliens with other species of aliens, also seems likely. Even the idea there may have been a prehistoric nuclear war seems to be a distinct possibility.

Finally, we have shown that since aliens do seem to exist, are carrying on "their" business on a daily basis, and aren't omnipotent, that they must have bases. Again, using the Principle of Occam's Razor, we've shown the most likely places for these bases are on the Moon and perhaps also in our seas. Not being all-powerful, the aliens are limited by logistics, and those logistics require bases from which they can come forth and influence our lives and world.

By referring to what some people have said who've worked at NASA, or for it in some fashion as an affiliate of some type, and by referring to the following lengthy and in-depth report, **NASA Technical Report R-277 *"Chronological Catalog Appendix of Reported Lunar Events"*** U.S. Government Publication, we have clearly demonstrated something very strange is going on. That strangeness seems to center on our Moon and has for a very long time!

The vast amount of evidence in the form of literally hundreds of thousands of sightings of UFOs and USOs, combined with the thousands (perhaps over a million?) reports of abductions, together with a tremendous number of animal mutilations, we believe amply supplies the need for "extraordinary evidence for extraordinary claims." As we've said earlier, it's either the simplest explanation for all this, according to the Principle of Occam's Razor, or everyone throughout history who claimed seeing these things is wrong, or finally, the perpetration of an incredibly and unbelievably massive hoax and conspiracy to hoodwink the entire human race is being conducted. Moreover, this conspiracy/hoax must have been going on for at least centuries!

Since these last two just seem unlikely in the extreme, we have to conclude the alien phenomenon is real. We also have to conclude, given the vast amount of evidence in this regard, that the aliens seem to have, at the very least, an amoral attitude toward us as individuals and as a race. At the worst, they've been horrific in their "culling" of our species for their own hidden and ultimate goals, and interfering with us as individuals repeatedly.

This means that you, as an individual, could be in danger from all this. In a prior chapter, we explained what steps a reasonable and rational person might take to protect themselves, as best they can. If you are wealthy enough and have the money to spare, we'd suggest building a bunker, as so many around the world are doing. If you aren't wealthy, take those normal precautions you'd take for the possibility of any major emergency, as outlined in this book. This is just a practical and rational thing to do.

Above all, we have to say this one last time; if you are alone on an empty road at night and a strange light or object starts seemingly to track your vehicle. Seek shelter at once! If you see a strange craft on the ground in the woods, in some isolated location, think twice before approaching it, at least, not without a Geiger counter of some sort. Take pictures and video only if you can do so without jeopardizing your safety.

We mean this! Don't let your natural inclination to be curious and to explore the unknown lead you into what may be a patently unsafe situation! Be cautious, and take precautions. That's our considered advice. Frankly, if you see a UFO coming your way, rather than standing out in the middle of your yard to gawk at it like a tourist, you might just want to run for cover!

And when in the night you happen to glance up at the old companion of Earth, that ancient orb of the Moon, just remember, "somebody" there may be looking back at you and scrutinizing you closely. And from what we've researched, they aren't regarding you in a very compassionate or kind way!

Our further advice is to use the many links provided in this book and at the end of it to further research all this for yourself. Hiding your head in the sand, as the proverbial ostrich does, just isn't the answer. To be "forewarned and informed is to be forearmed" and to have knowledge you can use in an emergency is paramount. So study the situation more. Give it some real consideration. Then, as an informed person on the subject, you can make your own decisions.

And despite our personal conclusions about all this; believe us when we say we hope we are wrong. We desperately want to be way off base on all of this and that's the truth. After all, life would be much nicer, much more pleasant that way, and for all of us, wouldn't it?

Unfortunately, after years of research on the subject, after looking at all the available evidence and sifting painstakingly through it over more than two decades, we just don't think we are wrong. Moreover, because of that, we think you should take care, be watchful, and implement certain simple and basic safeguards as any rational human would and should. And if you think the aliens are our friends, please think again! Our opinion is that they most definitely are not our friends, and may well be our enemies.

So, beware, know that there is a darker side of the moon in many respects, and that "they," in all likelihood, are watching us! Just why, remains to be seen. Let's hope we don't find out anytime soon…

AUTHORS' NOTE: For scientists, we wish to state for the record we feel they should stop disregarding the plethora of UFO and USO reports as just being "nonsense," the claims of abduction, etc., as being just "hoaxes," and actually, "really" investigate such things. We know there is a tremendous disincentive from the government, from colleagues, educational institutions, from many sources, against them doing this. But for the life of us, if someone claims to be a true scientist, he or she should at least attempt to sift through the available evidence and attempt to arrive at some conclusions, and not just summarily dismiss it all as "swamp gas," "mass hallucinations," "manifestations of neuroses," etc.

Dr. Josef Allen Hynek, a former UFO skeptic, and one who acted as a scientific advisor to Project Bluebook, the U.S. Air Force investigation of UFOs, was a scientific convert. After personally reviewing much of the "evidence," this skeptic then became an adherent of the idea aliens and UFOs exist. And he was a scientist with all the appropriate degrees and education.

In any case, isn't it a scientist's job to investigate such things? The UFO phenomena, whether real or false, is still a huge phenomenon, impacts hundreds of millions, whether real or imagined, and so certainly should be worthy of a scientist's time in investigating just why this is so. Whether real or a sociological phenomenon, it is definitely worthy of attention.

As for our readers, we strongly advise you to read the entire NASA report at some point. The evidence is there. It's clear. It's in abundance. And as we've stated, although some of it can be put down to various natural phenomena, certainly not all of it can be, by any means. The only way one could do this (as scientists themselves admit), is to invoke a number of explanations for strange natural phenomena whose causes are not yet known to our science. This is an unwieldy and unlikely solution.

As always, by using the Principle of Occam's Razor, the simple answer is that "someone" is responsible for many of these odd events on our Moon. And the strange preponderance of sightings around certain areas of the Moon, and by so many observers, over so many centuries, is telling evidence in itself, and forms a "preponderance of evidence" to justify our "extra-ordinary claim."

ABOUT THE AUTHORS:

Rob Shelsky is an avid and eclectic writer, and averages about 4,000 words a day. Rob, with a degree in science, has written a large number of factual articles for the former *AlienSkin Magazine*, as well as for other magazines, such as *Doorways, Midnight Street* (U.K.), *Internet Review of Science Fiction* (*IROSF*), and many others. While at *AlienSkin Magazine*, a resident columnist there for about seven years, Rob did a number of investigative articles, including some concerning the paranormal, as well as columns about UFOs, including interviews of those who have had encounters with them.

Along with George Kempland, both authors have often and over a long period, explored the UFO question together, making investigative trips to research such UFO hotspot areas as Pine Bush, New York, Gulf Breeze, Florida, and other such regions, including Brown Mountain, North Carolina, known, for the infamous "Brown Mountain Lights, as well as investigating numerous places known for paranormal activity.

With over 20 years of such research and investigative efforts behind them, Authors George Kempland and Rob Shelsky are well qualified in the subject of UFOs, as well as that of the paranormal. Where Rob Shelsky tends to be the skeptic, and insists upon being able to "kick the tires" of a UFO, to ascertain their reality, George Kempland is the theorist, constantly coming up with possible explanations for various such phenomena. Together, they make a powerful investigative team when it comes to tackling the hard questions about UFOs and what they might mean for us all.

For links to other books written, please go to:

http://home.earthlink.net/~robngeorge/

Or: http://www.smashwords.com/books/search?query=rob+shelsky

Or: http://robshelsky.blogspot.com/

Or:

http://www.amazon.com/gp/search/ref=sr_tc_2_0?rh=i%3Astripboo

ks%2Ck%3ARob+Shelsky&keywords=Rob+Shelsky&ie=UTF8&qid=1298820526&sr=1-2-ent&field-contributor_id=B002BO9RIE

APPENDIX

NASA Technical Report R-277 *"Chronological Catalog* Appendix *of Reported Lunar Events"* U.S. Govt. Pub.

Date & Time	*Feature or Location; Duration*	*Description*	*Observer*	*Reference*
1540 Nov 26, ~05h00m	**Region of Calippus**	Starlike appearance on dark side	**Observers at Worms**	**Hess 1911**
1587 Mar 5	**Dark Side**	"A sterre (star) is sene in the bodie of the Moon upon the (blank) of Marche, whereat many men merueiled, and not without cause, for it stode directly betwene the pointes of her hornes, the mone being chaunged, not passing 5 or 6 daies before."	**Anonymous**	**Harrison 1876; Lowes 1927**
1668 Nov 26	**Dark Side**	Bright starlike point	**Several New Englanders**	**Josselyn 1675; Mather 1714; Lowes 1927**
1671 Oct 21	**Pitatus**	N/A	**N/A**	**Bode 1792a; Lalande 1792 (1966)**
1671 Nov 12	**Pitatus**	Small whitish cloud	**D.Cassini**	**Bode 1792a; Lalande 1792 (1966)**
1672 Feb 3	**Mare Crisium**	Nebulous appearance	**D.Cassini**	**Bode 1792a; Lalande 1792**

				(1966)
1673 Oct 18	**Pitatus**	White spot	**D.Cassini**	**Bode 1792a; Lalande 1792 (1966)**
1685 Dec 10, ~22h28m	**Plato**	Reddish streak on crater floor seen during eclipse (lunar)	**Bianchini**	**Bianchini 1686; Klado 1965**
1706 May 12	**N/A**	Three sparkling spots	**N/A**	**Bode 1792a**
1715 May 3, ~09h30	**N/A**	"Lightning" on the face of the Moon. De Louville explained this as storms. Halley reference uses Old Style date.	**Louville, Halley**	**Louville 1715; Halley 1715; Schroter 1791; Houzeau and Lancaster 1964 ed.**
1725 Aug 16	**Plato**	A track of ruddy light, like a beam, crossing the middle of the obscure (shadowed) area (crater in darkness)	**Bianchini**	**Hesp. Phos. Phaenom. 1728; Sirius 1887; Wilkins 1958**
1738 Aug 4, 16h31m	**N/A**	During solar eclipse, appearance like lightning on the face of the Moon (Partial eclipse)	**Friend of Weidler**	**Phil. Trans. 1739**
1751 Apr 22	**Plato**	Yellow streak of light across crater floor while crater was in darkness	**Short, Stephens, Harris**	**Sirius 1887**
1772 Oct 11, ~17h13m	**N/A**	Bright spot on disk of fully eclipsed Moon	**Beccaria's nephew and niece**	**Beccaria 1781; Klado 1965**
1774 Jul 25	**Mare Crisium**	Four bright spots. Peculiar behaviour of terminator	**Eysenhard**	**Webb 1962 ed., pp. 106-107**

1778 Jun 14, ~15h38m	**N/A; 1 1/2 min**	During solar eclipse, observed spot near lunar limb almost as bright as sun	**Ulloa**	**Ulloa 1779, 1780; Houzeau and Lancaster 1964 ed.; Klado 1965**
1783 Mar 18 or Sep 10	**N/A**	Moving glows around middle of disk during lunar eclipse	**Messier**	**Liais 1865; Pop. Astr. 1894-95**
1783 Mar	**Near Aristarchus**	Bright points seen during observation of star occultation	**W.Herschel**	**Schroter 1791**
1783 May 4	**Aristarchus, vicinity**	Red spot, 4th mag, diameter <3"	**W.Herschel, Mrs Lind**	**Herschel 1912**
1784	**Aristarchus**	Nebulous bright spot of light	**Schroter**	**Schroter 1791**
1785	**Aristarchus**	Nebulous bright spot of light	**Schroter**	**Schroter 1791**
1786 Dec 24	**Aristarchus**	Extraordinarily bright	**Schroter**	**Schroter 1791**
1787 Mar	**Dark side**	Three bright spots	**W.Herschel**	**Schroter 1791**
1787 Apr 19	**Dark side**	Three "volcanoes." The brightest, 3'57"3 from N limb, the other two much farther toward the center of the Moon	**W.Herschel**	**Herschel 1787, 1912**
1787 Apr 20	**Dark side**	Brightest "volcano" even brighter and at least 3 miles in diameter	**W.Herschel**	**Herschel 1787, 1912**
1787 May 19-20	**Aristarchus**	Extraordinarily bright	**von Bruhl**	**Bode 1790; Schroter 1791; Herschel 1912**
1787 May 22	**Helicon**	N/A	**Villeneuve**	**Lalande 1792 (1966)**
1788 Jan 11	**Near Plato**	Bright spot on dark side	**Observers in**	**Schroter**

			Mannheim	**1791**
1788 Mar 9-10	**Dark side**	Bright spot	**Schroter**	**Schroter 1791**
1788 Mar 13	**Riccioli**	Bright spot	**Schroter**	**Schroter 1791**
1788 Mar 13	**Helicon**	Lunar "volcano" like 6th mag star	**Nouet**	**Schroter 1792; Bode 1792a; Lalande 1792 (1966**
1788 Apr 9	**Aristarchus; 1 hr**	Extraordinarily bright	**Bode**	**Bode 1792b**
1788 Apr 9-11	**Aristarchus**	Bright spot 26" N of crater rim	**Schroter, Bode**	**Schroter 1789, 1791, 1792a, 1792b**
1788 May 8	**N/A**	Bright spots	**Mechain**	**Lalande 1792 (1966)**
1788 May 8-9	**N/A**	Bright spots	**Bode**	**Bode 1792b**
1788 Aug 27	**N/A**	Bright spot	**Schroter**	**Schroter 1791**
1788 Sep 26, 4:25am	**N edge of Mare Crisium**	Small nebulous bright spot	**Schroter**	**Rozier 1788, 1792; Schroter 1791**
1788 Sep 26	**1'18" SE of Plato; 15 min**	Whitish bright spot shining somewhat hazily and 4" to 5" in diameter, 5th mag, SE of Plato in bright moiuntainous region bounding Mare Imbrium	**Schroter**	**Schroter 1789, 1792a, 1792b; Sirius 1888**
1788 Sep 26	**Near Aristarchus; 30 min**	Bright spot 26" N of main crater	**Schroter**	**Rozier 1788, 1792; Schroter 1791**

1788 Dec 2, 5:35am	**Aristarchus**	Extraordinarly bright, like star	**Schroter**	**Schroter 1791**
1788 Dec 11	**Plato**	Bright area, like thin white cloud	**Schroter**	**schroter 1791**
1788	**Aristarchus**	Brilliant spots	**Bode**	**Bode 1792b; Houzeau and Lancaster 1964 ed.**
1789 Jan 10	**N/A**	Lunar "volcano"	**Seyffer**	**Seyffer 1789; Houzeau and Lancaster 1964 ed.**
1789 Mar 29-30	**Grimaldi, and near Riccioli**	Two flickering spots on E edge of Grimaldi, and near Riccioli on dark side of Moon a bright spot	**Schroter**	**Schroter 1789, 1791; Houzeau and Lancaster 1964 ed.**
1789 Mar 29-31	**Aristarchus**	Nebulous bright area	**Schroter**	**Schroter 1791**
1789 Mar	**Near Aristarchus**	Brilliant spots near Aristarchus; luminous spots on dark side	**Bode**	**Bode 1788-89, 1789, 1793; Houzeau and Lancaster 1964 ed.**
1789 Apr	**Near Aristarchus**	Brilliant spots near Aristarchus; luminous spots on dark side	**Bode**	**Bode 1788-89, 1789, 1793; Houzeau and Lancaster 1964 ed.**
1789 May	**Near Aristarchus**	Brilliant spots near Aristarchus; luminous spots on dark side	**Bode**	**Bode 1788-89, 1789, 1793; Houzeau and**

				Lancaster 1964 ed.
1789 Sep 26	Mont Blanc; 15 min	Small speck of light at foot of mountain, like 5th mag star	Schroter	Pickering 1902; Webb 1962 ed., p.113
1790 Jan 17	Aristarchus region	Small, hazy spot of light	Schroter	Schroter 1791
1790 Feb 15-18	Aristarchus region	Small, hazy spot of light	Schroter	Schroter 1791
1790 Mar 19	Aristarchus region	Small, hazy spot of light	Schroter	Schroter 1791
1790 Oct 22	N/A	During total eclipse, Herschel saw at least 150 small, round, bright, red luminous points. (Mid-eclipse, lunar, Oct 23, 00h41m.)	W.Herschel	Herschel 1912 ed.; Klado 1965
1792 Feb 24	N/A	Cusps of Moon showed signs of atmosphere	Schroter	Webb 1962 ed., p.97
1792	Aristarchus	Many ocassions; special appearance	Bode	Bode 1792a
1792	Dark side	Brilliant spots	Schroter	Schroter 1792a, 1792b
1794 Mar 7	Dark side; 15 min	Appearance of light like a star seen in dark part of the Moon	W.Wilkins, Stretton	Wilkins 1794; Stretton 1794; Maskelyne 1795; Moore 1953; Houzeau and Lancaster 1964 ed.
1797 Mar 2	Promontorium Heraclides, vicinity	"Observations of a volcano on the Moon"	Caroché	Caroché 1799; Houzeau and Lancaster 1964 ed.

1797 Jul 2	**Mare Vaporum**	Vapors resembling mountain	**Schroter, Olber**	**Klein 1879**
1799	**Dark side**	Bright spots on dark side, seen during five different lunations	**Piazzi**	**Piazzi 1800; Houzeau and Lancaster 1964 ed.; Treanor and O'Connell 1965**
1820 Oct 17	**S of Sinus Iridum**	Brilliant spots in Mare Imbrium S of Sinus Iridum	**Luthmer**	**Luthmer 1824**
1821 Feb 5-6	**Aristarchus, vicinity**	Luminous appearance on dark side; 6th to 7th mag, 3' to 4' diameter	**Kater, Olbers, Browne**	**Kater 1821; Olbers 1822, 1824; Gauss 1874; Houzeau and Lancaster 1964 ed.**
1821 Apr 7	**Posidonius**	Appeared without shadow	**Gruithuisen**	**Webb 1962 ed., p.110**
1821 May 4-6	**Aristarchus, vicinity**	Bright spot on dark side, <1' diameter	**Ward, Baily**	**Ward 1822; Baily 1822**
1821 Jul 25	**Dark side**	Brilliant flashing spots	**Gruithuisen**	**Gruithuisen 1824**
1821 Nov 28, ~20h00m	**Dark side**	Variable bright spot like 6th mag star	**Fallows**	**Fallows 1822**
1822 Jan 27	**Aristarchus, vicinity**	Bright spot like 8th mag star	**F.G.W. Struve**	**Struve 1823**
1822 Jun 22-23	**Aristarchus**	Lunar "volcano"	**Ruppell**	**Ruppell 1822**
1822	**N/A**	"Volcanoes" on the Moon; several occasions	**Flaugergues**	**Flaugergues 1822**
1822	**N/A**	Lunar "volcano"	**Zach**	**Zach 1822**
1824 May 1	**Near Aristarchus**	Blinking light, 9th to 10th mag on dark side	**Gobel**	**Gobel 1826**
1824 Oct 18	**Aristarchus,**	Mingling of all kinds of colors	**Gruithuisen**	**Gruithuisen**

	vicinity	in small spots in the W and NW of Aristarchus		**1824; Fauth 1899**
1824 Oct 20, 05h00m	**Dark side, Mare Nubium**	Bright area 100 x 20 km	**Gruithuisen**	**Flammarion 1884; Azevado 1962**
1824 Dec 8	**Plato**	Bright fleck in SE part of crater	**Gruithuisen**	**Sirius 1879**
1825 Apr 8	**Plato**	W part of crater brighter than E part	**Gruithuisen**	**Sirius 1879**
1825 Apr 22	**Aristarchus and vicinity**	Periodic illumination	**Argelander, Gobel**	**Argelander 1826, Gobel 1826**
1825 Dec 1, 23h45m	**Ptolemaeus**	Bright spot	**Schwabe**	**Sel.J. 1880**
1826 Apr 12, 20h00m	**Mare Crisium**	Black moving haze or cloud	**Emmett**	**Emmett 1826; Capron 1879**
1826 Apr 13, 20h00m	**Mare Crisium; 1 hr**	Cloud less intense	**Emmett**	**Capron 1879**
1832 Jul 4	**Mare Crisium**	Speckled with minute dots and streaks of light	**T.W. Webb**	**Astr.Reg. 1882; Webb 1962 ed., p.105**
1832 Dec 25	**Aristarchus, vicinity**	Bright spot	**C.P. Smyth**	**Smyth 1836**
1835 Dec 22, 18h30m	**Near Aristarchus**	Bright spot, 9th to 10th mag	**C.P. Smyth**	**Smyth 1836**
1836 Feb 13	**Messier**	Two straight lines of light; a band between covered with luminous points	**Gruithuisen**	**Sci. Amer. Supp. Vol.7**
1839 Jun 24	**Grimaldi**	Smoky-gray mist	**Gruithuisen**	**B.A.A. Mem. 1895**
1839 Jul 7	**South Pole**	Twilight	**Gruithuisen**	**B.A.A. Mem. 1895**
1839 Jul 19	**Schroter**	Dark mist	**Gruithuisen**	**B.A.A. Mem. 1895**
1842 Jul 8, 07h02m	**N/A**	During solar eclipse, Moon's disk occasionally crossed by	**N/A**	**Wullerstorff 1846;**

		bright streaks		Zantedeschi 1846
1843 Jul 4	Peak S of Alps	On terminator saw an unusually bright spot that glowed like a fixed star	Gerling	Gerling 1845; Sirius 1888
1844 Apr 25	SW of Pico	A bluish glimmering patch of light, not quite within the night side of the Moon	J.Schmidt	Sel.J. 1878
1847 Mar 18, 19	Dark side	Large luminous spots on dark side	Rankin, Chevalier	Rankin 1847; Houzeau and Lancaster 1964 ed.
1847 Dec 11, 18h00m	Teneriffe Mts.	A bright spot about 1/4-ang diam of Saturn was perceived which, though it varied in intensity like an intermittent light, was at all times visible (dark side)	Hodgson	Hodgson 1848
1848 Mar 19	N/A	During eclipse rapid changes in .... (*wording illegible*)	Gorjan	M.N. 1847-48
1849 Feb 11	Posidonius	Without normal shadow	J.Schmidt	Webb 1962 ed., p.110
1854 Dec 27	Teneriffe Mts. (near Plato); 5 hr	Two luminous fiery spots on bright side. "... an appearance I had never seen before on the surface of the Moon though I have observed her often these last 40 years .... It appeared to me from the brightness of the light and the contrast of colour to be two active volcanoes or 2 mouth of one in action."	Hart	Hart 1855
1855 Jun 20	N/A	Traces of twilight seen. Webb gives low weight to observation "for want of better optical means."	Webb	Webb 1962 ed., p.97
1862 Jun 12, 06h19m	N/A	"During [lunar] eclipse, the E [IAU:W] side dark brick red and something seemed to oscillate before it." At the mid-eclipse on the S side, "a very small meniscus was seen nearly the color of the uneclipsed Moon."	N/A	Liais 1865

1864 May 15 and Oct 16	**Mare Crisium, E of Picard**	Bright cloud	**Ingall**	**Ingall 1864**
1864	**N/A**	Bright spot	**Birt**	**Birt Birt 1864**
1865 Jan 1	**SE of Plato; 30 min**	Bright spot like 4th mag star slightly out of focus. Bright speck remained changeless for 30 min, and its light was steady.	**Grover**	**Grover 1866; Webb 1962 ed., p.114**
1865 Apr 10	**Mare Crisium, E of Picard**	Point of light like star. Whole of Mare Crisium intersected with bright veins, mixed with bright spots of light. Aperture 4-1/2 in.; 4 hr before full Moon	**Ingall**	**Astr. Reg. 1866**
1865 Sep 5	**Mare Crisium, E of Picard**	Point of light like star, with misty cloud	**Ingall**	**Astr. Reg. 1866**
1865 Nov 24	**Carlini; 1 hr 30 min**	Dark side, distinct bright speck like 8th mag star	**Williams and two others**	**Webb 1962 ed., p.125**
1865	**Mare Crisium**	Dots and streaks of light	**Slack, Ingall**	**Webb 1962 ed., p.105**
1866 Jun 10	**Aristarchus**	Starlike light	**Tempel**	**Denning, Tel.Work p.121**
1866 Jun 14-16	**Aristarchus, vicinity**	Reddish-yellow	**Tempel**	**Tempel 1867**
1866	**Dark side**	Bright spots	**Hodgson**	**Hodgson 1866**
1867 Apr 9, 19h30m - 21h00m	**Aristarchus, vicinity; 1 hr 30 min**	Bright spot on dark side, 7th mag, becoming fainter after 20h15m UT	**Elger**	**Elger 1868**
1867 Apr 12, 07h30m - 08h30m	**Aristarchus, vicinity; 1 hr**	Bright spot on dark side, 7th mag.	**Elger**	**Webb 1962**
1867 May 6-7	**Aristarchus; at least several hours each night**	Left side of crater, very bright luminous point, appearing like a volcano	**Flammarion**	**Flammarion 1884**
1867 May 7	**Aristarchus,**	Reddish-yellow, beacon-like	**Tempel**	**Tempel**

	vicinity	light		**1867; Astr. Reg. 1868**
1867 Jun 10	**Sulpicius Gallus**	Three blackish spots	**Dawes**	**The Student Vol.1**
1867	**Dark side**	Bright spots	**W.O. Williams**	**Williams 1867**
1870 May 13	**Plato**	Bright spots, extraordinary display	**Pratt, Elger**	**Rept. Brit. Assn. 1871**
1870	**N/A**	White spots on the Moon, "lightning".	**Birt**	**Birt 1870**
1870	**Godin**	Purplish haze illuminating floor of crater, still in shadow	**Trouvelot**	**Trouvelot 1882; Moore 1963**
1871	**Plato**	Streak of light across floor visible while crater in shadow	**Elger**	**Sirius 1887**
1871	**W of Plato**	Fog or mist	**Elger, Neison**	**Flammarion 1884**
1872 Jul 16	**Plato**	NE portion of floor hazy	**Pratt**	**Capron 1879**
1873 Jan 4	**Kant**	Luminous purplish vapors	**Trouvelot**	**Trouvelot 1882; Flammarion 1884; Moore 1963**
1873 Apr 10	**Plato**	Under high sun, two faint clouds in W part of crater	**Schmidt**	**Sirius 1879**
1873 Nov 1	**Plato**	Unusual appearance	**Pratt**	**Capron 1879**
1874 Jan 1	**Plato**	Unusual appearance	**Pratt**	**Capron 1879**
1877 Feb 20, 09h30m - 10h30m	**Eudoxus; 1 hr**	Fine line of light like luminous cable drawn W to E across crater	**Trouvelot**	**Flammarion 1884; l'Astron. 1885**
1877 Feb 27, 19h19m	**N/A**	Lunar eclipse. Flickering light on lunar surface	**Dorna**	**L'Opin. Nazion. 1877**
1877 Mar 17, 06h45m	**N/A**	Moon's horns showed traces of atmosphere. Moon 2d16h old (2.75 in. reflector)	**Dennett**	**Eng. Mech. 1882**
1877 Mar 21	**Proclus**	Brilliant illumination	**Barrett**	**Eng. Mech. 1882**

1877 May 15, 20h30m and May 29, 00h35m	**E of Picard**	Bright spot	**N/A**	**Eng. Mech. 1882**
1877 Jun 17, 22h30m	**Bessel**	Minute point of light (seen with 2.75 in. reflector)	**Dennett**	**Eng. Mech. 1882**
1877 Jul 29	**Plato**	S of center of crater, bright streak, disappeared at 2:30am	**Gray**	**Flammarion 1884**
1877 Aug 23-24, 23h10m	**N/A**	Lunar eclipse. (1) Unusual spectrum with strong absorption in yellow. (2) Two patches of crimson light of short duration	**(1) Airy; (2) Capron, Pratt**	**(1) Sirius 1878; (2) Capron 1879**
1878 Feb 2, 08h16m	**At limb**	Changes in spectrum during solar eclipse suggesting lunar atmosphere	**Observers at Melbourne, Australia**	**Sirius 1878**
1878 Mar 10, 19h20m	**Mare Crisium**	White patch E of Picard badly defined	**Noble**	**Sel. J. 1878**
1878 Oct 5, 21h40m	**Plato**	Faint bright shimmer like thin white cloud	**Klein**	**Klein, Woch. fur Astr.; Sirius 1878**
1878 Oct 21	**3 hr**	Half of Moon's terminator obliterated	**Hirst**	**Capron 1879**
1878 Nov 1	**Messier**	Obscuration of Messier	**Klein**	**Pop. Astr. 1902**
1878 Nov 9, 21h00m	**Plato**	Faint but unmistakable white cloud, not seen before	**Klein**	**Sirius 1878**
1878 Dec 4	**Agrippa, Klein's Object and the oval spot nearby**	"Odd misty look as if vapour were in or about them."	**Capron**	**Capron 1879**
1878	**E of Picard**	White patch	**Birt**	**Eng. Mech. Vol 28**
1878	**Interior of Tycho**	Cloudy appearance	**Birt**	**Eng. Mech. Vol 28**
1880 Jan 18	**Whole of Mare Nectaris**	Foggy. Fog extended into the floor of Fracastorius. Gruithuisen said that the seeing was unsatisfactory.	**Gaudibert**	**Gaudibert 1880**

1881 Feb 3, 19h00m	**Aristarchus (on dark side, limb area)**	Very bright (~8.0 mag star) with pulsations	**"Gamma"**	**Sirius 1881**
1881 Jul 4, 00h30m	**N/A**	"Two pyramidal luminous protuberances appeared on the Moon's limb .... These points were a little darker than the rest of the Moon's face. They slowly faded away ...."	**Several observers**	**Sci. Amer. 1882**
1881 Aug 6-7	**Aristarchus region**	Whole region between Aristarchus and Herodotus and S part of Great Rille (Schroter's Valley) appeared in strong violet light as if covered with fog	**Klein**	**Klein 1902**
1881 Dec 5, 17h09m	**Aristarchus**	During eclipse, Aristarchus was a white spot in the coppery disk and continued so. (Lunar eclipse)	**S.J. Johnson**	**Johnson 1882; Fisher 1924**
1882 Jan 29, 17h00m - 17h30m	**Eudoxus; 30 min**	Unusual shadow	**N/A**	**Sirius 1882**
1882 Feb 27, 18h30m - 19h30m and 20h30m - 20h45m	**Eudoxus; 1 hr, and 15 min**	Unusual shadow (on Feb 25, the shadow was normal)	**N/A**	**Sirius 1882**
1882 Mar 27, 18h45m	**Plato**	Floor glowed with milky light	**A.S. Williams**	**Williams 1882**
1882 Apr 24	**Near Godin and Agrippa**	Shadows blurred and oscillating. Shadows in Aristoteles steady. Intervals between obscurations, ~10 min	**Ridd**	**Proc. Liverpool Astr. Soc. 1883**
1882 May 19	**Just E of Mare Crisium against Prom. Agarum**	Cloud, not less than 100 mi x 40 or 50 mi; no trace seen on May 20	**J.G. Jackson and friends**	**Eng. Mech. 1882; Strol. Astr. 1966; B.A.A. Lunar Sec. Circ. 1966, 1, No.8**
1882 Jul 17	**Just E of Mare Crisium,**	Feathery mist or cloud	**J.G. Jackson**	**Strol. Astr. 1966**

	against Prom. Agarum			
1882 Nov 7, 09h00m	Dark limb	Line of light around dark limb, attributed to atmosphere, well seen, equally bright throughout length. Age of Moon 26.5 days	Hopkins	Sirius 1884
1883 Mar 12, 20h00m	Dark limb	Line of light (see 1882 Nov 7) well seen	Hopkins	Sirius 1884
1883 Mar 12	Taruntius and environs	Peculiar blurred appearance. Unmistakable variations in the sharpness of the shadows of the ring plain	Davies	Proc. Liverpool Astr. Soc. 1883; B.A.A. Lunar Sec. Circ. 1966, 1, No 10
1883 May	Edge of Mare Crisium	Light mist or cloud	J.G. Jackson	Flammarion 1884
1883 Nov 5, ~18h00m	Aristarchus	Very bright (~7.0-8.0 mag star)	"R"	Sirius 1883
1884 Feb 5	Kepler	Illumination in Kepler	Morales	l'Astron. Vol.9
1884 Oct 4, ~22h03m	Tycho	During eclipse, bright spot like a star of the 2nd mag. (Lunar eclipse)	Parsehian	Parsehian 1885; Fisher 1924
1884 Nov 29, 19h00m - 21h00m	Aristarchus; 2 hr	Nebulous at center; elsewhere features well defined	Hislop	Sirius 1885
1885 Feb 19	Small crater near Hercules	Small crater was dull red with vivid contrast	Gray	l'Astron. Vol.4; Knowledge Vol.7
1885 Feb 21	Cassini	Red patches	Knopp	l'Astron. Vol.4
1885 Jun 10	Aristarchus	Starlike light	Tempel	Pop. Astr. 1932
1886 Sep 6	Plato	Streak of light on dark floor of crater in shadow (67 mm refl.)	Valderama	Sirius 1887
1887 Feb 1,	Plato	Appearance of light in crater	Kruger	Sirius 1887

~17h00m				
1887 Feb 2	**La Hire**	Intense yellow streak that cast shadows around neighbouring features	**Klein**	**Sirius 1903**
1888 Jul 15	**S edge of Alps on dark side of Moon**	"Lunar volcano"; ~1 mag star. Yellow light tinged with red from refractor's secondary spectrum	**Holden**	**Sirius 1888**
1888 Nov 23, 17h15m	**45 min**	A triangular patch of light (seen with 3 1/2 in. refractor and 180 x mag)	**von Speissen and others**	**Sirius**
1889 Mar 30	**Copernicus**	Black spot	**Gaudibert**	**l'Astron. 1889**
1889 May 11	**Gassendi**	Black spot on rim	**N/A**	**l'Astron. 1889**
1889 Jun 6, 22h00m	**Plato B and D (Schmidt's designation)**	Two extremely bright spots (8 in. refractor)	**Evon Lade**	**Sirius 1889**
1889 Jul 12, ~20h52m	**Aristarchus**	During lunar eclipse, brilliance in surrounding gloom was striking	**Krueger**	**Krueger 1889; Fisher 1924**
1889 Sep 3	**Alpetragius; 30 min**	"Central peak, its shadow and all the floor seem to be seen through haze."	**Barnard**	**Barnard 1892**
1889 Sep 13	**Plinius**	White spot over central peak	**Thury**	**Thury 1889a, 1889b**
1889 Oct 3-4	**Alpetragius**	Hazy	**Barnard**	**Barnard 1892**
1890 Oct 3, ~22h00m	**Posidonius**	Unusual shadow	**Meller**	**Sirius 1890**
1891 May 23, ~18h20m	**Aristarchus region**	Lunar eclipse, half hour before end of totality, Aristarchus and region immediately N of it became conspicuous and increased in brightness from that time on	**W.E. Jackson**	**Jackson 1890-91; Fisher 1924**
1891 Sep 16	**Schroter's Valley**	"Dense clouds of white vapour were apparently arising from its bottom and pouring over its SE [IAU:SW] wall in the direction of Herodotus."	**W.H. Pickering**	**Pickering 1903**

1891 Sep 17, 18, 23, 25	**Schroter's Valley**	Apparent volcanic activity	**W.H. Pickering**	**Pickering 1903**
1891 Oct 14	**Schroter's Valley**	Apparent volcanic activity	**W.H. Pickering**	**Pickering 1903**
1891 Nov 7	**Aristarchus**	Very distinct luminous point	**d'Adjuda**	**l'Astron. Vol.11**
1892 Mar 31	**Thales**	Pale luminous haze	**Barnard**	**Barnard 1892**
1892 May 10	**Schroter's Valley**	Apparent volcanic activity	**W.H. Pickering**	**Pickering 1903**
1892 May 11, ~22h53m	**N/A**	During partial lunar eclipse, extension of earth's shadow beyond the cusps	**N/A**	**Sirius 1892**
1893 Jan 30	**Schroter's Valley**	Apparent volcanic activity	**W.H. Pickering**	**Pickering 1903**
1893 Apr 1	**N/A**	Shaft of light	**de Moraes**	**l'Astron. Vol.13**
1894 Feb 23	**Henke (now Daniell) and N wall of Posidonius**	Strong brownish-red coppery hue in Henke and also on N wall of Posidonius	**Krieger**	**Sirius 1895**
1895 Mar 11, 03h42m	**N/A**	During lunar eclipse, very striking color in SE quadrant	**Foulkes**	**B.A.A. Mem. 1895**
1895 May 2, (1)~20h45m; (2)~23h30m	**Plato; (1)~12-14 min**	(1) Streak of light. (2) Bright parallel bands in center	**(1)Brenner; (2)Fauth**	**(1)Sirius 1895, 1897; (2)Sirius 1896, 1897**
1895 Sep 25	**N/A**	Shaft of light	**Gaboreau**	**l'Astron. Vol.13**
1896	**Macrobius**	Penumbral fringe to shadow	**Goodacre**	**Firsoff 1962 ed., p.90**
1897 Jun 14	**Schroter's Valley**	Apparent volcanic activity	**W.H. Pickering**	**Pickering 1903**
1897 Sep 21, 23h00m	**Aristarchus**	Glimmering streaks	**Molesworth**	**Goodacre 1931**
1897 Oct 8, 10, 13, 15	**Schroter's Valley**	Apparent volcanic activity	**W.H. Pickering**	**Pickering 1903**
1897 Dec 9	**Wm. Humboldt**	Light chocolate border to shadow on E wall	**Goodacre**	**B.A.A. Mem. 1898**

1898 Jan 8, 00h30m	**Tycho region**	About mid-eclipse, shadow so dense that details of surface disappeared entirely, except that bright ray extending SSW from Tycho was clearly visible throughout its whole extent and continued so throughout eclipse. (Lunar eclipse)	**Chevremont**	**Chevremont 1898; Fisher 1924**
1898 Apr 6-8	**Schroter's Valley**	Apparent volcanic activity	**W.H. Pickering**	**Pickering 1903**
1898 Jul 3, 21h47m	**Proclus**	Half hour after mid-eclipse, the crater shone with reddish light in shadow. (Lunar Eclipse)	**Moye**	**Moye 1898; Fisher 1924**
1898 Dec 27, ~23h38m	**Aristarchus**	During eclipse, Aristarchus brilliant (Lunar eclipse)	**Stuyvaert**	**Niesten and Stuyvaert 1898-99; Fisher 1924**
1901 Oct 25	**Marius**	A number of light streaks noticed on the crater floor. (Usually none are seen)	**Bolton**	**Bolton 1901**
1902 Aug 13, 00h50m	**Near Lambert**	(1) Brilliant starlike point; (2) completely round bright area, on dark side of Moon's terminator, mag 3 or 4	**Jones**	**(1) Pickering 1902; (2) Sirius 1903**
1902 Oct 16	**Theaetetus**	Cloud near Theaetetus	**Charbonneaux**	**Charbonneaux 1902**
1903 Mar 1	**Aristarchus**	Intermittent light "like a little star"	**Rey**	**Rey 1903**
1903 Mar 3	**Aristarchus**	Intermittent light "like a little star"	**Gheury**	**Bull. Soc. Astr. France**
1904 Jul 31	**Plato**	Bright hazy object 2" diameter on crater floor	**Pickering**	**Pickering 1906**
1904 Oct 2, 13h00m; 16h00m	**Plato**	Total or partial obscuration of crater floor	**Elger, Klein, Hodge, Goodacre**	**Goodacre 1931; Webb 1962 ed.; Green 1965**
1905 Feb 19, ~19h03m	**Aristarchus**	During eclipse, bright spot shining in the dark as a little star. (Lunar eclipse)	**Moye**	**Moye and Russell 1905; Fisher 1924**

1905 Aug 15, ~03h39m	**Tycho**	Visible, even brilliant during eclipse	**Rey**	**Sforza 1905; Fisher 1924**
1906 Aug 4, ~12h58m	**Aristarchus**	Shone conspicuously during lunar eclipse	**Ward**	**Ward 1906-07; Fisher 1924**
1906	**Mare Humorum**	N/A	**Flammarion**	**Azevado 1962**
1906	**Mare Serenitatis**	N/A	**Dubois, Flammarion**	**Azevado 1962**
1906	**Lichtenberg**	N/A	**Flammarion**	**Azevado 1962**
1906	**Alphonsus**	N/A	**Flammarion**	**Azevado 1962**
1907 Jan 22	**Plato**	Glow of light in part of Plato	**Fauth**	**Fauth 1907**
1909	**Tycho**	False dawn	**Mellish**	**Mellish 1909**
1909	**Mersenius**	Dimly lighted zone W of shadow	**Merlin**	**Merlin 1909**
1912 Apr 1, ~22h15m	**Tycho**	Visible like a bright spot standing out in the dark slate-gray shadow. Only Tycho was seen during the lunar eclipse	**LeRoy**	**LeRoy 1912; Fisher 1924**
1912 May 19	**Dark side**	Small red glowing area noticed on shadow side of Moon	**Valier**	**Valier 1912**
1912 May 20	**Leibnitz Mts. area**	Glowing line of light into dark side	**Franks**	**Franks obs. book**
1912 Sep 25	**Pico B**	Haze spreading from W end of crater	**Pickering**	**Rawstron 1937**
1913 Mar 22, ~11h57m	**N/A**	During eclipse totality, there remained visible to the NW only a luminous point not much larger than the planet Mars and of the same color (Lunar eclipse)	**G.Jackson**	**Jackson 1913; Fisher 1924**
1913 Jun 15	**South**	Distinct small reddish spot	**Maw**	**Webb 1962 ed.**
1915 Jan 31	**Littrow**	Seven white spots arranged like a Greek gamma	**Burgess**	**Eng. Mech. Vol. 101**

1915 Apr 21	**S of Posidonius**	Noticed special occurrence S of large circle Posidonius which he took as evidence of water vapor	**Houdard**	**Houdard 1917**
1915 Apr 23	**Clavius**	Narrow, straight beam of light from crater A to crater B	**Cook**	**B.A.A. Mem. 1916**
1915 Dec 11	**Mare Crisium**	Particularly bright spot like star on N shore	**Thomas**	**Eng. Mech. Vol.103**
1916 Oct 10	**Plato**	Pickering's craterlet No.59 involved in reddish shadow and disappeared. Usually distinctly seen under similar illumination.	**Maggini**	**Sci. Amer. 1919**
1917 Jan 8, ~07h45m	**Dionysius**	Point on rim of crater shone like a small star for sometime after entering the eclipse shadow (Lunar eclipse)	**W.F.A. Ellison**	**Ellison 1917; Fisher 1924**
1919 Nov 7, ~23h45m	**Tycho, vicinity**	Long ray in direction of Longomontanus remained visible glowing in weak gray-green light during whole eclipse (until clouds stopped observation) (Lunar eclipse)	**Fock**	**Fock 1920; Fisher 1924**
1920	**Near Vitruvius**	Some peaks varied considerably in brightness	**Franks**	**Wilkins and Moore 1958**
1922 Nov 28	**La Hire; 20 min**	Shadow cut through by white streak	**H.P. Wilkins**	**Wilkins 1954**
1927 May 12	**Peirce A (Wilkins' Graham)**	Complete obscuration of crater	**H.P. Wilkins**	**Moore 1953; Green 1965**
1927 Dec 23, 22h00m	**Peirce A (Wilkins' Graham)**	Invisible	**H.P. Wilkins**	**H.P. Wilkins obs. book**
1931 Feb 22	**Aristarchus**	Reddish-yellow	**Joulia**	**Joulia 1931**
1931 Mar 27	**Tycho**	Central mountain gray although crater interior was in full shadow	**Barker**	**Moore 1953; Green 1965**
1931	**Aristarchus**	Bluish glare	**Goodacre, Molesworth**	**Goodacre 1931**

1932 Apr 15, 06h57m	**Plato**	Sudden appearance of white spot like cloud	**Goddard and friend**	**Pop. Astr. 1932**
1933 Mar 30	**Aristarchus region**	White	**Douillet**	**Douillet 1933**
1933 Sep 1	**Neighbourhood of Pico, and Pico B**	Haze observed	**Rawstron**	**Rawstron 1937**
1933 Oct 1	**Neighbourhood of Pico, and Pico B**	Haze observed	**Rawstron**	**Rawstron 1937**
1936 May 4	**Eratosthenes**	Detected small bright spots on crater floor	**Martz**	**Haas 1942**
1936 Oct 4	**Eratosthenes**	Many small bright spots on crater floor, some of which Martz detected, but Johnson drew bright bands in their positions	**Haas**	**Haas 1942**
1936 Oct 25	**Eratosthenes**	Small bright spots on floor of crater	**Haas**	**Haas 1942**
1937 Feb 14	**Cassini**	Bright spot	**Andrenko**	**Azevado 1962**
1937 Sep 17	**Aristarchus**	Bright streak	**H.M. Johnson**	**Haas 1942**
1937 Sep 28	**Riccioli**	Color of dark area was deep purple; next night same with vivid hue	**Haas**	**Haas 1942**
1937 Oct 26	**Alphonsus, Herschel, and Ptolemaeus**	Milky floors	**Alter**	**Alter 1959**
1937 Dec 12	**Plato**	Strongly marked streak of orange-brown on E wall	**Barker**	**Barker 1940**
1938 Jan 16-17	**Plato**	Brownish gold-veined surface of color irregularly laid on smooth floor of crater	**Barker**	**Barker 1940**
1938 Feb 14	**Plato**	Golden-brown spot on E wall very prominent, with a yellowish glow without a definite boundary spreading over floor of crater	**Fox**	**Barker 1940**

1939 Feb 23	**Aristarchus**	Bright spot	**Andrenko**	**Azevado 1962**
1939 Mar 29, 19h00m	**Copernicus; 15 min**	Central mountain group seen distinctly as diffuse light spot. Sunrise on peaks did not begin until 22h00m	**Wilkins**	**Wilkins 1954**
1939 Aug 2, 00h10m	**Schickard**	Dense fog	**Moore**	**Wilkins and Moore 1958; Firsoff 1962 ed., p.80**
1939 Oct 19	**Macrobius**	Floor of crater reddish-brown, a hue ordinarily absent	**Barcroft**	**Haas 1942**
1939 Dec 27	**Aristarchus**	Slight bluish tinge on the still brilliant W wall	**Barcroft**	**Haas 1942; Firsoff 1962 ed., p.84**
1940 May 20, 20h00m	**Schickard**	Whitish obscuration; less dense than 1939 Aug 2	**Moore**	**Moore obs. book**
1940 Jun 14	**Plato**	Two hazy streaks of medium intensity, much complex detail	**Haas**	**Haas 1942**
1940 Jul 14	**Tycho**	Curious faint milky-looking luminosity seen. Luminous marks in shadow were ragged-edged and irregularly shaped	**Haas**	**Haas 1942**
1940 Oct 19	**Lichtenberg area**	Pronounced reddish-brown or orange color around area. Found color less marked next night, and slight by Oct 22	**Barcroft**	**Haas 1942; Strol. Astr. 1951**
1940 Oct 29	**Cusps**	Prolongation of N horn by 15 degrees	**Vaughan**	**Firsoff 1962 ed., p.127**
1940 Dec 2	**Aristarchus**	Distinguished crater in dark hemisphere as a bright spot	**Vaughan**	**Haas 1942**
1940 Dec 9	**Tycho**	Found some luminosity on W crater rim of W outer slope	**Barcroft**	**Haas 1942**
1940 Dec 25	**Cusps**	"Each horn appeared prolonged by about 10	**Haas**	**Firsoff 1962 ed., p.127**

		degrees"		
1941 Jan 6	**Arzachel**	Anomalous shadow	**Barcroft**	**Azevado 1962; Wilkins 1954**
1941 Feb 6	**Conon**	Faint bright spot, not too definite in outline, seen on crater floor	**Vaughan**	**Haas 1942**
1941 Mar 6	**Cusps**	Prolongation suspected	**Barcroft**	**Firsoff 1962 ed., p.127**
1941 Mar 31	**Aristarchus**	Crater perceived by earthshine (Haas thought it must have been unusually brilliant)	**Barcroft**	**Haas 1942**
1941 Jul 10	**Gassendi, and near Hansteen**	Moving luminous speck near Hansteen; estimated diameter 0.1", mag +8 (lunar meteor?)	**Haas**	**Wilkins and Moore 1958, p.281; Azevado 1962**
1942 Feb 2, 18h20m - 19h15m	**W of Kepler; 55 min**	Whitish glow near earthlit limb	**Y.W.L. Fisher**	**Wilkins and Moore 1958, p.271**
1942 Aug 26	**Atlas**	Dark areas faded in crater	**Haas**	**Haas 1965**
1944 Apr 4	**Hyginus N (Klein N)**	Much darker than usual	**Wilkins**	**Moore 1953, p.144; Green 1965**
1944 Aug 12, 23h00m	**Plato**	Exceptional darkness of crater floor, three light spots noted at foot of E wall. Although no light streaks were visible, there was a large and conspicuous spot near the center. Since this spot has been noted as slightly but definitely rimmed all round, Wilkins suggested that temporary dark cloud or vapor may have covered true floor up to level of rim.	**Wilkins**	**Wilkins 1944**
1944 Aug 31	**Schickard**	Mist on crater floor	**Wilkins**	**Wilkins and Moore 1958**
1945 Oct 19, 11h23m50s	**Plato**	Bright flash on crater floor near E wall	**Thornton**	**Green 1965; Thornton 1945**

1945 Oct 19	**Darwin**	Three brilliant points of light on wall	**Moore**	**Wilkins 1954**
1947 Jan 30	**Eratosthenes**	Without normal shadow	**H. Hill**	**Wilkins and Moore 1958**
1947 Aug 28	**SE of Langrenus**	Mountain on limb very decidedly bluish	**Baum**	**Wilkins 1954**
1947 Nov 30	**Aristarchus**	Bright spots on inner W slopes	**Favarger**	**Wilkins 1954**
1948 Feb 17	**Dawes**	Central peak not seen, but cleft-like marking from SW crest towards E shadow	**Thornton**	**Contrib. by Moore**
1948 Apr 14	**N/A**	Prolongation of southern cusp	**Wilkins**	**Wilkins 1954**
1948 Apr 15	**30 degrees N of Grimaldi on W limb**	Bright spot on earthlit W limb 30 degrees N of Grimaldi and estimated equal to a 3rd mag star	**Vince**	**J.B.A.A. 1948**
1948 May 20	**NE of Philolaus; 15 min**	Red glow	**Baum**	**Firsoff 1962 ed., p.82**
1948 Jul 21-22	**Mare Crisium; several hours**	Almost featureless apart from Picard, Peirce	**Moore**	**Moore obs. book**
1948 Jul 27	**Promontorium Heraclides**	Blurred and misty	**Moore, Docherty**	**Moore obs. book**
1948 Aug 8	**Dark side**	A small bright flash on earthlit portion ... like a bright sparkle of frost on the ground	**Woodward**	**Moore 1953**
1948 Aug 16	**E of Picard; several hours**	Two areas E of Picard appeared featureless	**Moore**	**J.B.A.A. 1949**
1948 Oct 8	**Barker's Quadrangle**	Nebulous white patch in place of Quadrangle	**Moore**	**Moore obs. book**
1948 Oct 19	**Promontorium Heraclides**	Blurred	**Docherty**	**Contrib. by Moore**
1949 Feb 7, 18h00m	**Kepler**	White glow near Kepler	**Y.W.I. Fisher**	**Contrib. by Moore**
1949 Feb 9	**Barker's Quadrangle**	Quadrangle not seen ... appeared misty	**Moore**	**Moore obs. book**
1949 Feb 10	**Schroter's Valley near**	Diffuse patch of thin smoke or vapor from W	**Thornton**	**Wilkins and Moore 1958,**

	Cobrahead	side of Schroter's Valley near Cobrahead, spreading into plain; detail indistinct, hazy (surrounding area clear)		**p.263**
1949 Mar 3, 20h00m	**Barker's Quadrangle**	Whole area hazy	**Moore**	**Moore obs. book**
1949 May 1	**Aristarchus**	Visible in earthshine, glowing suddenly as diffuse light patch	**Wilkins**	**Wilkins 1954**
1949 Oct 7, ~02h54m	**Aristarchus**	Abnormally bright during lunar eclipse	**G.Brown, Hare**	**Contrib. by Moore**
1949 Nov 3, 01h06m	**Aristarchus**	Blue glare, base inner W wall	**Bartlett**	**Bartlett 1967**
1950 Jun 27, 02h30m	**Aristarchus**	Blue glare, base inner W wall	**Bartlett**	**Bartlett 1967**
1950 Jun 27	**Herodotus**	Bright point in crater	**Bartlett**	**Strol. Astr. 1962**
1950 Jun 28, 03h27m	**Aristarchus**	Blue glare, rim of W wall	**Bartlett**	**Bartlett 1967**
1950 Jun 29, 05h30m	**Aristarchus**	Strong bluish glare; E, SE wall	**Bartlett**	**Bartlett 1967**
1950 Jul 26, 02h52m	**Aristarchus**	Blue glare, base inner W wall	**Bartlett**	**Bartlett 1967**
1950 Jul 31, 04h50m	**Aristarchus**	Violet glare, E, NE rim	**Bartlett**	**Bartlett 1967**
1950 Aug 28, 04h25m	**Aristarchus**	Intense blue-violet glare; E wall bright spot, E, NE rim	**Bartlett**	**Bartlett 1967**
1951 Jan 21	**E of Lichtenberg**	Red patch	**Baum**	**Strol. Astr. 1951**
1951 Feb 4, 21h00m - 23h00m	**W of Endymion; 2hr**	Mist over peak	**Baum**	**Baum 1966**
1951 May 17	**Gassendi**	Bright speck of short duration	**Wilkins**	**Moore 1953, p.118**
1951 Aug	**W.H. Pickering**	Brilliant white patch inside crater	**Moore**	**Moore**

20	**(Messier A)**			**1953, p.147**
1951 Oct 20	**W.H. Pickering (Messier A)**	Bright circular patch	**Moore**	**Moore obs. book**
1952 Apr 3	**N/A**	Twenty-one spots were charted, one surrounded by a light area, while three streaks were seen in the NW quarter.	**Wilkins, Moore**	**Wilkins and Moore 1958**
1952 Apr 4	**Plato**	Obscuration of crater floor	**Cragg**	**Moore 1953, 1965**
1952 Sep 9, 23h00m	**Calippus**	Broad hazy band of light across floor (observer gave observation low weight	**Moore**	**Moore obs. book**
1952 Dec 24	**Theaetetus**	Hazy line of light	**Moore**	**Wilkins and Moore 1958, p.238**
1953 Apr 18	**N/A**	Faint extension of cusps	**Wilkins**	**Wilkins 1954**
1953 Nov 15, 02h00m	**Near Pallas**	Very bright spot on illuminated part near terminator seen and photographed	**Stuart**	**Strolling Astr. 1956; Stuart 1957**
1954 Mar 23	**Atlas**	Violet tint in Atlas	**Delmotte**	**Delmotte**
1954 May 10	**Crater in Ptolemaeus**	Flash	**Firsoff**	**Firsoff 1962 ed., p.53**
1954 May 11, 20h00m	**Eratosthenes**	Central mountain group invisible, though surrounding details very clear	**Cattermole**	**Contrib. by Moore**
1954 Jul 14, 04h39m	**Aristarchus**	E wall bright spot; violet glare	**Bartlett**	**Bartlett 1967**
1954 Jul 16, 05h35m	**Aristarchus**	Whole interior of strong violet ting; violet tint in nimbus and N and NE of crater	**Bartlett**	**Bartlett 1967**
1954 Jul 17, 07h05m	**Aristarchus**	Pale violet tint on surface NE of crater; no color elsewhere	**Bartlett**	**Bartlett 1967**
1954 Jul 24, 07h19m	**Aristarchus**	Crater filled with pale violet light	**Bartlett**	**Bartlett 1967**
1954 Aug 11, 22h00m	**Aristarchus**	Brilliant in red (filter), variable	**Firsoff**	**Firsoff 1966**
1954 Aug	**Aristarchus**	Brilliant blue-violet glare over E	**Bartlett**	**Contrib. by**

18		and NE walls		**Moore**
1954 Sep 8, 20h00m	**Proclus**	Brightness variation in blue light	**Firsoff**	**Firsoff 1962 ed., p.83**
1954 Oct 8, 10	**Timocharis**	Red glow	**Firsoff**	**Firsoff 1962, 1966**
1954 Oct 11, 04h57m	**Aristarchus**	Violet tint on floor, E wall and central peak; intermittent	**Bartlett**	**Bartlett 1967**
1954 Oct 12, 01h32m	**Aristarchus**	Pale violet radiance; S wal, SE, E, NE walls; central peak	**Bartlett**	**Bartlett 1967**
1954 Oct 12, 04h09m	**Aristarchus**	Strong violet tint E half of floor; very faint W half of floor and W wall. Dark violet in nimbus; pale violet on plateau	**Bartlett**	**Bartlett 1967**
1954 Oct 13, 02h00m	**Aristarchus**	Bright blue-violet glare, E rim; pale violet radiance within crater and around S wall bright spot. Dark violet in nimbus; pale violet on plateau.	**Bartlett**	**Bartlett 1967**
1954 Oct 13, 05h15m	**Aristarchus**	Scarcely perceptible violet radiance within crater; wall bands look faint	**Bartlett**	**Bartlett 1967**
1954 Oct 18, 06h47m	**Aristarchus**	Strong blue-violet glare, E wall bright spot, E wall and on central peak	**Bartlett**	**Bartlett 1967**
1954 Nov 5	**Copernicus**	Bright point	**Johnstone**	**Strol. Astr. 1962**
1954 Nov 7, 23h20m	**Kepler**	Bright point just outside E wall	**Lugo**	**J.B.A.A. 1955**
1954 Nov 12, 02h42m	**Aristarchus**	Blue-violet glare; E wall bright spot and whole length of E wall. Suspected violet tint in N and NE of crater; Certainly on plateau. Greatly faded by 05h07m	**Bartlett**	**Bartlett 1967**
1954 Dec 12, 02h44m	**Aristarchus**	Strong violet glare, E rim, changing to brown	**Bartlett**	**Bartlett 1967**
1955 Jan 8, 00h46m	**Aristarchus**	Strong violet glare whole length of E rim; brightest SE and around E wall bright spot	**Bartlett**	**Bartlett 1967**
1955 Jan 12, 04h54m	**Aristarchus**	Blue-violet glare; E wall bright spot, E, NE rim	**Bartlett**	**Bartlett 1967**

1955 Apr 2, 03h20m - 05h00m	**Straight-wall region; ~1 hr 40 min**	Small craters between Birt and fault invisible at times under excellent viewing conditions, while craterlets on E side were continually observed	**Capen**	**Capen 1955, 1967**
1955 Apr 5, 03h20m	**Aristarchus**	E wall and glacis; violet; uncertain	**Bartlett**	**Bartlett 1967**
1955 Apr 24	**Near Posidonius**	White flash of short duration N of Mare Serenitatis near Posidonius	**Wykes**	**Strol. Astr. 1955**
1955 May 5, 03h30m	**Aristarchus**	Pale violet tint in E half of floor; violet band at base, E side of central peak	**Bartlett**	**Bartlett 1967**
1955 May 7-8	**Lictenberg**	N/A	**Nicolini**	**Azevado 1962**
1955 May 24	**Near South Pole**	"Glitter" suggesting electrical discharge	**Firsoff**	**Firsoff 1962 ed., p.131**
1955 Jun 25, 20h30m	**Theophilus**	Mistiness; absent the next night	**Firsoff**	**Firsoff 1962 ed., p.84**
1955 Jul 3, 22h00m	**Schroter's Valley**	Starlike point	**Firsoff**	**Firsoff 1962 ed., Pl.X**
1955 Jul 13	**Aristarchus**	Brilliant in blue and green	**Firsoff**	**Firsoff 1966**
1955 Aug 3, 04h50m	**Aristarchus**	Plateau only; pale violet tint	**Bartlett**	**Bartlett 1967**
1955 Aug 3	**Manilius, Timocharis**	Manilius extraordinarily brilliant; Timocharis bright in blue, appears large and diffuse	**Firsoff**	**Firsoff 1966**
1955 Aug 26	**Near Carpathians; ~35 sec**	Bright flare on dark side similar to 2nd mag star	**McCorkle**	**Sky and Tel. 1955**
1955 Aug 30, 03h40m	**Aristarchus**	Floor, base inner W wall, NW wall; faint bluish glare	**Bartlett**	**Bartlett 1967**
1955 Sep 7, 03h20m	**Copernicus**	Brightened in blue	**Firsoff**	**Firsoff 1966**
1955 Sep 7, 04h52m	**Aristarchus**	Strong blue-violet glare; E, NE rim; also E base of central peak. Dark violet, nimbus.	**Bartlett**	**Bartlett 1967**
1955 Sep 8, 04h32m	**Aristarchus**	Strong bluish glare on E, NE wall, on S edge of E wall bright spot, and bordering both edges of the bright floor band, passing around	**Bartlett**	**Bartlett 1967**

		W of central peak. Dark violet tint in nimbus.		
1955 Sep 8	**Taurus Mountains**	Two flashes from edge of Taurus Mountains	**Lambert**	**Sky and Tel. 1955**
1955 Sep 9, 02h58m	**Aristarchus**	Floor; blue clay color	**Bartlett**	**Bartlett 1967**
1955 Sep 28, 23h00m	**Cobrahead**	Obscured by brown patch	**Bestwick**	**Contrib. by Moore**
1955 Oct 2, 05h42m	**Aristarchus**	Violet glare, E, NE rim. Over E wall bright spot resembled a violet mist. Crater itself was hazy; could not get sharp focus.	**Bartlett**	**Bartlett 1967**
1955 Oct 4, 04h55m	**Aristarchus**	Pale violet tint; E wall bright spot and whole length of E rim; dark violet in nimbus	**Bartlett**	**Bartlett 1967**
1955 Oct 4	**Aristarchus**	Spectrum enhanced in H and K region	**Kozyrev**	**Kozyrev 1957**
1955 Oct 5, 03h44m	**Aristarchus**	Intensely bright blue-violet glare; E wall bright spot, E, NE wall	**Bartlett**	**Bartlett 1967**
1955 Oct 31, 00h40m	**Aristarchus**	Bright blue-violet glare, E, NE rim; dark violet hue in nimbus; pale violet radiance over plateau	**Bartlett**	**Bartlett 1967**
1955 Oct 31, 04h50m	**Aristarchus**	Intense blue-violet glare, E, NE rim. Dark violet in nimbus; pale violet on plateau	**Bartlett**	**Bartlett 1967**
1955 Oct 31, 19h00m	**Cobrahead**	Dark blue obscuration	**Milligan**	**Contrib. by Moore**
1955 Nov 1, 03h18m	**Aristarchus**	Pale violet tint; E wall bright spot, E, NE rim, dark violet hue in nimbus	**Bartlett**	**Bartlett 1967**
1955 Nov 6, 05h50m	**Aristarchus**	Strong blue-violet glare, E, NE wall. Dark violet hue in nimbus	**Bartlett**	**Bartlett 1967**
1955 Nov 27, 02h48m	**Aristarchus**	Floor; blue clay color	**Bartlett**	**Bartlett 1967**
1955	**Plato**	N/A	**Sytinskaya**	**Azevado 1962**
1955	**Aristarchus**	N/A	**Sytinskaya**	**Azevado 1962**
1955	**Tycho**	N/A	**Sytinskaya**	**Azevado**

				1962
1956 Jan 24	**W edge of Cavendish; ~10 min**	Variable point of light	**Houghton, Warner**	**Strol. Astr. 1955**
1956 Jan 27, 01h18m	**Aristarchus**	Violet glare whole length of E wall and around E wall bright spot; violet tint N and NE of crater	**Bartlett**	**Bartlett 1967**
1956 Jan 28, 02h33m	**Aristarchus**	Pale violet radiance; E, NE rim	**Bartlett**	**Bartlett 1967**
1956 Mar 14, 19h00m	**N/A**	Twilight at S cusp traced 400 mi. beyond cusp. No trace of twilight at N pole. 6 1/2 inch reflector used. Moon 2 1/2 days old	**Firsoff**	**J.B.A.A. 1956**
1956 Mar 18	**N/A**	Anomalous dimming of Tau and 105 Tau before occultation	**Firsoff**	**J.B.A.A. 1956**
1956 Jun 20, 03h39m	**Aristarchus**	Blue glare, base inner W wall	**Bartlett**	**Bartlett 1967**
1956 Jun 26, 07h42m	**Aristarchus**	Intense blue-violet glare; on E wall bright spot. Dark violet in nimbus	**Bartlett**	**Bartlett 1967**
1956 Jun 28, 05h35m	**Aristarchus**	Intense blue-violet glare, E wall bright spot. Dark violet, nimbus. Pale violet N and NE of crater and on plateau	**Bartlett**	**Bartlett 1967**
1956 Jun 29, 06h10m	**Aristarchus**	Faint, blue-violet tint; E wall bright spot	**Bartlett**	**Bartlett 1967**
1956 Jun 30, 06h55m	**Aristarchus**	Vivid blue-violet glare; E wall bright spot, E, NE wall	**Bartlett**	**Bartlett 1967**
1956 Jul 28, 05h40m	**Aristarchus**	Vivid blue-violet glare on central peak, band across E floor to E wall bright spot; on E wall bright spot and E, NE wall. Absent by 07h20m.	**Bartlett**	**Bartlett 1967**
1956 Oct 16, 02h34m	**Aristarchus**	Blue glare, base inner W wall	**Bartlett**	**Bartlett 1967**
1956 Oct 20, 00h45m	**Aristarchus**	Bright blue-violet glare on E wall bright spot, E, NE rim. Dark violet in nimbus	**Bartlett**	**Bartlett 1967**
1956 Oct 26	**Alphonsus**	A suspected partial obscuration of the floor based on differences	**Alter**	**Alter 1956, 1959**

		in detail in infrared and ultraviolet photographs		
1956 Nov 15, 01h17m	**Aristarchus**	Faint blue radiance, base inner W wall	**Bartlett**	**Bartlett 1967**
1956 Nov 16, 03h33m	**Aristarchus**	Floor; bright bluish tint E of central peak; blue-gray W of central peak	**Bartlett**	**Bartlett 1967**
1956 Nov 17-18	**Aristarchus, Tycho, Kepler, Proclus, Manilius, Byrgius**	Extraordinarily bright	**Argentiere, et al**	**Azevado 1962**
1956	**Tycho**	N/A	**Dubois**	**Azevado 1962**
1956	**Mare Humorum**	N/A	**Vigroux**	**Azevado 1962**
1957 Mar 17, 06h24m	**Aristarchus**	Strong violet glare; E wall bright spot and whole length of E wall. Dark violet in nimbus; pale violet on plateau	**Bartlett**	**Bartlett 1967**
1957 Mar 18, 06h43m	**Aristarchus**	Strong violet glare; E wall bright spot, E wall. Very strong violet hue in nimbus	**Bartlett**	**Bartlett 1967**
1957 Jun 11, 04h48m	**Aristarchus**	Floor; uniform bluish radiance	**Bartlett**	**Bartlett 1967**
1957 Jul 11, 05h40m	**Aristarchus**	Pale violet radiance in crater and on plateau	**Bartlett**	**Bartlett 1967**
1957 Aug 18, 06h58m	**Aristarchus**	Pale blue tint on all walls; floor dazzling white	**Bartlett**	**Bartlett 1967**
1957 Oct 11, 03h15m	**Aristarchus**	Bright blue-violet; E wall bright spot, E, NE rim. Dark violet in nimbus	**Bartlett**	**Bartlett 1967**
1957 Oct 12, 02h40m	**Aristarchus**	Bright blue-violet glare; E wall bright spot, E, NE, N, NW walls. Dark violet nimbus	**Bartlett**	**Bartlett 1967**
1957 Oct 12	**Aristarchus; 1 hr**	Bright flash; then brownish eccentric patch	**Dachille and daughter**	**Cameron 1965**
1957 Oct 13, 04h00m	**Aristarchus**	Weak violet glare; whole length of E wall	**Bartlett**	**Bartlett 1967**
1957 Oct 13	**In or near**	Bright spot of light ("explosion")	**Haas**	**Haas 1957**

	Aristarchus			
1957 Oct 15, 05h45m	**Aristarchus**	Strong blue-violet glare, whole length of E wall	**Bartlett**	**Bartlett 1967**
1957 Oct 16, 06h00m	**Aristarchus**	Faint blue-gray tint; N, NW, W floor and walls	**Bartlett**	**Bartlett 1967**
1958 May 1, 03h00m	**Aristarchus**	Entire sunlit area of floor, bluish	**Bartlett**	**Bartlett 1967**
1958 May 4, 06h28m	**Aristarchus**	Blue-violet glare S side of E wall bright spot; dark violet in nimbus; pale violet on plateau	**Bartlett**	**Bartlett 1967**
1958 May 31, 03h40m	**Aristarchus**	Pale blue-gray floor; violet band E base of central peak	**Bartlett**	**Bartlett 1967**
1958 Jun 29, 04h04m	**Aristarchus**	Floor; very pale bluish tint	**Bartlett**	**Bartlett 1967**
1958 Jul 2, 06h29m	**Aristarchus**	Strong violet glare whole length of E wall, involving E wall bright spot; dark violet, nimbus	**Bartlett**	**Bartlett 1967**
1958 Jul 3, 07h06m	**Aristarchus**	Bright blue-violet glare; E, NE rim. Dark violet, nimbus; pale violet, plateau	**Bartlett**	**Bartlett 1967**
1958 Aug 2, 06h15m	**Aristarchus**	Strong violet glare; E wall bright spot, NE wall. Dark violet, nimbus. Strong violet, plateau	**Bartlett**	**Bartlett 1967**
1958 Sep 1, 07h27m	**Aristarchus**	Whole crater filled with pale violet radiance, especially bright on walls. Pale violet N and NE of crater and on plateau	**Bartlett**	**Bartlett 1967**
1958 Sep 23	**Piton**	Became enveloped in an obscuring cloud-like mist	**Moore**	**Moore obs. book**
1958 Oct 16	**N of Mare Crisium**	Bright spot in dark area of Moon	**Mayemson**	**Mayemson 1965**
1958 Nov 3, 03h00m	**Alphonsus**	Reddish glow, followed by effusion of gas	**Kozyrev**	**Kozyrev 1959, 1963; Green 1965**
1958 Nov 19, 04h00m - 04h30m	**Alphonsus; 30 min**	Diffuse cloud over central mountain	**Poppendiek, Bond**	**Alter 1959; Poppendiek and Bond 1959**
1958 Nov 19, 22h05m	**Alpetragius**	Portion of shadow in crater vanished	**Stein**	**Stein 1959**

1958 Nov 19	**Alphonsus**	Reddish patch close to central peak	**Wilkins, Hole**	**Wilkins 1959; Hole 1959; Moore 1965**
1958 Nov 22	**Alphonsus**	Gray spot	**Bartha**	**Moore 1965**
1958 Dec 19	**Alphonsus**	Reddish patch close to central peak	**Wilkins, Hole**	**Wilkins 1959; Hole 1959; Moore 1965**
1959 Jan 22	**Aristarchus**	Interior, light brilliant blue, later turning white	**Alter**	**Alter NASA report**
1959 Jan 23	**Aristarchus**	Brilliant blue interior	**Alter**	**Cameron 1965**
1959 Feb 18	**Alphonsus**	Red patch	**Hole**	**Moore 1965**
1959 Mar 24, 02h33m and 04h55m	**Aristarchus**	Strong blue and blue-violet glares; E wall, E wall bright spot, S wall bright spot; intermittent display. Observation at 04h55m of same phenomenon	**Bartlett**	**Bartlett 1967**
1959 Mar 25, 05h24m	**Aristarchus**	Intense blue-violet glare on whole length of E rim and on E wall bright spot; dark violet hue in nimbus	**Bartlett**	**Bartlett 1967**
1959 Apr 19	**W of Mare Humorum**	Bright point to W of mare	**McFarlane**	**Strol. Astr. 1959**
1959 Sep 5	**Aristarchus**	Irregular, intermittent starlike point of light, 8th to 9th mag, appeared within bright area. No color seen	**Rule**	**Rule 1959**
1959 Sep 13	**Littrow**	Obliterated by a hovering cloud (Feist disagrees with Bradford)	**Bradford**	**Contrib. by Moore**
1959 Oct 23	**Alphonsus**	Red glow seen. Spectrum showed unusual features	**Kozyrev**	**Kozyrev 1962**
1960 Jan 6	**Alphonsus**	Red spot	**Warner**	**J. Int. Lunar Soc. 1960**
1960 Nov	**Piton; ~30 min**	Red obscuration concealing peak	**Schneller**	**Cameron 1965**
1960 Dec	**Piton**	Red obscuration less intense than in November	**Schneller**	**Cameron 1965**

1961 Jan	**Piton**	Red obscuration less intense than in November	**Schneller**	**Cameron 1965**
1961 Feb 15, ~08h11m	**Aristarchus, Plato**	Seen as bright features during solar eclipse (on film of eclipse shown by BBC May 6, 1966)	**Sartory, Middlehurst**	**Contrib. by Middlehurst**
1961 May 30-31	**Aristarchus**	Enhancement of spectrum in UV	**Grainger, Ring**	**Grainger and Ring 1963**
1961 Jun 27-28	**Aristarchus, ray near Bessel**	Enhancement of spectrum in UV	**Grainger, Ring**	**Grainger and Ring 1963**
1961 Jun 29-30	**E of Plato**	Enhancement of spectrum in UV	**Grainger, Ring**	**Grainger and Ring 1963**
1961 Oct 18	**Eratosthenes**	Bright spot in crater	**Bartlett**	**Strol. Astr. 1962**
1961 Nov 26	**Aristarchus region**	Red glow seen. Anomalous spectra in red and blue	**Kozyrev**	**Kozyrev 1963**
1961 Nov 28	**Aristarchus region**	Red glow seen. Anomalous spectra in red and blue	**Kozyrev**	**Kozyrev 1963**
1961 Dec 3	**Aristarchus region**	Red glow seen. Anomalous spectra in red and blue	**Kozyrev**	**Kozyrev 1963**
1962 Sep 5	**Region of Walter near terminator; 7 min**	Faint point of light	**Chalk**	**Cameron 1965**
1962 Sep 16	**"Whole Moon"**	Spectrum showed UV emission, particularly in region of H and K lines by comparison with spectra of Sun, Mars and Jupiter	**Spinrad**	**Spinrad 1964**
1962 Oct 8	**Aristarchus; ~1 hr**	Activity	**Adams**	**Cameron 1965**
1963 Oct 5	**Aristarchus region**	Enhancement of 30 percent at 5450 A	**Scarfe**	**Scarfe 1965**
1963 Oct 30	**Aristarchus region**	Color changes; reddish-orange to ruby patches	**Greenacre, Barr**	**Greenacre 1963**
1963 Oct 30	**Cobrahead; 7 min**	Brightened area, 7th to 11th mag	**Budine, Farrell**	**Cameron 1965**
1963 Nov 1, 23h00m	**Near Kepler; 20 min**	Enhancement of large area in red light	**Kopal, Rackham**	**Kopal and Rackham**

				1964a, 1964b
1963 Nov 11	**Aristarchus**	Color changes	**Jacobs**	**Shorthill 1963; Gree 1965, p.409**
1963 Nov 28	**Aristarchus, Schroter's Valley; 1 hr 15 min**	Red spots, then violet, blue haze	**Greenacre, et al**	**Greenacre 1963**
1963 Nov 28	**Cobrahead; 35 min**	Pink spot on W side	**Tombaugh**	**Cameron 1965**
1963 Nov 28	**Aristarchus, Anaximander; ~1 hr**	Red spot in Aristarchus and also on N edge of Anaximander	**W. Fisher**	**Cameron 1965**
1963 Dec 28, 15h55m - 16h26m	**Aristarchus to Herodotus; 31 min**	Extensive red area	**9 students at Hiroshima, Japan**	**Sato 1964**
1963 Dec 29-30, 22h00m - 03h00m	**Aristarchus region; 5 hr**	Purplish-blue patch	**Doherty and others**	**Contrib. by Moore**
1963 Dec 30, ~11h00m	**NE limb; ~20 min**	During eclipse, anomalous reddish glow inside umbra (Lunar eclipse)	**Many observers**	**Sky and Tel. 1964**
1964 Feb 25	**Cobrahead; 3 min, Aristarchus; 1 min**	Red flashes, + 12 mag	**Budine**	**Cameron 1965**
1964 Mar 16	**Aristarchus**	Sudden red glow on SW rim	**Lecuona**	**Cameron 1965**
1964 Mar 18	**Aristarchus**	Flash	**Earl and brother**	**Cameron 1965**
1964 Mar 26, 00h37m	**Aristarchus**	Floor; blue clay color	**Bartlett**	**Bartlett, 1967**
1964 Mar 28, 01h59m	**Aristarchus**	Blue-violet glare, E wall and N wall; E wall bright spot; violet tinge in nimbus	**Bartlett**	**Bartlett 1967**
1964 Apr 22	**Near Ross D**	Bright spot	**Cross and others**	**Harris 1967**
1964 Apr 26	**Region of**	Surface brightening somewhat	**Hopmann**	**Hopmann**

	Censorinus	similar to Kopal-Rackham (1963 Nov 1) event		**1966**
1964 May 17	**Theophilus**	Crimson color on W rim, ~10 mag	**Dieke**	**Cameron 1965**
1964 May 18, 03h55m - 05h00m	**SE of Ross D; 1 hr 5 min**	White obscuration moved 20 mph, decreased in extent. Phenomenon repeated. Newtonians 8" f/7 and 9" f/7 used	**Harris, Cross and others**	**Cameron 1965; Harris 1967**
1964 May 20	**Plato; ~10 min**	Strong orange-red color on W rim of crater, + 10 mag	**Bartlett**	**Bartlett 1967**
1964 May 26, 04h22m	**Aristarchus**	Strong blue-violet glare, E wall and E wall bright spot; strong violet tinge in nimbus	**Bartlett**	**Bartlett 1967**
1964 May 28, 05h38m	**Aristarchus**	Blue-violet glare; E wall bright spot, E, NE walls. Dark violet, nimbus	**Bartlett**	**Bartlett 1967**
1964 Jun 6	**Aristarchus area; 50 min**	Spur between Aristarchus and Herodotus; red spots (glow) in Schroter's Valley	**Schmidling, St.Clair, Platt**	**Cameron 1965**
1964 Jun 17	**SE of Ross D**	Moving bright spot; 2 brief obscurations of part of wall. Newtonian, 19" f/7	**Cross, Harris**	**Harris 1967**
1964 Jun 20, 06h00m	**Aristarchus**	Nimbus only; dark violet hue	**Bartlett**	**Bartlett 1967**
1964 Jun 21, 03h43m - 05h44m	**S of Ross D; 2 hr, 1 min**	Moving dark area. Newtonian 19" f/7	**Harris, Cross, Helland**	**Harris 1967**
1964 Jun 23, 04h55m	**Aristarchus**	Blue-violet glare, NE rim; strong violet tinge in nimbus	**Bartlett**	**Bartlett 1967**
1964 Jun 25, ~01h07m	**Aristarchus**	Very bright during eclipse (direct photograph, lunar eclipse)	**Titulaer**	**Hemel en Dampkring 1967**
1964 Jun 25, 01h07m	**Grimaldi**	During lunar eclipse, white streak from Grimaldi toward limb	**Azevado**	**Letter to Moore**
1964 Jun 26, 05h24m	**Aristarchus**	Dark violet in nimbus; pale violet on plateau. Absent from crater	**Bartlett**	**Bartlett 1967**
1964 Jun 27, 05h48m	**Aristarchus**	Bright blue-violet; E wall bright spot, E, NE rim. Dark violet in nimbus	**Bartlett**	**Bartlett 1967**

1964 Jun 28, 06h44m	**Aristarchus**	Blue-violet glare; E wall bright spot, E, NE, N, NW walls	**Bartlett**	**Bartlett 1967**
1964 Jun 28	**S region of Aristarchus**	Reddish-brown tone observed	**Bartlett**	**Greenacre 1965**
1964 Jul 16	**SE of Ross D**	Temporary "hill," est 3 km diam and shadow seen	**Cragg**	**Harris 1967**
1964 Jul 17	**Plato**	Faint pink bands at base of inner W wall and on rim of N wall	**Bartlett**	**Greenacre 1965**
1964 Jul 18	**SE of Ross D**	Bright area moved and shrank. Extent greater with amber filter	**Harris**	**Cameron 1965; Harris 1967**
1964 Jul 18	**Plato; some minutes**	Pink tinge to W wall, 10th mag	**Bartlett**	**Cameron 1965**
1964 Jul 28, 04h43m	**Aristarchus**	Blue-violet glare; E wall bright spot. Dark violet in nimbus; pale violet on plateau	**Bartlett**	**Bartlett 1967**
1964 Jul 29, 05h50m	**Aristarchus**	Nimbus only; dark violet hue	**Bartlett**	**Bartlett 1967**
1964 Jul 31, 05h28m	**Aristarchus**	Pale blue tint; NE, N, NW walls and floor	**Bartlett**	**Bartlett 1967**
1964 Aug 16, 04h18m - 05h20m	**SE of Ross D; 1 hr, 2 min**	Bright area. Condensations varying with time	**Harris, Cross**	**Harris 1967**
1964 Aug 24, 04h22m	**Aristarchus**	Bright blue-violet; E wall bright spot, E, NE wall	**Bartlett**	**Bartlett 1967**
1964 Aug 25, 04h58m	**Aristarchus**	Bright blue-violet; E wall bright spot, E, NE rim. Dark violet in nimbus	**Bartlett**	**Bartlett 1967**
1964 Aug 26, 04h16m	**Aristarchus**	Blue-violet glare; E wall bright spot, E, NE rim. Dark violet hue in nimbus	**Bartlett**	**Bartlett 1967**
1964 Aug 26	**Aristarchus; ~1 hr**	Red and blue bands	**Gennatt, Reid**	**Cameron 1965**
1964 Aug 27, 04h37m	**Aristarchus**	Blue-violet glare; E wall bright spot, E, NE wall. Dark violet, nimbus; pale violet on plateau	**Bartlett**	**Bartlett 1967**
1964 Aug 28, 04h40m	**Aristarchus**	Faint blue-violet radiance, E wall bright spot and NE rim. Dark violet in nimbus	**Bartlett**	**Bartlett 1967**

1964 Sep 18, 01h15m	**Aristarchus**	Craterlet, base NW wall; bluish	**Bartlett**	**Bartlett 1967**
1964 Sep 20	**Aristarchus to Herodotus**	Several red spots in area	**Crowe, Cross**	**Cameron 1965**
1964 Sep 20	**SE of Ross D**	Bright obscuration	**Cross**	**Cameron 1965; Harris 1967**
1964 Sep 22, 03h03m	**Aristarchus**	Bright blue-violet glare; E wall bright spot and NE rim. Dark violet in nimbus	**Bartlett**	**Bartlett 1967**
1964 Sep 22	**Kunowsky; 1 hr**	Red area blinked in blinker	**Gillheaney, Hall, L.Johnson**	**Cameron 1965**
1964 Sep 23, 03h30m	**Aristarchus**	Blue-violet flare [glare?]; E wall bright spot, E, NE, N, NW wall	**Bartlett**	**Bartlett 1967**
1964 Sep 25, 04h05m	**Aristarchus**	Blue-violet glare; E wall bright spot. Dark violet on nimbus	**Bartlett**	**Bartlett 1967**
1964 Sep 25, 04h43m	**Aristarchus**	Blue-violet glare; E wall bright spot. Dark violet in nimbus; pale violet on plateau	**Bartlett**	**Bartlett 1967**
1964 Sep 26, 05h07m	**Aristarchus**	Moderately intense; E wall bright spot. Dark violet, nimbus	**Bartlett**	**Bartlett 1967**
1964 Oct 19, 02h02m	**Aristarchus**	Strong blue tint E half of floor; blue-violet glare, base E side central peak	**Bartlett**	**Bartlett 1967**
1964 Oct 22, 02h12m	**Aristarchus**	Blue-violet glare, E wall bright spot, E, NE wall. Dark violet hue in nimbus	**Bartlett**	**Bartlett 1967**
1964 Oct 24, 04h02m	**Aristarchus**	Blue-violet glare; E wall bright spot, E, NE rim Dark violet hue in nimbus	**Bartlett**	**Bartlett 1967**
1964 Oct 25, 04h17m	**Aristarchus**	Nimbus only; dark violet hue	**Bartlett**	**Bartlett 1967**
1964 Oct 25, 04h37m	**Aristarchus**	Blue-violet glare; E wall bright spot, E, NE wall. Faint violet tinge in nimbus	**Bartlett**	**Bartlett 1967**
1964 Oct 27	**Alphonsus**	Reddish-pink patch at base of sunlit central peak	**L.Johnson, et al**	**Cameron 1965**
1964 Nov 14	**Plato**	Peak on W wall very brilliant white. At foot of peak on inner	**Bartlett**	**Greenacre 1965**

		side, strong blue band. Immediately adjacent, on SE was a small, bright red spot		
1964 Nov 21, 01h57m	**Aristarchus**	Bright blue-violet glare; NE, N, and NW rims	**Bartlett**	**Bartlett 1967**
1964 Nov 23, 03h29m	**Aristarchus**	Strong blue-violet glare; N, NE, NW walls. Dark violet, nimbus	**Bartlett**	**Bartlett 1967**
1964 Nov 24, 04h50m	**Aristarchus**	Blue-violet glare, N rim. Dark violet in nimbus; pale violet N and NE of crater	**Bartlett**	**Bartlett 1967**
1964 Dec 19	**Aristarchus; 1 min**	Brightened by a factor of 5	**Budine, Farrell**	**Cameron 1965**
1964 Dec 19, ~02h35m	**N/A**	Anomalous bright area during lunar eclipse	**S. Hill and student**	**Hill 1966**
1964 Dec 19, ~02h35m	**Edge of Mare Nubium**	Photoelectric photometry showed strong anomalous enhancement of radiation during lunar eclipse	**Sanduleak, Stock**	**Sanduleak and Stock 1965**
1965 Mar 14, 07h40m	**SE of Ross D**	Crater wall partially obscured. Bright area. Cassegrain 12", f/15	**Cross**	**Harris 1967**
1965 Jul 1	**Aristarchus, dark side**	Starlike image	**Emanuel**	**Cameron 1965**
1965 Jul 2	**Aristarchus; 1 hr 21 min**	Bright spot like star on dark side, estimated mag 4	**Emanuel, et al**	**Greenacre 1965**
1965 Jul 3	**Aristarchus; ~1 hr 10 min**	Pulsating spot on dark side	**Emanuel, et al**	**Greenacre 1965**
1965 Jul 4	**Aristarchus; 1 hr**	Bright spot, no pulsations, on dark side	**Emanuel, et al**	**Greenacre 1965**
1965 Jul 7	**Grimaldi**	White streak extended toward limb	**Azevado, et al**	**Revista Astr. 1965**
1965 Jul 8	**Theophilus; 10 min**	Bright spot	**Cross**	**Cameron 1965; Greenacre 1965**
1965 Jul 9	**Aristarchus; 2 hr 6 min**	Starlike image	**Emanuel**	**Cameron 1965**
1965 Jul 31	**Aristarchus**	Starlike image	**Welch**	**Cameron 1965**

1965 Aug 2	**Aristarchus; ~1 min**	Starlike brightening, 8th to 9th mag	**Bornhurst**	**Cameron 1965**
1965 Aug 3	**Aristarchus; ~6 min**	Starlike image, 6th to 7th mag	**Bornhurst**	**Cameron 1965**
1965 Aug 4	**Aristarchus; ~2 min**	Starlike image, 6th to 7th mag	**Bornhurst**	**Cameron 1965**
1965 Sep 3	**SE of Ross D**	Ridge obscured	**Harris**	**Harris 1967**
1965 Sep 9, 13h20m	**Aristarchus**	Orange-red strip on floor	**Presson**	**Contrib. by Moore**
1965 Oct 10, 06h07m	**Aristarchus**	Pale violet radiance; whole of W interior; dark violet, nimbus; pale violet on plateau	**Bartlett**	**Bartlett 1967**
1965 Oct 11, 01h47m	**Aristarchus**	Whole crater, exclusive of S area, pale violet; dark violet in nimbus; pale violet on plateau	**Bartlett**	**Bartlett 1967**
1965 Oct 12, 02h20m	**Aristarchus**	Nimbus only; dark violet hue	**Bartlett**	**Bartlett 1967**
1965 Oct 13, 03h02m	**Aristarchus**	Pale, blue-violet tint on E wall bright spot and whole length of E wall; pale violet radiance in crater, exclusive of S region. Dark violet, nimbus	**Bartlett**	**Bartlett 1967**
1965 Nov 15	**Aristarchus**	Bright spots	**L.Johnson**	**Phys. Today 1966**
1965 Dec 1	**N/A**	Reddish glow followed by black obscuration	**Evrard and others**	**Gingerich 1966**
1965 Dec 4, 04h25m	**Ross D**	Obscuration of part of rim, also bright area 7-10 km diameter, not seen on following night (04h00m - 07h30m)	**Cross (Harris, Cragg on Dec 5)**	**Harris 1967**
1966 Feb 7, 01h10m	**Aristarchus**	Nimbus only; intense violet hue	**Bartlett**	**Bartlett 1967**
1966 Mar 29, 21h00m	**Archimedes**	Floor bands brilliant	**E.G. Hill**	**B.A.A. Lunar Sec. Circ. 1966, 1, No.6**
1966 Apr 2, 23h30m	**Aristarchus; 20 min**	Central peak very bright	**M. Brown**	**B.A.A. Lunar Sec. Circ. 1966, 1, No.7**

1966 Apr 3, 23h00m	**Aristarchus; 30 min**	Central peak very bright	**M. Brown**	**B.A.A. Lunar Sec. Circ. 1967, 1, No.7**
1966 Apr 12, 01h05m	**Gassendi; 18 min**	Abrupt flash of red settling immediately to point of red haze near NW wall. Continuous until 01h23m	**Whippey**	**B.A.A. Lunar Sec. Circ. 1967, 2, No.5**
1966 Apr 30 - May 2	**Gassendi**	Red glows	**Sartory, Moore, Moseley, Ringsdore**	**J.B.A.A. 1966; B.A.A. Lunar Sec. Circ. 1966, 1, No.6**
1966 May 1, 21h55m - 22h45m	**Aristarchus; 50 min**	Red patch	**Patterson**	**B.A.A. Lunar Sec. Circ. 1966, 1, No.6**
1966 May 1, 22h10m	**Aristarchus; 15 min**	Small intense white spot NW of crater wall	**M. Brown, Sartory**	**B.A.A. Lunar Sec. Circ. 1966, 1, Nos.6, 7**
1966 May 27, 21h10m	**Alphonsus; 50 min**	Faint red patches	**Sartory, Moore, Moseley**	**B.A.A. Lunar Sec. Circ. 1966, 1, No.6**
1966 May 30, 20h52m	**Gassendi; 7 min**	Blink, orange patch and obscuration	**Sartory**	**B.A.A. Lunar Sec. Circ. 1966, 1, No.6**
1966 Jun 1, 03h20m	**Aristarchus**	Entire sunlit area of floor, bluish	**Bartlett**	**Bartlett 1967**
1966 Jun 3, 06h10m	**Aristarchus**	Nimbus only, violet hue	**Bartlett**	**Bartlett 1967**
1966 Jun 26, 04h30m - 04h40m	**Alphonsus; 10 min**	Absorption band (4880 +- 50A) seen in spectrum of central peak	**Harris, Arriola**	**Harris 1967**
1966 Jun 27	**Plato; 15 min**	Inside SW wall of crater, blink	**Hedley Robinson, Sartory**	**B.A.A. Lunar Sec. Circ. 1966, 1, No.11**
1966 Jul 10, 02h00m	**Triesnecker; 1 hr**	Bright streak in crater	**Allen**	**B.A.A. Lunar Sec. Circ. 1966, 1, No.10**

1966 Aug 4-5, 22h37m - 23h30m and 02h32m - 02h58m	**Plato; 53 min, 26 min**	Red color, NE wall and floor	**Corvan, Moseley**	**B.A.A. Lunar Sec. Circ. 1966, 1, No.10**
1966 Sep 2, 00h00m	**Gassendi; 3 hr**	Reddish patches	**Moore, et al (8 observers)**	**B.A.A. Lunar Sec. Circ. 1966, 1, No.10; ibid 1966, 1, No.11**
1966 Sep 2	**Alphonsus; intermittent, 1 hr 2 min**	A series of weak glows; Final flash observed at 04h18m	**Whippey**	**B.A.A. Lunar Sec. Circ. 1966, 2, No.12**
1966 Sep 3, 03h55m	**Gassendi**	Blinks on NE, ENE walls and SW and W of central peak	**Moseley**	**B.A.A. Lunar Sec. Circ. 1966, 1, No.10**
1966 Sep 25, 20h20m	**Gassendi; 30 min**	Reddish patches	**Moore, Moseley**	**B.A.A. Lunar Sec. Circ. 1966, 1, No.11**
1966 Sep 25, 23h12m	**Plato; 3 min**	Blinks in crater	**Moseley**	**B.A.A. Lunar Sec. Circ. 1966, 1, No.11**
1966 Ot 25, 03h46m	**SE of Ross D**	Large bright area obscuring half of crater wall. Not present Oct 24. Newtonian 19" f/7	**Cross**	**Harris 1967**
1966 Oct 25, 22h30m	**Gassendi**	Red blinks, N wall	**Moore, Moseley, Sartory**	**B.A.A. Lunar Sec. Circ. 1966, 2, No.1**
1966 Oct 29, 00h45m - 01h30m	**Copernicus, N rim; 45 min**	Red spot	**Walker**	**Walker 1966**
1966 Dec 22, 06h00m - 06h30m	**Messier (W.H. Pickering); 30 min**	Blinks on floors of both craters	**Kelsey**	**B.A.A. Lunar Sec. Circ. 1967, 2, No.4**
1966 Dec 23, 05h15m - 07h10m	**Plato; 55 min**	Numerous light streaks on floor, three bright spots on floor, all showed blinks	**Kelsey**	**B.A.A. Lunar Sec. Circ. 1967,**

				2, No.4
1966 Dec 27, 06h30m - 07h05m	**Gassendi; 35 min**	Very faint blink on SW floor and another N of it on NW floor (observer considers observation very suspect)	**Kelsey**	**B.A.A. Lunar Sec. Circ. 1967, 2, No.4**
1967 Jan 21, 19h35m	**Gassendi**	Small blink and suspect faint colored patch in outer W wall in position of original observation of 1966 Apr 30	**Sartory, Moore, Moseley, Duckworth, Kilburn**	**B.A.A. Lunar Sec. Circ. 1967, 2, No.3; ibid 1967, 2, No.4**
1967 Feb 17, 17h47m - 18h12m	**Alphonsus; 25 min**	Blink just inside the SW floor of crater suspected on elevation NW of dark patch	**Moore, Moseley**	**B.A.A. Lunar Sec. Circ. 1967, 2, No.4**
1967 Feb 19, 20h30m - 20h40m	**Alphonsus; 10 min**	Bright red glow in position of suspected blink of 1967 Feb 17. Fading by 20h37m	**Moseley, Moore**	**B.A.A. Lunar Sec. Circ. 1967, 2, No.4**
1967 Mar 22, 19h40m	**Gassendi**	Red color and blink	**Moseley**	**B.A.A. Lunar Sec. Circ. 1967, 2, No.5**
1967 Mar 23, 18h40m	**Gassendi**	Red color under S wall	**Sartory, Farrant**	**B.A.A. Lunar Sec. Circ. 1967, 2, No.5**
1967 Mar 23, 19h45m	**Cobrahead**	Red color outside SE wall	**Moore, Moseley, Farrant**	**B.A.A. Lunar Sec. Circ. 1967, 2, No.6**
1967 Mar 23, 19h05m - 19h55m	**Aristarchus**	Red glows	**Sartory, Moore, Moseley**	**B.A.A. Lunar Sec. Circ. 1967, 2, No.5, 6**
1967 Apr 15, 19h15m - 21h00m	**Aristarchus (on dark side); 1 hr 45 min**	Aristarchus very bright. Seeing very good until 21h00m UT, after which seeing too bad to continue observing. On April 16 and 17 nothing special was to be seen.	**Classen**	**Hopmann 1967**
1967 Apr 21, 19h16m - 21h15m	**Aristarchus; 1 hr 59 min**	Bright points on S wall. Red patch to NE	**Darnell, Farrant**	**B.A.A. Lunar Sec. Circ. 1967, 2, No.7**

1967 Apr 21, 21h20m	**Schroter's Valley, Cobrahead**	Red color	**Darnell, Farrant**	**B.A.A. Lunar Sec. Circ. 1967, 2, No.7**
1967 Apr 22	**Aristarchus (on bright side)**	Aristarchus so bright that it could be seen with the naked eye	**Classen**	**Hopmann 1967**
1967 May 20, 20h15m and 21h05m - 21h20m	**Aristarchus; 15 min**	Red spots on south rim. Moon low	**Darnell**	**B.A.A. Lunar Sec. Circ. 1967, 2, No.8**
1967 May 20	**Gassendi**	Elongated blink in crater, SW part of floor	**Kelsey**	**B.A.A. Lunar Sec. Circ. 1967, 2, No.8**
1967 May 29, 06h40m - 07h25m	**Aristarchus; 45 min**	Red-brown color	**C.A. Anderson**	**B.A.A. Lunar Sec. Circ. 1967, 2, No.8**
1967 Jun 18, 21h10m - 22h30m and 22h50m - 23h59m	**Gassendi; 1 hr 20 min and 1 hr 9 min**	Faint redness outside the NW and SW wall of Gassendi	**Whippey**	**B.A.A. Lunar Sec. Circ. 1967, 2, No.8**
1967 Aug 13, 21h00m	**Alphonsus; 15 min**	Glow in interior of crater	**Horowitz**	**B.A.A. Lunar Sec. Circ. 1967, 2, No.10**
1967 Sep 11, 00h32m	**Mare Tranquilitaties; 8-9 sec**	Black cloud surrounded by violet color	**Montreal group**	**B.A.A. Lunar Sec. Circ. 1967, 2, No.12**
1967 Sep 11, 00h45m	**Sabine**	Bright yellow flash visible a fraction of a second	**Mrs P.Jean and Montreal group**	**B.A.A. Lunar Sec. Circ. 1967, 2, No.12**
1967 Sep 17, 02h05m	**Aristarchus**	Red color observed	**Delano**	**Kelsey 1967**
1967 Oct 10, 02h15m	**SE of Ross D**	Bright area moved 80 km/hr toward SSE and expanded as contrast reduced	**Harris**	**Harris 1967**
1967 Oct 19, 05h00m	**Kepler, Aristarchus**	High Moon, 19 after full, apogee. Kepler appeared at least one mag	**Classen**	**Classen 1967**

brighter than Aristarchus. On Oct 20 and 22 at 05h UT, relative brightness returned to normal

Endnotes

---

[i] http://math.ucr.edu/home/baez/physics/General/occam.html
[ii] http://www.unsolvedrealm.com/2011/12/03/why-are-witnesses-of-ufos-and-ghosts-dubbed-whacko/
[iii] http://www.huffingtonpost.com/2010/08/23/ufo-on-the-record_n_689518.html#s129374&title=The_Remaining_Incidents
[iv] http://en.wikipedia.org/wiki/Nick_Pope
[v] http://www.youtube.com/watch?v=eaGCw8ezYkw
[vi] http://articles.nydailynews.com/2010-08-05/news/27071845_1_ufo-sighting-ufo-related-letter-claims
http://www.telegraph.co.uk/news/newstopics/howaboutthat/ufo/7926037/UFO-files-Winston-Churchill-feared-panic-over-Second-World-War-RAF-incident.html
[vii] http://www.ufoevidence.org/topics/cometa.htm
[viii] http://www.ufoevidence.org/topics/belgium.htm
[ix] http://video.google.com/videoplay?docid=-440410516309790842
[x] http://www.youtube.com/watch?v=mUcYW-w21RA&feature=related
[xi]http://wiki.answers.com/Q/What_percentage_of_Americans_believe_in_UFO_visits_according_to_a_study_in_the_year_2000
[xii] http://www.ufoevidence.org/topics/publicopinionpolls.htm
[xiii] http://www.unexplained-mysteries.com/viewnews.php?id=179717
[xiv] http://www.worldometers.info/population/
[xv] http://www.ufoevidence.org/documents/doc969.htm
[xvi] http://en.wikipedia.org/wiki/James_E._McDonald
[xvii] http://www.abduct.com/features/f85.php
[xviii] Principle of Occam's Razor, Wikiepedia, http://en.wikipedia.org/wiki/Occam%27s_razor
[xix] http://www.indiana.edu/~ensiweb/lessons/percep.html
[xx] http://www.merriam-webster.com/dictionary/weltanschauung
[xxi] http://www.hyper.net/ufo/overview.html
[xxii] http://www.history.com/shows/ancient-aliens
[xxiii]http http://www.hyper.net/ufo/overview.html
[xxiv] http://en.wikipedia.org/wiki/Alfred_Wegener
[xxv] http://www.bigsiteofamazingfacts.com/why-was-the-darwin-wallace-theory-so-ridiculed-by-the-public
[xxvi] http://carm.org/extraordinary-claims-require-extraordinary-evidence

[xxvii] http://www.astroengine.com/2009/01/is-the-universe-a-holographic-projection/
[xxviii] http://science.discovery.com/tv/through-the-wormhole/
[xxix] http://superstringtheory.com/basics/basic4.html
[xxx] Legendarytimes.com. Feature Interview with Giorgio A. Tsoukalos, A.A.S. R.A. Chairman & Director of Research
http://www.legendarytimes.com/index.php?menu=journal&op=journal&func=show&id=3
Comment by Giorgio A. Tsoukalos, A.A.S. R.A. Chairman & Director of Research.
[xxxi] http://www.2012endofdays.org/more/Native-American-prophecy.php
[xxxii] http://www.eridu.co.uk/Author/human_origins/AAS_Intro2/Sitchin_Message/sitchin_message.html
[xxxiii] http://www.unmuseum.org/siriusb.htm
[xxxiv] http://www.uforesearchnetwork.proboards.com/index.cgi?board=ancient&action=print&thread=143
[xxxv] Ramayana and Mahabharata Texts
[xxxvi] http://bible.org/seriespage/sons-god-and-daughters-men-genesis-61-8
[xxxvii] http://www.johnpratt.com/items/docs/enoch.html
[xxxviii] http://home.comcast.net/~kevinr99/images/dead.html
[xxxix] Ancient Aliens, Who Do you Believe?
http://ancientaliens.wordpress.com/2011/05/
Referencing: Evidence of Iron Ore Mining in Southern Africa in the Middle Stone Age", R.A. Dart and P. Beaumont (1969)
[xl] https://www.forbiddenhistory.info/?q=node/10
[xli] http://www.rense.com/general82/nations.htm
[xlii] Ancient Aliens, Who Do you Believe?
http://ancientaliens.wordpress.com/2011/05/
Referencing: "Secrets of the Lost Races: New Discoveries of Advanced Technology in Ancient Civilizations", Rene Noorbergen (2001)
[xliii] http://www.rense.com/general82/nations.htm
[xliv] http://www.sacred-texts.com/nam/maya/cbc/cbc33.htm
[xlv] http://www.voxalien.com/attachments/alien-ancient-civilizations/96d1249890833-aliens-sculptures-petroglyphs-pictographs-cave-paintings-geoglyphs-ufotanzia2.jpg
[xlvi] http://www.world-mysteries.com/sar_1.htm
[xlvii] The Baghdad Battery

[xlviii] http://en.wikipedia.org/wiki/Baghdad_Battery
[xlix] http://www.starchildproject.com/
[l] http://discovermagazine.com/2009/the-brain-2/28-what-happened-to-hominids-who-were-smarter-than-us
[li] http://perdurabo10.tripod.com/warehouseb/id30.html
[lii] Definition of anomaly, The Free Dictionary, http://www.thefreedictionary.com/anomaly
[liii] http://superstringtheory.com/basics/basic4.html
[liv] http://policeufo.com/ArticleResearchPreamble.html
[lv] http://www.youtube.com/watch?v=O8oKEdwNzIs
[lvi] http://www.history.com/shows/ancient-aliens
[lvii] http://www.universetoday.com/20050/10-interesting-facts-about-the-moon/
[lviii] http://www.spacedaily.com/2002/021208051116.75xytpjz.html
[lix] http://ufocasebook.conforums.com/index.cgi?board=moon&action=display&num=1115439796
[lx] http://www.nature.com/news/2009/091217/full/news.2009.1149.html
[lxi] http://adsabs.harvard.edu/full/1982Metic..17Q.264O
[lxii] http://www.ianslunarpages.org/tlp.html
[lxiii] http://web.ics.purdue.edu/~nowack/geos105/lect9-dir/lecture9.htm
[lxiv] http://en.wikipedia.org/wiki/Atmosphere_of_the_Moon
[lxv] http://www.thelivingmoon.com/43ancients/41Group_Lunar_FYEO/02files/FYEO_Lunar_02.html
[lxvi] https://www.google.com/search?q=cherenkov+radiation&hl=en&client=firefox-a&hs=cLk&rls=org.mozilla:en-US:official&prmd=imvns&tbm=isch&tbo=u&source=univ&sa=X&ei=lHcLT9TPDYLqtgfg9-GoBQ&ved=0CDkQsAQ&biw=1024&bih=581
[lxvii] http://news.discovery.com/space/this-moon-was-made-for-mining-helium-3.html
[lxviii] http://news.discovery.com/space/this-moon-was-made-for-mining-helium-3.html
[lxix] Wikipedia Reference: Time Magazine, Friday, Jul. 25, 1969 "A GIANT LEAP FOR MANKIND"
[lxx] http://www.youtube.com/watch?v=O8oKEdwNzIs
[lxxi] http://ufos.about.com/od/nasaufos/p/ufosMoon2.htm

[lxxii] http://ufos.about.com/od/nasaufos/p/ufosmoon2.htm
[lxxiii] http://www.ufos-aliens.co.uk/airbrush.htm
[lxxiv] http://www.youtube.com/watch?v=dvPR8T1o3Dc
[lxxv] http://ufocasebook.com/Astronaut.html
[lxxvi] http://www.syti.net/UFOSightings.html#anchor355602
[lxxvii] http://www.syti.net/UFOSightings.html#anchor355602
[lxxviii] http://ufocasebook.com/Astronaut.html
[lxxix] http://ronrecord.com/astronauts/mchatelain.html
[lxxx] http://www.unexplained-mysteries.com/forum/index.php?showtopic=87349
[lxxxi] http://library.thinkquest.org/28170/221.html
[lxxxii] http://www.ufoevidence.org/cases/case486.htm
[lxxxiii] http://www.ufoevidence.org/cases/case486.htm
[lxxxiv] http://www.fsr.org.uk/fsrart4.htm
[lxxxv] http://darnellwilliamsword.blogspot.com/2011/04/ufos-in-puerto-rico.html
[lxxxvi] http://www.ufoconspiracy.com/reports/zetareticuli_star_sys.htm
[lxxxvii] http://www.nasa.gov/topics/moonmars/features/LOIRP/
[lxxxviii] http://en.wikipedia.org/wiki/Spaceship_Moon_Theory
[lxxxix] http://www.iris.edu/hq/files/publications/brochures_onepagers/doc/Lenticular.pdf
[xc] http://en.wikipedia.org/wiki/Earth#Moon
[xci] http://science.howstuffworks.com/space/aliens-ufos/angel-hair-ufo.htm
[xcii] http://science.howstuffworks.com/space/aliens-ufos/angel-hair-ufo.htm
[xciii] https://www.google.com/search?q=images+of+vimanas&hl=en&client=firefox-a&hs=oqL&rls=org.mozilla:en-US:official&prmd=imvns&tbm=isch&tbo=u&source=univ&sa=X&ei=X3QMT-_ILdK7tgfepeTgBQ&ved=0CCEQsAQ&biw=1024&bih=581
[xciv] http://rt.com/usa/news/porn-bunker-pink-visual-479/
[xcv] http://www.december212012.com/articles/news/Russians_Shelters_2012.htm
[xcvi] http://www.examiner.com/finance-examiner-in-national/terror-threats-rising-as-fema-orders-1-billion-dehydrated-food
[xcvii] http://schott.blogs.nytimes.com/2010/05/25/survival-condos/
[xcviii] http://globalresearch.ca/index.php?context=va&aid=23503

xcix

http://www.pathsofdevotion.com/zoroastrianism/zoroastrian_apocalypse.html

c

http://2012supplies.com/what_is_2012/mother_shipton_prophecy_2012.html

CPSIA information can be obtained at www.ICGtesting.com
Printed in the USA
LVOW121910151112

307520LV00020B/50/P